Arthur Edward Waite

FORGOTTEN ESSAYS

Book Second

Darrell Jordan

EX LIBRIS

Arthur Edward Waite - Forgotten Essays: Book Second
Compiled with graphics and edits by Darrell Jordan
Copyright © First Edition 2024. All rights reserved.

Library of Congress Cataloging-in Publication Data
Names: Wait, Arthur | Jordan, Darrell
Title: Arthur Edward Waite - Forgotten Essays: Book Second
Description: First U.S. edition. | Coeur D'Alene, Idaho: Athenaia [2024]
Identifiers: LCCN (pending) | ISBN 979-8-88556-050-4 (First Edition hardcover)
Subjects: OCC016000: BODY, MIND & SPIRIT / Occultism |
HI036000: PHILOSOPHY / Hermeneutics |
REL047000: RELIGION / Mysticism
LCCN record available at https://lccn. loc.gov

On the internet: Parallel47North.com/collections/esoteric-books
Managing Editor: Darrell Jordan
Original Author and Essay: Arthur Edward Waite
Executive Producer: Yuka Jordan
Book Cover Art and Illustrations: Jessica Naomi
Image Credits: Arthur Waite's and Darrell Jordan's personal collections

Printed and bound in the United States

Publisher: Athenaia, LLC
2370 N Merritt Crk Lp, Ste 1
Coeur D'Alene, ID 83814 , The United States
Enquiry@Athenaia.Co

Arthur Edward Waite
FORGOTTEN ESSAYS
Book Second

Darrell Jordan

Dedication

To those who Search for Truth and a Path with Heart.

Seat of Knowledge

An Inprint of Athenaia, LLC

"Employ your time in improving yourself by other men's writings so that you shall come easily by what others have labored hard for."

Socrates

Contents

FORWARD

Book Second - THE MYSTICISM OF A. E. Waite

I T happens that when one seeks for the three writers of the most important and significant books on mysticism recently published in England, one immediately calls to mind Dean Inge, Miss Evelyn Underhill, and Mr. A. E. Waite. The first two have in common with one another more than either has with the third. Employing a loose classification, the attitude of Dean Inge towards mysticism may be termed philosophic, that of Miss Underhill scientific, and that of Mr. Waite sacramental. Both Dean Inge and Miss Underhill are associated with the Established Church, but Mr. Waite, while he stands apart from all formal religion, is avowedly sympathetic towards Roman Catholicism.

The importance of youthful influences may have been overstressed in recent years, but anyone who attempts to define Mr. Waite's position in the literature of mysticism and neglects to give due consideration to the early influences of this writer is willfully throwing away an important key. It cannot be denied that Dean Inge, although the severest critic of the modern age, with the possible exception of Mr. Chesterton, is nevertheless as much a product of it as Mr. Wells or Mr. Shaw; while of Miss Underhill, it can be said that she is perfectly at ease with current scientific and philosophic speculations. But Mr. Waite stands apart from the life of to-day. His spirit, inasmuch as it pertains to any historical period, unmistakably belongs to the Middle Ages.

A conception of the Middle Ages which assumes this period to have been wholly one of superstition and unreason is current. Such a false conception is not intended here. It is not contended that the mind of Mr. Waite lacks logic, nor that he is incapable of analytic and synthetic thought. Indeed, the purpose of this essay is to indicate that Mr. Waite's most important achievement is his acute analysis of the mystic's position. The contention is that, although the method of scientific thought is employed by Mr. Waite, the general outlook of modem man is undeniably foreign to him. His mind is calmer, more reposeful than that of the modem mind, and above all he has certitude and conviction.

We are told that Mr. Waite was scarcely out of his teens when one day, while browsing around a second-hand bookseller's, he came across a copy of Eliphas Levi's Dogme et Rituel de l'haute magie. No one who has read this amazing concoction of truth and charlatanism, written in a cunning and fascinating style, can doubt the nature of the impression which it made upon the sensitive mind of Arthur Waite. The glamour of magic is incomprehensible to those who have not sensed it, but to those others who have come under its spell, the very symbol suggests unseen worlds. There can be little speculation as to the effect which magic had upon Mr. Waite in these early days, but it is only necessary to study his writings to discover the extent to which his thought was bound up with ancient magic.

Mr. Waite is a voluminous writer and has produced many scholarly and illuminating books, but those which are the most significant and certainly the most relevant to my present purpose are two—The Occult Sciences and Lamps of Western Mysticism.

The Occult Sciences was published first in 1891, when Mr. Waite was just over thirty. A secondary title might well be The Magician's Vade-mecum. In the space of under three hundred pages, all phases of magic are discussed, and in so critical yet earnest a manner as must have startled the world when this book was first given to it. There is no other work on the subject of a corresponding size which is at the same time so exhaustive, complete, critical and serious.

Whatever truth there may be in magic, it is certain that romantic imaginings about it are most undesirable; and those who possess the greatest knowledge of the subject will agree that in this direction lies its greatest danger. In this way, magic can fascinate, confusing and eventually destroying the mind. Investigation undertaken in a critical and scientific spirit alone is the correct approach to this subject.

There is no doubt that, when he first published this book, Mr. Waite believed that in magic he had found the surest way to the stars; in fact, he declares in its pages that experimental magic is a valid means of attaining the mystic's end. There remains this difference, however, between Mr. Waite and almost any other modem practitioner of magic—it is difficult to believe that personal experience in practical magic is unknown to him—that, even in the early days of his investigations into magic, his sole aim was mystical, and not an attempt to extend his knowledge of worlds either natural or supernatural. But if it did happen that he came across secrets regarding the nature of the universe, this was accidental and merely incidental to his quest for God. It is in this respect that Mr. Waite differs from the majority of occultists, and it is because he has sought a divine Being by the path of magic that he differs from Dean Inge and Miss Underhill.

Only those who have passed through a similar schooling can realize the nature of the temptations which besiege those who adopt this method. It is one of the greatest tributes to Mr. Waite's sanity, and to the validity of his inspiration, that he has succeeded in emerging unscathed from his journeying in the realm of magic.

Many have found themselves called upon to lead the mystic's life at one period or another of their earthly existence, but few have received that call so early, or obeyed it so whole-heartedly, as Mr. Waite has done. No one who has studied his work even but slightly can doubt that the sole aim and illuminant of his life is his desire for divine union. Nor can they overlook the fact that with a richer experience his attitude towards magic has changed, and that method which he once considered the mystic way par excellence is now held by him not only as being invalid, but rather a way of illusion and self-deception.

"Mysticism," like most words descriptive of mental states and conditions, has received an undue amount of abuse and maltreatment. It is impossible to obtain a clear definition of the word from dictionaries, and most other books of reference are equally useless. It cannot be denied that this term has been employed by some to indicate vagueness of thought; but that these are as incorrect as those who regard it as a synonym for occult science or magic is demonstrated by the fact that mysticism definitely leads to a condition beyond thought. It dispenses with thought, and on this account is systematically opposed by those who maintain that, if reality can be comprehended, it is only by the normal faculties of the mind that this is possible. Mysticism does not solve world problems, does not give knowledge of other planes of existence. It does not claim to give knowledge—in the accepted sense of the word—of reality, unless by this phrase is implied Divine Union.

Mysticism from which the added superfluities of formal religion have been removed resolves itself into this: Mysticism is the attempt of the human mind to effect communication with God. From this desire to come in contact with Infinity, all religion has sprung, and on its realization, all religious truth depends.

Mysticism is not a creed, but an experience, and Mr. Waite is not propounding a theory, but speaking from experience, when he says that he who seeks out a Divine Being does not search in vain, but is rewarded by certitude and the knowledge of whence he has come and whither he is going. Mr. Waite has defined the mystic's position in the simplest terms; he has as clearly declared what it is not. He has sundered mysticism and occultism, and has indicated that, whatever truth there may be in spiritism, it has nothing to teach the mystic, for he knows that sooner or later he must return whence he came, and is therefore not concerned with intermediary stages of being. That there are various states of mystical experience is admitted, but all are experiences of joy. Whether the final experience can come to man while still in the flesh—that state of consciousness perhaps beyond consciousness in the accepted sense, which is termed divine union, and which is truly said to "pass all understanding"—is a question Mr. Waite is unable to answer.

The day has passed when competent psychologists can overlook the problems raised by the mystical experience; in fact, it is a subject which increasingly demands their attention. But psychology is still a young science, which has not yet fully emerged from its elementary stage: its methods are still uncertain and its conclusions tentative, while mysticism is the oldest art practiced by man. Psychology has shown, however, that the mystic's experience is one of a definite and unique kind, which cannot be confused with other experiences exhibiting similar, but superficial, resemblances. It is, however, in their interpretations of this experience that psychologist and mystic differ; for the psychologist maintains that "the still, small voice," the apparent divine response, the mystic senses, is nothing more than one section of the brain, the whole being in a condition of dissociation, responding to the other. But psychologists bear witness to the intense ecstasy of the experience, and are of the opinion that it is perhaps the most beneficial which one can participate in, for it appears to possess the power of re-establishing order and bringing harmony to the mind. The competent investigator realizes that mysticism cannot lightly be dismissed, and whether the mystic's experience is valid according to his interpretation or not, it seems probable that therein lies the solution of a large number of our modern mental problems.

Under many different symbols, and in a multitude of myths and legends, Mr. Waite has spoken of the mystic's experience. He has seen glimmerings of it in many unlikely places, and has discovered references to it in the legend of the Holy Graal, in Alchemy, in the Rosicrucian Order, in ancient Israel, and in Freemasonry. Whatever interpretation one may finally give to his experiences, one cannot deny their depth and intensity. One cannot doubt that he has passed far on the mystic's way, for he has spoken of it as clearly as words will avail him, and now that it would appear that he has passed to a deeper state beyond the power of normal language, he has been compelled to resort to symbolism and fable.

Pure mysticism is unconcerned with world problems, and those who seek in the writings of A.E. Waite a solution to the enigma of the universe must be disappointed. He is not interested in general religious problems. He is not a great moral teacher, for morals do not enter into his sphere. He does not speak of the future; he does not prophesy a spiritual revival, or the contrary. His sole concern is with the attainment of the mystic's goal. This does not imply coldness or selfishness on his part. In innumerable books, he has given the most valuable help which any man can give in these matters; while those who are favored with his friendship testify to his warmth and generosity of spirit. For him, the world is a symbol, and life a sacrament, "an outward and visible sign of an inward and spiritual grace." He is in the great tradition of mystics, and, like his great predecessors, he has borne witness to states of consciousness unknown to us who are less gifted, less spiritually refined. He has freed mysticism from the shackles of formal religion, and has given it to us in its pure form. He has set an example to be followed, and has indicated how this may be most easily achieved. He has found the Infinite, and if this be illusion, it is the Great Illusion.

Illusion or reality, the experience remains, and the testimony of Mr. Waite proves that it is one which may well be described as ecstatic. The path has been shown to us, and it depends on us whether we follow it or turn aside. It is only one possessed of great courage, sincerity, discernment and refinement who could have achieved what Mr. Waite has done, who could have followed the path of the mystics in these modern days, and who, avoiding illusion, can speak so lucidly and so fearlessly of his experiences.

Luis Trew

FREEMASONRY AND THE FRENCH REVOLUTION

September, 1911

IT may seem extravagant to say that among associations which are called secret, that must be the most secret of all which (a) exists in the open face of day; (b) has always paraded its objects; (c) gives everywhere proof palpable that its affirmed objects are those with which it is concerned essentially and only; (d) occasionally prints its proceedings so far as the business side of its meetings is concerned; (e) tolerates the printing of its rites and ceremonies, in unauthorized and often fraudulent versions; and yet is other than it claims to be, (1) in the opinion of its hostile critics and (2) also—but for far different reasons—in that of a select few who are in it, are of it, and believe that they have penetrated to its inmost essence. It may seem extravagant, but it is a little difficult to set aside when the subject is that of Freemasonry. The critical opinion which I have mentioned—though not in the sense of approval—would consent out of hand, and might add that the witness of Masonic history is quite definite as to its real apart from its assumed character, although it is concealed so deeply that its own members know nothing for the most part. The select few would consent, and they also might add—but in a contrary sense entirely—that the witness of symbolism and ritual is quite definite as to the real objects of the institution, though those who work and those even who expound them, for the most part, know nothing.

There is a concern on the surface of Masonry which is real after its own manner and is represented by the ethical side—the side of brotherly love and universal beneficence, with all that is implied therein. But there is a witness beneath the surface to another kind of concern, by virtue of which it is connected with the instituted mysteries and secret doctrine of the past, of Egypt, Greece and Rome. It carries on by its ritual procedure the same memorials of experience in spiritual birth, inward life, mystic death and resurrection in the spirit. It is this deeper testimony by means of symbolism to exotic states attainable in consciousness that is not realized by the great body of those who belong to it, but who are yet excellent and earnest Masons after their own manner. These intimations of experience are disguised in the vestures of an art of emblematic building, by which the Order is connected with another form of secret doctrine, being that of Kabalism. I am not now concerned with questions of origin, but as it is usually held that the rough mystery of reception into the old building guilds was spiritualized in the seventeenth century and that Emblematic Masonry resulted, the point is that those who did the work were acquainted with theosophical tradition in Israel. I am speaking of the Craft Grades, and the kind of Kabalism which these embodied had Christian implicits, as at the period was inevitable. They led at a later period to the construction of what is called High Grades, of which those in the true line of succession are designed to show how Jewish secret doctrine was completed by Christianity.

It follows that in root-purpose, as in ritual development, Masonry has no political aspect. In England, where it originated, and in English-speaking countries, no one suspects that it has, but when it entered the Continent France was already with child, and the child which had to be born was the French Revolution.

Adam Weishaupt.

I do not think that anything contributed so little to that birth as Masonry; I know that all the evidence to the contrary is the work of false or imbecile witnesses; but it was a secret society maintaining the natural equality and brotherhood of all mankind; as such, it lies under suspicion, and it naturally tended to draw those who held kindred views independently and aspired to put them into practice. There was also in Germany one definite attempt to appropriate Masonry in the interests of a propaganda which aimed at religious, political and social revolution. The Illuminati of Bavaria was an order founded in 1766 by a young man named Adam Weishaupt, who had conceived a scheme of universal reform and apparently regarded any means as justified by such an end. He was not a Mason at the time, but he sought initiation subsequently and began to incorporate Masonic elements into his system of Degrees. Of these, there were three classes—the first preparatory, the second Masonic, the third containing the ultimate secrets of the Order. His collaborator in the construction of the last series was Baron von Knigge, a Mason of considerable standing and one who has been praised by almost every writer as a person of great amiability and many intellectual gifts. At the celebrated Masonic Convention of Wilhelmsbad, held in 1782, under the auspices of the Duke of Brunswick, von Knigge sought and failed to obtain recognition for the Order; but, his zeal notwithstanding, he became dissatisfied with Weishaupt's propaganda and abandoned the Illuminati, shortly before their forcible suppression by an electoral edict in 1784. In its complexion, the Order was anti-Christian, in the sense of aggressive Deism; it was anti-monarchical certainly; and those who describe it as an anti-social movement are not far from the mark, if we admit the validity of their implicits in the use of the term. It was an attempt to embody in association a spirit of the age, which was represented individually by, e.g., the German bookseller, C. F. Nicolai. The latter was a Mason also and is useful to remember as epitomizing the set of intellectual, moral and religious feelings which brought about such experiments as the Illuminati. The Masonry of Southern Germany was included for a time in their downfall, and some of the disbanded associates are reported, on very poor authority, to have entered France and to have been received into a few of its Lodges, where they quickened the spirit of revolution. I have given here an example of the grounds on which continental Masonry in the eighteenth century is supposed to have had political aspects and concerns in the worst sense of the expression. The connexion of the Illuminati with the older institution is simply that they stole some of its Degrees and pressed them into their own service. The other materials of hostile criticism and accusation are of similar value, but they served for those who used them. At the head of the criticism and condemnation, there stands, for what it is worth, the Holy Roman Church; yesterday, today and forever it neither changes nor falters. From the moment that it began, within its own limits, to understand the institution, the voice of condemnation sounded. It has been always the same sentence, though the counts of the indictment have not been the same precisely. The variations, such as they are, may be found in papal bulls and allocutions; but for the general purpose they may be regarded as summarized and perhaps even extended, by the findings of the Anti-Masonic Congress held at Trent some fifteen years ago.

ADOLF FREIHERR VON KNIGGE.

I have covered this ground previously and I am not now actually returning upon it, though there is always a new reason. Very few serious persons trouble about Rome at this day in respect of Freemasonry; we know exactly how its hostility arose and how it has helped in continental countries to create the situation of which it is its province to complain.

There is, of course, another side to the question, and I must not say that the briefs for the defense are much better than those of the accusers, save in respect of good faith. The task is easy—in a sense—to dispose of Robison in England, of Barruel and Deschamps in France, of Eckert in Germany and his French translator, Abbé Gyr. Though easy, it is scarcely sufficient; but the work of destruction is either carried no further or it passes at the next stage into simple generalities. It remains that, personally speaking, I do not think that Masonic erudition or keenness has appeared to any special advantage; and supposing it to have obtained a verdict, this would be rather on the bad faith of the witnesses than on the merits of its own pleadings. In one sense, there is no verdict to give and in another, it has been given long ago. There is none, because public opinion in all parts of the world does not consider that any question is seriously at issue; or, alternatively, it has been given, as I have said, because Rome has pronounced, and for those who look to Rome, the only course is concurrence. Here again, therefore, there is no question for settlement.

But it so happens that from time to time some new writer arises sporadically who does think that there is a case to go to the jury, supposing that a jury were impaneled; the question is therefore with us, and it is desirable to see whether the last witness has carried matters further. Miss Una Birch, who wrote not long ago a life of Anna Von Schurman, which offered a remarkable instance of patient research into a subject of little consequence or interest, has reprinted recently from current periodical literature a few essays under the title of Secret Societies and the French Revolution.

FR. NICOLAI.

Here, on the contrary, the subject is of great interest, but when we turn to the evidence of research, we find that she has read a good deal beforehand along the ordinary and obvious lines, but more than this, nothing. It should be said that her keenness remains over many points of detail, and thus in her study of the Comte de St. Germain, there are a few new items, or new at least to myself. They do not really help us to understand better his personality or his mission, but they determine his occupations at given periods of his life. There is another study, this time on Mme. de Stael, which is exceedingly fresh, highly informed and of great charm in its treatment. It deserves well at the hands of the conventional reviewer, but in this case, it is no part of my subject. Miss Birch's first essay is that which is embodied by the title given to the series and it attempts to trace the hand of Masonry in the work which led ultimately to the French Revolution. The keynote is in a quotation from Lord Acton, who said that in this upheaval the "appalling thing" was "not the tumult, but the design . . . The managers remained studiously concealed and masked; but there is no doubt about their presence from the first." The thesis of Miss Birch is that the mask was Masonry. On the affirmative side she cites five familiar deponents, including some of those whom I have mentioned, and though she terms them special pleaders, it is on them that she is chiefly dependent. She appears reasonably dissatisfied notwithstanding and complains that "no unprejudiced person outside Masonry" has attempted to explain "the greater activity of Lodges of all Rites" during the years which preceded the Revolution, and the sudden disappearance of those Lodges in the early months of 1789. As one who is practically and intimately acquainted with every Rite and Grade produced during the period and subsequently, as also with every Ritual, I can assure her that the cause of activity is to be sought in the surface claim of the Rites and in the vistas which they opened into the unknown, while their sudden disappearance in the vortex of the social cataclysm is explained by the vortex itself. When comparative tranquility was restored, many of the Rites reappeared, but many also had dissolved or been transmuted prior to the Revolution. It is, however, to deal with these points that Miss Birch's essay has been compiled, and I think that the course pursued is a typical instance of the kind of fortune that befalls "the unprejudiced person outside Masonry" when he or she attempts to adjudicate on a subject so deeply involved. She has followed—as she could do no otherwise, without years of research—the familiar authorities and the special pleaders, as a consequence of which her account deals with inventions and not with facts. It may be scarcely worthwhile in itself, but it is requisite in a serious notice to specify a few of the pitfalls into which she has entered unawares.

(a) She believes that Jacobite Lodges in France were responsible primarily for the spread of Masonry in that country; but almost every statement concerning this form of conspiracy is a late and idle product of fantastic minds. Practically speaking, there were no Jacobite Lodges. The story arose out of the claims of Baron von Hund and his Rite of the Strict Observance; it falls with these. (b) She affirms that both the Pretenders instituted Masonic Rites to accomplish their own restoration. She has been misled again by von Hund and by writers like Clavel. There is no reason to suppose that either of the princes in question were ever made Masons, and one of them certainly denied it when he had no ulterior purpose in so doing. (c) In her account of the origin of Emblematic Masonry—which, it may be said, is quite beside the mark—she states that Francis Bacon was a Rosicrucian. This fiction is, I think, referable to Ragon, no statement of whom on any Masonic subject can be accepted without careful verification. (d) She speaks of the Chevalier Ramsay's strenuous Masonic life and thinks that he "managed to popularize Masonry and exalt it into a fashionable pursuit." His activity was confined to a lecture of a few pages; he never established any Rite, as Miss Birch supposes, nor did he claim to derive anything from Godfrey de Bouillon. (e) She is mistaken in like manner as to the Masonic interests of Swedenborg, who had no concern in the movement, whose supposed initiation is no doubt another fiction. Reghellini da Scio is thought to have manufactured this particular story. (f) She is deceived also about the Rite of Pasqually, which only came into existence towards 1770, when it had no concern with iliuminism, as that term would have been understood by Weishaupt. (g) In respect of Saint-Martin she is egregiously deceived by Robison as to the trend of Des Erreurs et de la Vérité. (h) She is no less mistaken as to the Lodge of the Philalethes, which was founded for the investigation of Masonic origins and history. (i) As much may be said of her views concerning the Brotherhood connected with the name of Abbé Pemetti at Avignon; but the elucidation of this difficult question has been accomplished only in recent days. (j) Finally, the Order of the Strict Observance was not suspended by the Convention of Wilhelmsbad. Its reformation at Lyons was ratified; it existed after the Revolution, and it exists still.

Miss Birch's authorities outside those whom I have cited are Le Couteulx de Canteleu and the modem Martinist, Papus. It may surprise her to learn that the former, whose Tombeau de Jacques de Molay is a worthless tract, altered his views subsequently and became a Mason. The latter's pretensions have been reduced to their real value by the anonymous translator of Franz von Baader's little work on the Secret Teachings of Pasqually. It is regrettable that a paper so open to criticism should occupy the chief position and furnish the title to a volume in which many of the later pages do honor to the capacity of the writer and encourage the opinion that she is likely to produce work in the future which will be of permanent historical and also literary value.

ROBERT FLUDD: PHILOSOPHER AND OCCULTIST

January, 1912

THERE is every opportunity for the ordinary literate reader to know something at the present day, in a preliminary sense, concerning Robert Fludd, of Bersted by Maidstone in Kent, born in 1574, a reputed Rosicrucian and mystic. If a student of animal magnetism, the literate reader may come across his name and a summary account concerning him in Joseph Ennemoser's attempt to explain the whole history of magic by means of the force which Mesmer found or recovered at the close of the eighteenth century. If drawn alternatively to investigate the origin of the Masonic Fraternity, he will have seen some dubious and rather sensational references to Fludd in that fantastic exposition which Thomas de Quincey adapted from the German Buhle, under the title of Rosicrucian's and Freemasons. But if his interest has been rather towards the mysterious and elusive brotherhood who united the Rose and Cross in a single symbol, he may have met with Fludd's literary and philosophical portrait at much greater length in my own history of the Rosicrucian's, or with the connexion between Fludd and alchemy in my lives of the alchemists and elsewhere. Finally, he may have gone much further—but this almost suggests a sense of dedication—to the excellent monograph on Doctor Robert Fludd, by the Rev. J. B. Craven, of whose care and sympathy it is good to say a word in recognition.

I have mentioned here the available sources of information in what is practically a chronological order, and those who would pursue the subject must have recourse to the philosopher's writings, which are buried—with one exception—in Latin of the seventeenth century and are mostly books in folio.

PORTRAIT OF ROBERT FLUDD

They perplexed the scholars of their own period and they perplexed rare readers in later generations, till it came to be understood tacitly that the author might be mentioned but not consulted. Yet a good deal of curious lore has accreted about his name and he now stands somewhat as a figure of philosophical romance. Mr. Craven has dealt as he could with Fludd's involved system, taking the texts successively, and I do not propose to confuse my own readers by extracting from the biographer's pages or atoning for his reasonable omissions. The works treat of life, death and resurrection; the macrocosmos, or greater world; the world in little, or the microcosm; Mosaical cosmogony; the universal medicine; the claims put forward by Rosicrucian's and the recognition due to these. In the words of his own letter, addressed to King James I, Fludd was a seeker in all things for "the unknown basis of true philosophy and the supreme secret of medicine." At the beginning of the seventeenth century, as it did for some time afterwards, this quest signified the Kabalistical interpretation of the universe and the pursuit of alchemy. The theosophical tradition of Israel—represented by the word Kabalism—was a great intellectual puzzle and wonder of that time, and Fludd was one of its students, so far as its literature had passed into the Latin tongue. William Postel had translated the Book of Formation. Riccius, Reuchlin and Archangelus de Burgo Nuovo had brought back glad tidings from Hebrew and Aramaic texts. Portent and comet of a season, Picus de Mirandula had flashed much earlier across the horizon of Europe and passed too soon. But he had left his Theses Cabbalisticac and the report of Zoharic MSS. which embodied all mysteries of Israel from the days of the patriarch Abraham. Like all those who preceded him. Fludd construed the tradition in the light of Christian revelation. As to the alchemists whom he followed, "their voices were in all men's ears." Both subjects belonged to the romantic mind of the period, and so far as England was concerned in the days of James, it was this romance which has taken name and shape about Fludd. It was not a time of tolerance, as people may know if they read or remember history; but the Reformation meant qualified liberation, here and in Germany.

MILGATE HOUSE, THE BIRTHPLACE OF ROBERT FLUDD.

The horizon was extending everywhere; the study of different philosophies, of theosophical systems more than these, and above all of Nature, working in her secret laboratories, gave escape from the narrow measures of reform in official doctrine and practice without rejecting the reform and without ceasing to be "a true Protestant in the best sense of the Church of England," or of Luther.

It was further a period of great claims in the occult world, and not long after Robert Fludd "was at length returned to his Fatherland" after those "years of travelling beyond seas" mentioned on his monument at Bersted, the star of Rosicrucianism rose over the German world. Its story is known, and this is no place to repeat it; but, in a word, it purported to be an association of masters keeping guard over those very possessions to which Fludd himself aspired—the basis of philosophy and the supreme secret of medicine. They were the healers of their day and though they concealed, by repute and their own hypothesis, many mysteries beneath their cloak, their agreement was this—that they should profess only to "heal the sick, and that gratis." Robert Fludd espoused their cause and supported it through the rest of his life, either on the faith of their statement or because he had reason to know that the sodality was not a fable and a jeux d'esprit. He was acquainted familiarly with one of the two persons whom there is a colorable excuse for connecting with the society itself at its headquarters, assuming its corporate existence. This was the alchemist, Michael Maier. His own integration has been assumed, but an evidential basis is wanting, and the subject on several sides has been—as usual—in the worst critical hands. Even Mr. Craven reads an evasive statement of the work called Summum Bonum into an admission of Fludd's membership, whereas it is obviously the device of one who speaks but says nothing. The Tractatus Apologeticus, which Fludd addressed to his not too worthy sovereign, that he might be cleared of suspicion in that over-suspicious mind, contains an autobiographical memorial in two sentences. First among these is that which mentions his dedications. I have quoted it already; it is eloquent, as I feel, in simplicity and a little more than eloquent in gracious restraint. The second describes his manner of life as a Christian gentleman, who—for reasons which do not transpire—never entered into the bonds of wedlock; he affirms, in the sight of God and of his Majesty, that he has always lived as virgo immaculate. Was it because in undertaking to defend the Rosicrucian's he modelled himself on the rule of the first members, who were all bachelors and of vowed virginity? Was it because he was incorporated and living under their rule? The question must be answered, according to personal predilection, because again there is no evidence. It is possible—and I think on my own part—that, as time went on, the brotherhood was for him more and more spiritually understood, and that he aspired, under his best lights, to be one of the "living stones" in its spiritual temple.

I have indicated that Fludd was born in the sunny and typical Kentish village of Bersted. The event took place in a lovely manorial house, which was standing some few years ago, much as it did in Jacobean days. I give the picture as I saw it in 1894, when I had an opportunity to visit it from roof even to basement. The church is also, as it was in the philosopher's days, pleasantly situated on the pleasant slope of a hill above the village. We can picture the figure of Fludd traversing the path over meadows between the place of worship and that of his home-life.

CHURCH OF THE HOLY CROSS, BERSTED, THE BURIAL-PLACE OF ROBERT FLUDD.

We can picture him also at his city dwelling in Coleman Street, close by the headquarters of the Masons' Company, and we may remember—in this connection—that other dream which has allied him to the speculative fellowship. What we do know is that he practiced as a physician in London, and it is said that he was eminent in his medical capacity. It was in Coleman Street, also that he died, though he was buried in his native place. In what large sense Fludd is to be understood as an occult philosopher, his works remain to show. He has been called also a mystic, which is not one of his titles. I am sure, however, that he sought the divine ends, and we may agree, as regards his passing, with the words of his memorial inscription, that he "exchanged death for life on the 8th day of the month of September, A.D. 1637, in the 63rd year of his age."

THE SHRINE OF A THOUSAND BUDDHAS

April, 1912

THE voices are mighty that swell from the past, and not the least among those mighty are the voices of the old travelers. Speaking of our own era, from the days of Marco Polo to those of the Abbé Hue, they come to us from the centuries behind, some of them with a sense of remoteness almost past thought, but all like horns of enchantment. Perhaps at the present day, amidst our knowledge of the ends of the earth and so much that lies between them, the appeal is not exactly in that which the old voices say to us, but in that for which they stand—the great voyages and the great ventures, the quest of the unknown, the attainment, whatever it may have been—much or little— standing for that great experience in which the unknown passes into the known. It is "the dream of doing and that other dream of done," and it is the spirit which strives in the dream. For us, in our modem world, there are two distinctions in this kind of questing, and of these, at the actual moment, we have two examples before us, very brilliant and very precious, standing in their different ways on two peaks of achievement. This, at least, is how I see them, whose travels are in the mind only. The record of the one—and it is a monument in the very outer aspect of its volumes—has appeared almost coincidently with an announcement of the magnificent fact in respect of the other. The distinctions which I have mentioned are the call to that which is undiscovered, with the achievement therein, and the call to that which awaits rediscovery—the call of the past and its records. The whole question of association and its value is here involved, and it seems worthwhile to contrast for a little moment the kinds of dedication which took M. Aurel Stein to his field of exploration in Central Asia, Westernmost China, all that we understand by the magic word Cathay, and Amundsen into the polar night—the one to unearth great treasures of art and knowledge, out of all expectation but his own, in the Temple of the Thousand Buddhas, and the other to penetrate where no man has reached previously, in the land which is no-man's-land. The dedications are one at heart, for the quality of spirit is one, and that which lies so forgotten as to be beyond our ken is near enough in its status for the mind to that which is till now unknown.

There is no reason to suppose that our great explorer of the Southern Pole is a poet; but he comes before us in that light which is said never to be on land or sea because it abides really in the heart. Dr. Stein is no poet indeed, but he is the unconscious maker of atmospheres in which some of us may very nearly see that heart's light just mentioned shining over all his paths. For myself, I call his expedition an Argonautic quest, and he has come back to us with a ship full of wonders which are suggestive of a thousand golden fleeces. He is a man of learning, well and properly prepared beforehand, besides being an intrepid and resourceful traveler; he knows all the value of his treasures—by which I do not mean their price actual in the commercial market of the world, but their worth, beyond price, in the world of mind. Is he satisfied, therefore, perchance? I think not; the call of Cathay and its deserts is still ringing in his ears; there is more yet to be achieved and the last question which he asks is: "When may I hope that the gate will open for work in those fields to which cherished plans have been calling me ever since my youth, and which still remain unexplored?" Frost-bite and mortification have maimed one of his untiring feet, but he can still climb mountains, and we know that the "noble heart" which is "with child of glorious, great intent" can never rest until it has brought forth the "glorious brood" of its purposes into fair fulfillment.

Meanwhile, it will be a matter of years before his discovered manifestation of Cathay treasures can be appraised properly; he has told us all that he can, and, whether we are likely to be satisfied or not ourselves—who perhaps are also "with child" of hopes and longings without number—we can see that he has made us rich beyond expectation, if not beyond the dreams of avarice. It comes about, therefore, that we rest for the time being "in the face of what is won" by him, for us and for the extension of our knowledge. The zeal of our loving congratulation and wonder goes out to Amundsen, who has stood where all the lines of longitude meet at the Southern Pole; it is good to know the fact, and the glory of all nothingness which isolates that fastness of the world is like the thrill of the void itself; but Dr. Stein, from the place of a thousand Buddhas, has returned laden and over-laden: I know therefore in which research I would have been—if God had given me to be prepared for either—however equally I offer due honor to both.

Rows of Cave Temples, showing Decayed Porches, near Middle of Southern Group, "Thousand Buddhas" Site.

Let my readers—sitting as I now sit—but not perhaps with these great volumes before them—take any good map of the Chinese Empire. It will show them, above India and Burmah, the great region of Tibet. Above Tibet, they will see the locality in chief of Dr. Stein's pioneer work, which is Chinese Turkestan. They will identify with no pains the place called Khotan and the Taklamakan desert around it and far away to the East. It was amidst the sand-buried ruins of this spot that Dr. Stein made his first explorations in what he terms "a virgin field for antiquarian research." This was, once upon a time, "the main channel for the interchange of the civilizations of India, China and the classical West," through which Buddhistic art passed under Greek influence, as the remains of the past testify. The account of what he then accomplished is contained, firstly, in a popular work, published in 1903, and, secondly, in a detailed report establishing the scientific results. His present story starts in the valleys of the Indo-Afghan border, entering Chinese Turkestan by a new route, "across the Hindu-Kush to the uppermost Oxus valley and the Afghan Pamirs." It will serve no purpose here to map out the progress, nor am I concerned with anything but the record in chief of discoveries. I shall therefore allude but lightly to things which preceded the great find of all. The shrines of Khadalik, in the district of the desert of Chira, gave rich yields to excavation—coins of the eighth century, remains of stucco relievos, Tibetan records on wood, tablets inscribed in Brahmi, painted panels, Chinese Brahmi rolls and Buddhist texts. The ruins of Niza offered another post of vantage, rich in remains of the Græco-Buddhist style, wooden tablets inscribed in the ancient Kharoshthi script, previously so little known and so difficult to decipher, but above all records from a hidden archive, amounting to nearly three dozen perfectly preserved documents. The LopNor site was another place of marvels, including a small strip of paper in an unknown writing, afterwards increased by a "great find of complete letters in the same script." Another stage of discovery was the ruined fort of Miran, rich in Tibetan records—more than 1,000—on paper and wood. But apart from documents, the Temples had remains of colossal figures of Buddhas, frescoes of delicately painted cherubic winged figures, a dado of angels, a great cycle of festive figures, Buddhist legends in fresco composition and mural painting.

I come now to the real business of this notice, which is the Tower of the Thousand Buddhas, to the south-east of Tun-Huang, or Sha-Chou, as it is called on popular maps. The reader will see it on his own map, occupying roughly a middle point between Lop-Nor on the West and Su-Chou on the east. The caves are a host of grottoes "tenanted, not by Buddhist recluses, however holy, but by images of the Enlightened One himself." Each grotto is a shrine and together they form a bewildering multitude, apart from all order or arrangement, some high, some low, one above the other, with "rough stairs cut into the cliff and still rougher wooden galleries" serving as approaches to the higher caves. In the topmost rows, the shrines are evidently inaccessible. The adornments are frescoes and stucco sculptures. The best of the former belongs to the times of the T'ang dynasty, while the others "faithfully combine the traditions of that period."

Throughout, but especially in the figures of the Buddhas, there is the preservation of "the type of face, pose and drapery as developed by Graeco-Buddhist art." As regards the sculptured remains, most of the shrines had a seated figure of Buddha, which might be colossal in its proportions, surrounded by standing Bodhisattvas and divine attendants.

To the one thousand Temples, Dr. Stein came forewarned concerning "a great hidden deposit of ancient MSS.," which accident had discovered some years previously in one of the grottoes. With what care he proceeded so that nothing in deficiency of skill should imperil his access to this house of treasure; after what manner he dealt with the priestly guardian; the delays and expectations; the great investigation at last inaugurated and the successful consummation—these things constitute a real chapter—and one of surpassing interest—in the romance of archeology. The initial difficulties at length overcome, the Hidden Chapel was opened—truly like the Temple of a most secret and holy Rite in the Instituted Mysteries. There, "heaped up in layers, but without any order, appeared in the dim light of the priest's little lamp a solid mass of MS. bundles rising to a height of nearly ten feet, and filling, as subsequent measurement showed, close on 500 cubic feet."

STUCCO IMAGE GROUP, REPRESENTING BUDDHA BETWEEN DISCIPLES, BODHISATTVAS, AND DVARAPALAS, IN CAVE-TEMPLE CH. III., "THOUSAND BUDDHAS" SITE.

Dr. Stein believes that the deposition is referable to about the middle of the ninth century. The contents included (1) Buddhist texts in Chinese translations; (2) Texts in Indian Brahmi script; (3) Tibetan texts in roll form; (4) Paintings on fine gauze-like silk; (5) Silk banners showing beautifully painted figures of Buddhas and Bodhisattvas; (6) Ex-votos in all kinds of silk and brocade; (7) MSS. in Sanskrit and in one or other of the unknown tongues used by Turkestan Buddhism; (8) Above all, old Chinese block prints. As regards these, Dr. Stein says that they offer "conclusive evidence that the art of printing books from wooden blocks was practiced long before the conventionally assumed time of its invention . . . and that already in the ninth century the technical level had been raised as high as the process permitted."

The triumph of the whole story, in respect of its hero, is that ultimately, he brought away from this secret shrine of the centuries, twenty-four cases of MS. acquisitions, "while the paintings, embroideries and other miscellaneous relics filled five more." They are now deposited safely in the British Museum. It is obvious that the study of the MSS. will be the work of years, but Dr. Stein gives an interesting chapter of summary account. The Sanskrit MSS. contain texts of considerable interest for the critical history of the Sanskrit Canon of Northern Buddhism. The texts in what is called the unknown language, once current in the Khotan region, include translations of Buddhist texts available in their Sanskrit originals, so that the key to this mysterious tongue is now found. The Sogdian MSS. offer proof of Iranian influence much further eastwards than was known previously, and they contain translations of the canonical literature of Buddhism. There are also Turkish translations of canonical works, while the Tibetan MSS. belong presumably to the Tibetan Buddhist Canon. Finally, there are two unique finds: (1) A text in Syriac scripts, recognized as the characteristic writing of the Manichaeans and containing the confession of their laymen in its early Turkish version. (2) An original composition of more than 100 pages in Turkish, and in that form of almost unknown writing called Runic Turki.

It is obvious that the star of the treasure-trove has set westward once more; our thanks therefore to the finder; our gratitude also to the wise foresight of the British Museum, which united with the Indian Government to make such a journey possible. It is now rewarded by the possession of jewels which every center of learning must covet with laudable yearning. Health and God speed, in fine, to Dr. Aurel Stein, in view of his further researches, and when he returns again to tell us another story, may I still be one of the listeners.

WOMAN AND THE HERMETIC MYSTERY

June, 1912

THERE is an old Rosicrucian romance which is called the Chymical Marriage of Christian Rosy Cross, and those who have read it in the quaint English version of the seventeenth century may remember that very strange nuptials were celebrated therein amidst much joy and the emblazonments of a long pageant. It took place in a great mystical palace which was thronged by adepts of both sexes, and if it may be regarded, under necessary reserves, as an allegorical story of the Fraternity and its concerns at the period, there can be little question that Rosicrucianism in and about the year 1615 had thrown open its Temples and Sacred Houses of Initiation to members of both sexes; as it does at the present day. I am not pretending to put forward an historical thesis in offering this suggestion, for there is very sound evidence otherwise that the romance is romance simply and was written by a Lutheran theologian as a jeu d'esprit when he was still of tender age. The historical aspects apart, any question of origin signifies very little, for the Chymical Marriage was taken seriously enough by all who believed that early Rosicrucian documents were issued for the information of Europe by an illuminated secret Order which had been established for considerably more than a century.

The point with which I am concerned is to indicate in a few words, the hand of womanhood in the traditions of Hermetic practice, almost from the beginning of the experiments, which are connected with the idea of alchemy. And at the end, it is my design to suggest that behind the simple facts of the case, there is the suggestion of a great mystery. The legends of the art make mention of Semiramis, Queen of Egypt or rather of Nineveh, as the first woman who had attained the secret of transmutation, unless we assign a superior antiquity to Miriam, the prophetess and sister of Aaron, who was also an adept, according to a similar tradition, and who has indeed by repute bequeathed a tract on alchemy to the later followers of the quest. Passing from the region of mythos and coming to the fourteenth century of the Christian era, there is the case of Nicolas Flamel and his wife Peronella or Pemelle, who worked together on the hieroglyphical book of Abraham the Jew and were finally rewarded by the attainment of the entire secret. Another example, and apparently in this case a worker in solitude, was Leona Constantia, Abbess of Clermont, who according to a very curious testimony was received as a "master" into the Order of the Rosy Cross in the year 1736. It follows that at this period there were Sorores Rosea Cruets.

The most interesting evidence is contained, however, in the silent corroboration of picture-symbols. In the year 1677 there was published at Rupella a work entitled the Mutus Liber, or Dumb Book, the Book of the Silence of Hermes, wherein, as the title says, the whole Hermetic philosophy is represented by hieroglyphical figures apart from all letter-press. In the quaint Latin of the title, it is consecrated to the thrice-great-est and most merciful God, and it is dedicated to the Sons of the Art by an author whose assumed name is Altus. According to Lenglet du Fresnoy, it had great vogue among students, and it was faithfully re-printed by Mangetus in his folio collection entitled Bibliotheca Chymica Curiosa. He affirms in his analysis of contents that it is most evidently an opening of the mysteries of alchemy to the elect of that doctrine, and it consists of fifteen magnificent copperplates. The point which concerns us in the present connection is that the alchemist is represented working throughout in conjunction with a woman of the art: they begin and they attain together. The stages of the process are delineated in the succes-sive plates, and various symbolical personages appear to the workers for their encouragement and guidance, but more frequently to the woman than to the man, as if it were her task especially. One of them has the moon upon its left breast; another is Mercury manifesting.

I am reproducing four of the designs to illustrate the present text, and it will be seen that they are of singular interest. The first represents the symbolical ladder of Jacob, with angels descending thereon; they are in the act of sounding trumpets to awaken one who is asleep on the ground beneath, thus symbolizing the quickening of an artist who is called to the Great Work. The second plate shows that he has responded forthwith and has entered into consultation with a female collaborator, who is regarded as his wife. The metaphysical sun of philosophy is shining in the mid-heaven, and beneath it are two angels, having one foot on the land and another on the water, presumably to indicate that dryness and moisture both enter into the work. They are supporting a vessel in which the figures of the sun and moon appear in human form, with the god Vulcan seated between them, because the work is one of fire. At the bottom are the student of the art and his wife, kneeling on either side of a furnace and praying for success in their enterprise. The lamp at the base of the furnace indicates the gradual heat applied to the contents of the vessel suspended above. The third plate seems to put forward the theory of the work. The alchemical king is shown in the clouds of heaven, far out of human reach; below is the circle of research and the mode of operation therein. The sun and moon are like watchers on either side of the circle. The fourth and last plate is the completion, and it will be noted that Jacob's ladder, symbolizing the path of ascent from the earth of ordinary life to the heaven of philosophy, is now laid upon the ground because the work is done. The alchemical king of the third plate has been brought from heaven to earth; his flight is restrained by a rope which the adepts hold between them, and they are again kneeling, for they behold his glory with their eyes.

I regard this remarkable pictorial tract as perhaps the work of a Rosicrucian, though the surface evidence is only the appearance of roses in the symbolism. In 1788, a work entitled The Teaching of the Rosicrucian's in the Sixteenth and Seventeenth Centuries, published at Altona, contains a description of the alchemical practice which reads like an explanation of the second plate reproduced in this article. At the date in question, Rosicrucianism had been passing through a reform period and it is possible that there were two branches, one connected with Freemasonry and the other independent of that movement, though not disassociated therefrom in respect of its source. The first branch is represented by the evidence of a writer concealed under the name of Magister Pianco and also by the evidence of its rituals, which are still extant. They are positive proof that women were not admitted into this section of the Brotherhood. The evidence of the second branch is contained in a certificate concerning the admission of Dr. Sigismund Bacstrom into the Society of the Rosy Cross on September 12, 1794, his initiator being the Comte de Chazal and the place being Pampelavuso in the Island of Mauritius. The fourth clause of the postulant's undertaking certifies that worthy women are admitted as apprentices and as masters, if they possess the work practically and have accomplished it themselves. The grounds are (1) the manifestation of redemption to mankind by means of the Blessed Virgin and (2) the fact that there is no distinction of sexes in the spiritual world, neither among blessed angels nor rational immortal spirits of the human race. The document adds that the Rosicrucian's separated from the Freemasons in 1490.

The evidences with which we have been dealing concern solely the physical work of alchemy and there is nothing of its mystical aspects. The Mutus Liber is undoubtedly on the literal side of metallic transmutation; the memorials of Nicolas Flamel are also on that side; the Bacstrom certificate seems to contain no higher intimation, and he who was initiated on the date it bears is well known among students in England as a seeker of the physical mystery who has left many manuscripts behind him. I have further in my possession certain secret documents concerning the Comte de Chazal which seem final as to his dedications. There are, however, other intimations, and there is one which I will quote as most important of all, for it belongs to the Great Work on its mystical side. It is on record that an unknown master testified to his possession of the mystery, but he added that he had not proceeded to the work because he had failed to meet with an elect woman who was necessary thereto. I suppose that the statement will awaken in most minds only a vague sense of wonder, and I can merely indicate in a few general words that which I see behind it. Those Hermetic texts which bear a spiritual interpretation and are as if a record of spiritual experience present, like the literature of physical alchemy, the following aspects of symbolism: (a) the marriage of sun and moon; (b) of a mystical king and queen; (c) a union between natures which are one at the root but diverse in manifestation; (d) a transmutation which follows this union and an abiding glory therein. It is ever a conjunction between male and female in a mystical sense; it is ever the bringing together by art of things separated by an imperfect order of things; it is ever the perfection of natures by means of this conjunction. But if the mystical work of alchemy is an inward work in consciousness, then the union between male and female is a union in consciousness; and if we remember the traditions of a state when male and female had not as yet been divided, it may dawn upon us that the higher alchemy was a practice for the return into this ineffable mode of being. The traditional doctrine is set forth in the Zohar and it is found in writers like Jacob Boehme; it is intimated in the early chapters of Genesis and, according to an apocryphal saying of Christ, the kingdom of heaven will be manifested when two shall be as one, or when that state has been once again attained. In the light of this construction, we can understand why the mystical adept went in search of a wise woman with whom the work could be performed; but few there be that find her, and he confessed to his own failure. The part of woman in the physical practice of alchemy is like a reflection at a distance of this more exalted process, and there is evidence that those who worked in metals and sought for a material elixir knew that there were other and greater aspects of the Hermetic mystery.

Arthur Edward Waite - Forgotten Essays: Book Second

SIDE-LIGHTS ON JACOB BOHME

July, 2012

B LESSED are those who come in the name of the Lord, whatever capacity they fill. It is assuredly in no lesser name that Mr. C. J. Barker has undertaken his epoch-making reissue of the works of Jacob Böhme. One is thankful to know that it is proceeding duly and regularly on the course of publication. After the Threefold Life of Man, the Three Principles of the Divine Essence and the Forty Questions of the Soul, we are promised Aurora; and there is now little question that the noble venture will be carried to its term in triumph. The reissue is based on the best English version, being that of Sparrow, and not on the later, less intimate rendering which appeared anonymously and has often been attributed erroneously to William Law. But it has been throughout more than a mere reprint, and the later volumes are having the advantage of emendation by a lady—Mrs. D. S. Hehner—who has, I believe, been almost a life-long student of Böhme and is, moreover, familiarly acquainted with the German text. One is reminded of this important fact in turning over the leaves of a volume which has been included judiciously in the enterprise. It contains the contributions to the study of Jacob Böhme, which we owe to the zeal and insight of the late Mrs. A. J. Penny. She was also a lifelong and untiring student of the Teutonic Mystic; but her contributions to the subject were scattered through periodicals, one of which is no longer in existence, while that which remains among us is, of course, out of print in respect of issues belonging to the far past. It is dutiful rather than graceful to mention the journal in question—our contemporary Light—which, with an un-stinted liberality of spirit, gave space to Mrs. Penny's contributions at a period when students of Böhme among spiritualists could have been comparatively but very few. It is indeed to Light in the main, or more specifically to the insight and perhaps the personal interest of the Rev. Stainton Moses and Mr. E. Dawson Rogers, that we owe the existence of these papers, for in the days of Mrs. Penny there was practically no other periodical through which they could have been published Mr. Barker, in his preface, gives us the few facts which it is necessary to know concern-ing the writer, and he adds a memorial notice by the late C. C. Massey which seems to me an admirable specimen of that interesting mystic's style, outside the appeal of its subject in the present connection.

For my own restricted purpose, it must be sufficient to say that Mrs.

Penny was born in 1825, being a daughter of the Rev. Walter Brown, prebendary of Canterbury. She was first introduced to the works of Jacob Böhme in 1855; they became and remained her constant companions till her death in 1893—or a period of thirty-nine years. Her husband, Edward Burton Penny, was also an ardent student, and is remembered as the first translator of Saint-Martin. The writings here collected cover the years 1881 to 1892. Some of them are of considerable length and are elaborate studies or essays; others are occasional contributions which arose out of matters of current interest or consideration in the columns of Light. The statement suggests that the latter may be somewhat scrappy, but Mrs. Penny was thorough in her workmanship and it can be said that the least of her papers is a luminous presentation of Böhme doctrine on the subject which gave occasion to her pen. My friend the Rev. G. W. Allen is making a valiant and successful attempt in the pages of The Seeker to present the root matter of Böhme in intelligible terms to unfamiliar readers; and I am sure that he will agree with myself in regarding Mrs. Penny's two contributions toward the same end as of singular excellence within less comprehensive measures than his own. They are Jacob Böhme's Writings and Why are not Jacob Böhme's Writings Studied? Prefatory to both, there is an account of the German mystic, on the personal side, and this is of interest in its own degree.

The three papers open the present volume, and they should be taken in connection with Mrs. Penny's admirable criticism of Bishop Martensen's Life and Teaching of Jacob Böhme. Of the collection as a whole, unpremeditated as it is throughout, one can say that it will enable many to see better and further into Böhme's depths; I speak naturally of those who have not been searching for students of his work. It may seem at first sight that Mrs. Penny had taken into her heart a deliberate intention to make any and every occasion serve as a pretext for unfolding some view of her master, by hook or by crook, in the one available medium. Here it is "experiences in open vision," there a theory of "influx"; again, it is the Second Advent, a suggestion about "buried treasures," or a point of Hermetic interpretation arising from a book of my own. Well, if it were true that she worked in this way, it would have to be acknowledged that she worked well, for she leads up to her points with considerable natural skill. But the fact is, that Böhme took the universe at large for his subject, and whether a discussion of the moment in the columns of a weekly journal happens to be "unconscious creation," "spiritual evolution," the trance of life or "resurrection bodies," the lamp which he carried is somehow sure to cast light. One direction in which criticism does obtain is the extraordinary seriousness with which Mrs. Penny seems to have taken rather negligible and even illiterate correspondents. Her too easy recognition of certain exponents of false mysticism is another point. As regards the source of Böhme's revelation concerning revelation, Mrs. Penny's hypothesis may seem at first sight to be a spiritualistic explanation, however highly exalted. It was "one of the most remarkable cases of spiritual mediumship, in the highest sense"; he wrote "at the urgent dictate of an invisible guide"; he "wrote what was communicated to him."

The truth is, however, that in her view, and as she says indeed elsewhere, he was "a medium for the Holy Spirit." It was not, therefore, a personal guide who inspired him, in the sense that the Poughkeepsie seer and the ordinary trance-speaker have guides and controls, according to the testimony which their experience offers to themselves. Böhme himself understood the leading as that of God's Spirit. When it was with him, he wrote; in so far as it remained with him, he understood that which he wrote. When it left him, he not only wrote no more, but could understand nothing that he had expressed previously. "I know not my own labor and am made a stranger to the work of my hands." So, I presume, is anyone who is taught of the Spirit—whether mystics in the authorized sense or poets. It seems to me indeed that vestiges of the state in which Böhme received so much that it was given him to unfold in mighty books, is no uncommon thing. How many of us, "walking one day in the fields," as he did, or turning the comer of a street—it matters nothing—have found the mystery open suddenly and have known in a moment that which has baffled our thought previously. But we are not all of us such vessels of election as he was, and we receive enough only to show us how "the spark" does fall from heaven into the heart and mind of man; it is for few only that there is heaven's great flood of light.

A GATE OF ALCHEMY

October, 1912

I N an article on "Woman and the Hermetic Mystery," I gave some account of a Liber Mutus, Dumb Book, or Book of the Silence of Hermes, which claimed to expound in a series of copper-plate engravings the whole mystery of alchemy, apart from any thesis in writing. It was that branch of the mystery which belongs to the physical side, or the art of transmuting metals, and whether the most prepared of students could ever have attained the particular term of the Mastery by help of such kind on the path, must be left an open question. The work is very curious, and besides being curious is important on other considerations than its problematical value as a key of metallic regeneration. I indicated also that it is not the only record which has had recourse to instruction through the eye dwelling on pictorial symbols, either in the total absence of letterpress or making use of the latter only in an accessory sense. Another experiment of the kind, but this time, as we shall see, embodying mystical indications, is called Janitor Pansophus, and it appeared in the year 1578 as a section in fine of Museum Hermeticum Reformatum, a very important collection of Hermetic tracts, with an English translation of which I was concerned in 1893. It consists (a) of four folding plates, which the skill of the engraver has been able to reproduce in the present place by a careful process of reduction, and (b) of annotations thereon, being citations of scriptural passages and extracts from alchemical books, Janitor Pansophus signifies The All-Wise Doorkeeper, and the title further affirms that the four pictures exhibit analytically "the Mosaico-Hermetic science of things above and things below." It appears to have been prepared especially for its place in The Hermetic Museum, for there is no trace of separate publication.

The first question which arises concerning it is after what manner we are to understand its claim to unfold alchemical or indeed any other science. It is easy to see the intention on the surface of the plates, without invoking the help provided by the brief annotations. The first represents the Archetypal World, the ineffable abode of the Trinity, encompassed by the nine choirs of the Celestial Hierarchy. It is not exactly a Hermetic scheme, in any ordinary sense of the expression; it is rather representative of Dionysius the Areopagite so-called, and might be placed as a frontispiece to John Heywood's Hierarchy of the Blessed Spirits.

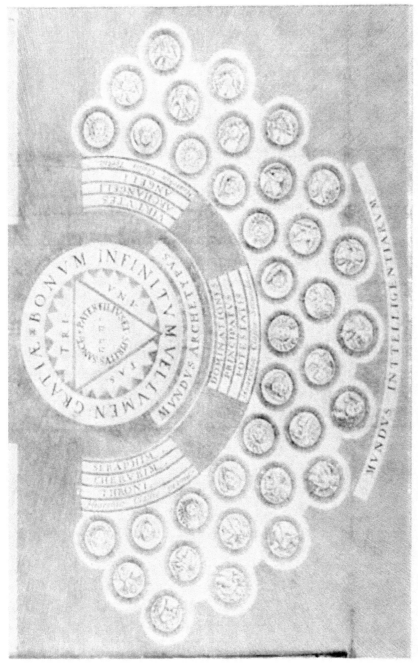

PLATE I The Archetypal World and World of Intelligences The Celestial Hierarchy encompassing the manifested Light of Divine Grace and Intimate Goodness. The Beatific Vision of the Trinity.

Persons who are acquainted with the fact that four worlds are recognized in Kabalism might speculate that they were presented figuratively in the four plates, when the one now under notice would correspond to Atziluth, the World of Deity, supposing that Kabalism were rectified, as it has often been, in one of the Christian alembics. There is, of course, a very obvious analogy for those who are unversed in the subject, but there is no real correspondence. It should not be necessary to add that— the text itself notwithstanding—the diagram is no more Mosaic than Kabalistic; it is the Christian scheme of the angelical world, which world is seen to be encompassing that Divine Center from which emanates the light, glory and rapture of the Blessed Vision. It is the doctrine of St. Thomas Aquinas projected in the form of a symbol. It will be seen that the angelical figures, each shining like a sun, but unquestionably as reflections from the Central Divine Sun, are presented in a number of aspects, the succession of which seems to follow a certain order; but it would be unwise to suggest that a particular emblematic meaning is to be sought in the variations.

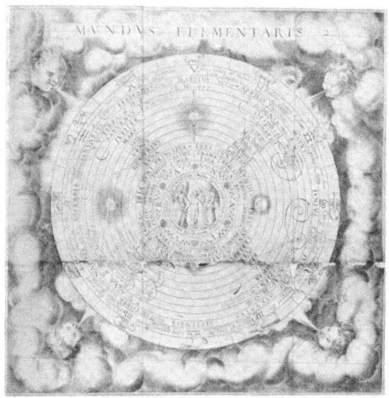

PLATE II.—The Elementary World, having Man in the centre, under the guard of Angels. The World of Nature and the Three Principles which operate therein. It is encompassed by the belt of the Zodiac.

The explanation is more probably to be found in the general conventionalism of design. The second plate represents the Elementary World, as it was understood by old cosmology, and its analogies are numerous enough in writings, like those of Robert Fludd. Again, they are surface analogies, for there are also important, almost essential, distinctions. It embodies the Hermetic concordance between the greater and lesser worlds, while its indications are valuable because of their comprehensive character. In the center of all is a human figure, having an angel on either side, surrounded by a Latin inscription which sets forth the doctrine of angelical custodians. The implicit is that God is the Centre of the archetypal world but man of that of the elements, and this is illustrated further by the third plate, which exhibits the development of creation in the symbolism of ten circles, beginning with the Divine—as it passes towards the activity of manifestation—and ending with the two aspects of humanity, male and female. The implicit is that God is the eternal Source, and man the term of creation. It should be observed that the two figures bear in their middle part the signs of the sun and moon, or the alchemical gold and silver, as if the Hermetic Mystery in its transcendence were a mystery behind sex, and as if the Great Work were the generation between them of that most perfect subject which is called the Son of the Sun in some allegories of the Art. The fourth plate furnishes the theory of alchemy, and it will be seen that the archetypal Adam and Eve again appear—not only bearing on their bodies the symbols already mentioned, but holding them in their hands, as if the work which they were meant to accomplish had been carried to its term. To indicate that it is a Divine work, the Eternal Father, represented by the Name Tetragrammaton, is shown at the apex; on one side is the Eternal Son, represented by the symbol of His incarnation—a lamb bearing a pennon; and on the other is the Eternal Spirit in the state of manifestation—that is, as a dove flying. Each human figure is held by a rope fastened to one of the wrists, and these bonds signify their attachment to the Divine in that supernal operation, which is depicted in summary above them.

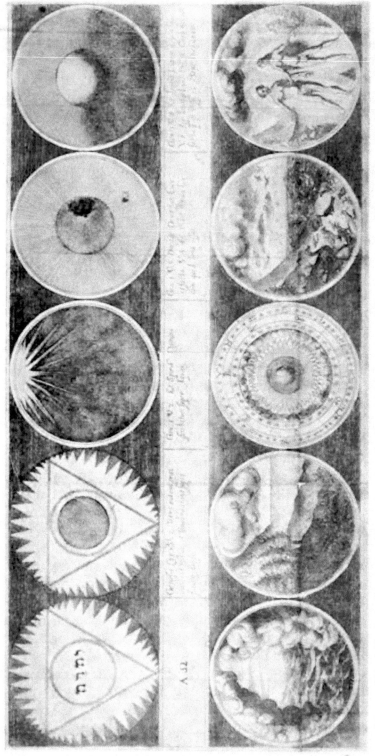

Plate III. The Development of Creation, showing how all things come forth by the *fiat of God*, with man as the object of all. The Scriptural references are to Genesis I. 2-14.

Like the Altus Liber Mulus, it is again a work accomplished between the man and the woman; but whereas in the latter hieroglyphics, the male and female characters are German alchemists of their period, they are here the catholic emblems of humanity at large, as if the design were to exhibit the true purpose of creation and the order which should have obtained. The two emblematical books are thus in an undesigned way the complement one of another, this representing the doctrine of the whole subject and that a particular sense in which it was attempted and fulfilled by two prepared students. But the analogy thus instituted will again be held to fail, because the pictures of the Liber Mutus are an allegory of the physical work, whereas these are mystical only; but it should be remembered that the work of metallic transmutation has been compared by the alchemists to that of God in creation, and that the stages of the one are affirmed to be an exact reproduction or counterpart of the other. We should remember also that alchemy in all its departments is dealing with matter which, ex hypothesi, is fallen, and that this is true indifferently of so-called base metals and of humanity in the base life. The thesis is that regeneration is an analogous process in every kingdom—that metals are reborn, transmuted, or redeemed, and that what happens in their case is not wanting in correspondence with the higher work of God in the soul.

The cryptic literature has not as yet been de-coded on the mystical side any more than on that of the physical; the broad and general lines are clear, but there is a veil over all the details; and I am almost the only investigator in this most difficult of fields. I am not, therefore, pretending to explain every feature in the diagrams with which I am dealing, and the attempt would take me far beyond the limits of a brief paper. The state of Adam and Eve in the tenth circle of the third plate must be compared with that of the fourth plate. They are clothed in the one with the Hermetic robe of glory, which means that they are in the state of Paradise; they are in the sublunary state in the other. The primary intention of the third plate is to show after what manner and for what reason man came forth from God; that of the fourth exhibits him, still indeed on this earth, but having undone the Fall therein. There is, however, another sense in which the third plate represents the stages in the conversion of the inward man, by which he passes from the natural chaos to the perfect order and union—opus catholicum indeed—great and catholic work—as Khunrath would term it.

I pass now to the Latin inscriptions which accompany the text of the pictures. The first is illustrated by a quotation from Marcellus Palingenius Stellatus, who wrote a Latin hexameter poem, once famous under the name Zodiac of Life. The extract is an appeal to the Creator of all things, that the suppliant may be directed in the right way. It reminds us of the Latin aphorism, which is also Hermetic: Laborare est orare.

To the second plate is appended a citation from Enchiridion Physicac Restitutae of Jean d'Espagnet, a tract which has always been held to be of great consequence in the records of alchemy. It regards Nature as the constant expression of the Divine Will.

PLATE IV.—The Theory of Mystical Alchemy.

The paradisical state is the true Nature, and its attainment is God's will in respect of humanity. The third plate is accompanied by a moving prayer of George Ripley, to whom Eirenaeus Philalethes owed so much of his light and leading. It asks for grace to know the blessedness and goodness of God, this being the only path to a "Knowledge of the Blessed Stone." All things were made by God "out of one chaos," and the artist seeks to evolve the microcosm of alchemy out of one substance, having three aspects, veiled by the names, magnesia, sulfur and mercury. The annotation to the fourth plate is the Emerald Tablet of Hermes, the doctrine of correspondence between things above and below, and the affirmation of the one substance wherein is "the glory of the whole world."

Alchemy is a secret science, using a veiled terminology, and it is not to be expected that these indications will prove intelligible on the surface. The true path of progress, or right way of Palingenius, in the mystic work, is that by which the seeker after eternal life becomes, by interior training, that which is Nature itself—an expression of the Divine Will, according to Jean d'Espagnet. The purpose is knowledge of God, in the sense that alchemists of either school spoke of knowledge of the Stone. It is possession in either case. The analogy instituted by Ripley between primeval chaos and the substance of art makes a harmony between the third and fourth plates of Janitor Pansophus. We see in the third how God's work proceeded in the making of the greater world, with triune man as the outcome; in the fourth, we see the same term attained by mystic alchemy. What is implied but not expressed in the two diagrams is that the transmuted state depicted in Plate IV is reached through successive inward stages comparable to those of Plate III. I must be content to summarize these in a single aphorism: The work of God in the soul is like that of God proceeding to the creation of Nature. On another occasion, and in connection with other forms of symbolism, I hope to explain these stages.

It would seem that the keeper of this particular "door of wisdom" bears the same testimony as other wardens of the portal, showing forth in his own manner that the intention of Nature is to make gold on all the planes of manifestation. He assists us to recognize, with every disciple of Hermes, that the same thing is everywhere—the same truth, the same possibility, the same grace of attainment and the same witness always in the world.

A HERMETIC APOCALYPSE

January, 1913

THE name of Heinrich Khunrath is rather a vague portent to most of us here in England, for his record in Hermetic archives was either in the Latin or German language, while he was somewhat disposed to the disastrous literary fashion set a few years previously by Paracelsus; that is to say, he interspersed his Latin with German, so that in his chief work he is a crux to the reader of either language only. When, therefore, the time came for his most important memorial to be put into a French vesture—now some years ago—I do not on my own part envy the competent translator to whom the task was committed. That rendering is unknown here, except by a very few indeed, and the rumor regarding Khunrath depends either from intimations given by myself or from references by Eliphas Levi, most of which I have been responsible for putting into English. The reader may be aware possibly that he was an alchemist, but of a strange, exotic kind, and it has been suggested, with a certain temerity, that he belonged to the Fraternitas R.C.. Eliphas Levi says that he is worthy in all respects to be saluted as a Sovereign Prince of the Rosy Cross, but this has to be understood in the symbolical and not the historical sense, as if it were a point of fact. The brilliant French occultist indeed specifies that he applies it scientifically or mystically, much as it might be conferred on himself. The title was, in any case, unknown to Rosicrucianism of the seventeenth century and is borrowed from a Masonic High Grade, belonging to a period which was very generous in the distribution of exalted dignities.

Khunrath was an illuminated Christian Kabalist, and insofar as the secret doctrine of the brotherhood may have set forth then, as later, the mystic theosophy of Israel under the light of the New and Eternal Covenant, so far the author of the Amphitheatre of Eternal Wisdom is on common ground with Rosicrucian's, with whom he has been for such reason identified. Being also, as I have said, an alchemist, though bizarre in his manner of expression, so far as the fraternity included Hermetic Mysteries among its implied possessions—which it did indeed and certainly—so far it was in a near relationship with the German philosopher.

THE ORATORY OF THE ALCHEMIST.

But Khunrath was born in or about the year 1560; he died in 1601, before Rosicrucianism had appeared on the horizon of history; and there is no evidence (a) that he was concerned in any secret movement which led up to its foundation, or alternatively (b) that he caused its antecedent existence to transpire, supposing that it is much older than the available records show. One student of the subject with whom I was once in correspondence—Dr. George Cantor, of Halle—even went so far in the opposite direction as to suggest that there is a veiled attack upon Khunrath in the Confessio Fraternitatis R.C., under the disguise of a stage player "with sufficient ingenuity for imposition." This tract belongs to the year 1615, when the death of the supposed subject of reference should have tended to shield his memory, while the period of time that had elapsed would have removed all point from the allusion, which is obviously to some man of the moment. Moreover, the mystical aspect of alchemy, which was the particular concern of Khunrath, should have drawn rather than repelled a society which protested against "ungodly and accursed gold making."

THE GATE OF ETERNAL WISDOM.

There is some evidence in his books that the alchemist was irascible enough, and abusive like Thomas Vaughan, in dealing with those from whom he differed, but there is nothing tangible to show that he made a figure at his period. How obscure he was is indeed evident from the few facts which have transpired concerning him. He was a native of Saxony who led the wandering life of so many struggling physicians before his day and after. Having taken his degrees at Basle, he made a certain stay at Hamburg and ultimately settled at Dresden, where he is said to have died in poverty at about 42 years of age. He published three small tracts in 1599; one was entitled Symbolum Physico Chemicum; another was on the Catholic Magnesia of the Philosophers; and the third was on the alchemical Azoth, by which he understood the First Matter of creation, otherwise, the Mercury of the Wise. One of them at least was reprinted in the eighteenth century, but there is nothing to suggest that they were important at their own epoch, in the opinion of that epoch. His really great work did not appear till 1609. He is to be distinguished from Conrad Khunrath, another writer on alchemy, who began to publish about 1605 and may have been his kinsman, but I have no particulars concerning him.

It is the Amphitheatre of Eternal Wisdom which occasioned some glowing panegyrics by Eliphas Levi, who also chose for the motto on the title-page of his enchanting History of Magic the definition which Khunrath gives of his own book, opus hierarchicum et catholicum—a catholic and hierarchic work. He points out, however, that in the matter of official religion, the German theosopher was a resolute Protestant, adding that herein he was "a German of his period rather than a mystic citizen of the eternal kingdom." Perhaps this is more an aphorism than an apology; but Levi recognized assuredly that on another side of his nature Khunrath abode in the freedom of the spiritual Zion and not under the aegis of reform, in Germany or otherwise. I have long felt that his apocalyptic presentation of the Kabalistic and Hermetic Mystery should be known among Students of the Doctrine in England, but the brief notice which is possible in the present place can only summarize the design.

I offer to the consideration of my readers three reduced plates out of the total series of nine most curious engravings on copper which form an integral part of the work with which I am concerned. They represent (1) the Oratory of an Alchemist, the device belonging to which is laborare est orare; (2) the Gate of Eternal Wisdom, being that of the Knowledge of God; and (3) the sum and substance of the whole work, termed by Eliphas Levi the Rose of Light; but this is the explanation of one symbol in the terms of another. It is the central point of all wisdom, human and Divine, which point is Christ. The suggestion of the designs as a whole is that the work of the alchemist belongs to the path of devotion, notwithstanding (a) the material vessels with which the kneeling figure is surrounded in the first and on which his back is turned somewhat significantly; (b) the message of the Latin dictum—that work is prayer. I conclude that here inward work is adumbrated. The suggestion of the second plate is that the Gate of Wisdom is one which is opened by prayer, but the latter is not to be understood in any formal and conventional sense. It opens in the darkness and seems like a journey to the center, meaning the inward way and the great path of contemplation.

The third design indicates that Christ is not only the Way but the Truth, understood centrally, and the very Life itself. This is the Christ of Glory, no longer the Man of Sorrows and acquainted with infirmity. Yet is He still in the human likeness, not the Mystic Rose in the center of the Macrocosmic Cross.

THE VISION AT THE CENTRE.

The reason is that as what is called theologically and officially, the scheme of redemption is an operation within humanity, for the manifestation of a glory to be revealed, so in its utmost attainment humanity is not set aside. The Christ manifest is not apart from the Lord of glory, and the Christ within is ever the Son of man in us. So also, our great Exemplar in Palestine could not do otherwise than come to us in human form, or He would have been never our pattern and prototype. He could not do otherwise than speak in the clouded symbols of our earthly language, or He would have brought us no message. There seems no question that in the opinion of Khunrath the knowledge of Christ gave that of the Philosophical Stone, in the ordinary alchemical understanding of this term, for a medicine of metals and of human nature, but he deals on his own part only with the mystic side of attainment, though in such language that it shall preserve the likeness of alchemy. Many of the old seekers may have sought to understand him literally and went astray accordingly.

The thesis is veiled under the guise of a new translation, with commentary, of certain passages extracted from the Book of Proverbs and the Apocryphal Book of Wisdom, the versicles being arranged so that there shall be one for each day of the year, and each with its annotation might well afford food for thought even at this time and amidst all the hurry of our ways. The new rendering—as such—is, I think, negligible, but it is printed side by side with the Vulgate. The commentary explains that in alchemy, as in religion, Man is the Matter which must be purified, the physical part being brought into subjection by that which is within and above. God is the soul which vivifies; the Holy Spirit is the bond of union that leads to the Everlasting Kingdom and gives admission therein through the work of regeneration. The part of co-operation which lies with the alchemist must be performed in the deeps and solitude of his own spirit, separated from sensible things, as by a withdrawal into God. The way of contemplation and Divine colloquy will open the Book sealed with Seven Seals—which is the Divine Book of the Scriptures, Nature and the Self. The end is a marriage of Divine Wisdom with the soul, and therein is the Blessed Vision wherein all things are beheld.

In addition to the allegorical plates, the text already mentioned and the commentary, there are some curious tables, and the significance of one is likely to escape the penetration of all but the most careful reader. It is a summary of the whole subject; and it suggests that those who are called to the work should realize, under Divine leading, that the knowledge (a) of God, (b) of Christ Whom He has sent, (c) of the greater world, (d) of the Self within each of us, and (e) of the Stone sought by the Wise under so many names, is one knowledge which is attained by one gift within ourselves, as in a clear mirror or fountain.

Such was mystic alchemy at the beginning of the seventeenth century and on the threshold of the Rosicrucian Mystery.

A MODERN MAGUS

February, 1913

T HERE is probably no name in the annals of modern occultism to compare in repute and celebrity with that of Eliphas Lévi, the so-called Abbé Constant. So far as England, America and the English-speaking colonies and dependencies are concerned, I suppose also—if it be worthwhile to do so—that the writer of these lines has been the instrument-in-chief for the diffusion of that knowledge which exists concerning him. As a result, Lévi is more familiar among us than in foreign countries, his own France excepted. I am registering a fact, not claiming a title of honor. Before I took him in hand for translation, he had been the subject of casual reference in Isis Unveiled, in Nineteenth Century Miracles, and the list is almost exhausted by these works. In periodical literature, Kenneth Mackenzie had printed what may be called an interview in some Transactions of the Masonic Rosicrucian Society; an old issue of Temple Bar had derided him in a kind of review, and this again is, I think, all. At the present moment, readers of occult literature might almost say that he is "familiar in our mouths as household words." I am not intending to exaggerate the esteem in which he is held, for such esteem varies, while if I am to be classed among those who love his memory, it is known that I am not his disciple and that when presenting him in an English vesture I have taken care that he should appear in a true light respecting his attainments, position and claims. Among his old disciples in France—for example, Dr. Papus—he remains an acknowledged master; masters seem necessary there as a kind of hall-mark which serves to classify, while it also provides status. There are, however, occasional Messiahs—prophets of modes to come—and these are content with precursors. Of such was Lévi, and Hoene Wronski, who discovered the Absolute in 1839, and endeavored to sell it much above the market-price recognized in houses of exchange, was unconsciously his John the Baptist. A few people at the present day are beginning to wake up in England to the fact of poor Wronski and to discover that he was remarkable after his own manner. I made a dip in the old days into his particular lucky-bag of mysteries. The experiment was unprofitable personally, and I might have sought consolation in Balzac's Recherche de l'Absolu; but I came upon the Messiah Constant, and, so long as I dwelt in the kingdom of occult science, to go further was not to fare better.

I have called him at the head of this article, a Modern Magus. He is to the manner born absolutely. Desbarolles read his hand and said that it bore every sign and seal by which his kind of dedication is revealed under the light of chiromancy. I had no need for its instruction when I met with the Doctrine and Ritual of Transcendental Magic. But the literary precursor of Eliphas Lévi was Alphonse Louis Constant—otherwise, his own self—in books which have now perished; and they prove him a magus in words before, in his own opinion and that of many others, he became a magus in science.

ELIPHAS LÉVI.

There are passages in Le Bible de la Liberté and Les Trois Malfaiteurs which contain spells of enchantment very curiously woven. His occult works are jeweled with talismans of this kind. One of my critics—it was The Saturday Review, if I remember rightly—said that he was never happy unless he was wrapping up a paradox in an epigram; this has a side of truth, but still more numerous are the epigrams which convey insight; while if these are gems, let me add that there are also stars, by which I mean his great luminous dicta on great and pregnant subjects—on eternal truths of morality, on the higher aspirations of the soul, on the large and gracious charity of the enlightened mind. Where I called upon to do one more book about Lévi, I should like it to be his Golden Book. I should forget that he had written upon Magic, upon things called Kabalah and Tarot; I should give his wise aphorisms, his doctrines of light in the heart, his religion of the liberated mind. It would not be a big book, but it might prove one for all time; I think that it should be printed in gold on skins of vellum and bound in white linen, like "the righteousness of saints." I am concerned, however, with another enterprise, and one of sufficient magnitude, being a complete translation of Lévi's History of Magic, rendered and annotated by myself. Publication will take place under the auspices of Messrs. William Rider & Son prior to the March issue of the Occult Review. It realizes a project which has been rather long in my mind. In The Key to the Tarot, published in 1910, I said that it was "the most comprehensive, brilliant, enchanting History of Magic which has ever been drawn into writing." Here is justification enough, according to all canons, and yet it is not my reason, though an excellent setting for this. No book written with authority so presents the claims of its subject that it is possible for the mystic to join hands with the magus over his explanation of facts. This is the reason which has prompted me. The facts of Magic, results which follow evocations, witchcrafts, the darksome processes of Grimoires and Keys of Solomon are neither explained by Levi as mere imposture nor elevated to the plane of veridic phenomena. Most are delusion, and that delusion is largely of the self-induced kind; but there remains a proportion to be accounted for in another manner—by the exteriorization of the psychic body, above all, by ¡an occult force postulated under the name of the Astral Light and held to be put in motion either by the will of the magus or through the abnormal gifts of mediums, as the case may be. What does not happen in either case is that the dead return to testify, or that communication is established with angels, demons, elementaries or planetary spirits. These are findings of research, and on this basis, the author gives his construction of Magic throughout the centuries. It is with this that I, as a mystic, am in substantial agreement; it is so much proof that those in search of certitude over spiritual things will only lose their time in the region of occult phenomena. In justification to myself, I have wished to make this point clear, lest the question should arise why I, as a mystic, have undertaken such a task. I have therefore written the present notice as a kind of Advertisement from Eleusis concerning the forthcoming work.

It may be reviewed in the usual way after publication in these as in other pages, and I hope that the fact will be remembered. I have made it plainer in the preface, where I have taken further occasion to dwell upon the value of the testimony, the general importance of the book, and to distinguish those matters over which I differ from Levi. He believed, like myself, in the existence of a secret tradition and that Kabalistic literature was one of its channels; but we are not in concurrence over the nature of the tradition or the date of its records. Readers of the History of Magic will be guided by their own judgment, and there are some who may be captivated by the glamor of the author's imaginative views rather than by my critical modifications, especially on certain points. Among numerous plates in the volume, I have chosen certain designs to illustrate this article.

THE SEVEN WONDERS OF THE WORLD.

Arthur Edward Waite - Forgotten Essays: Book Second

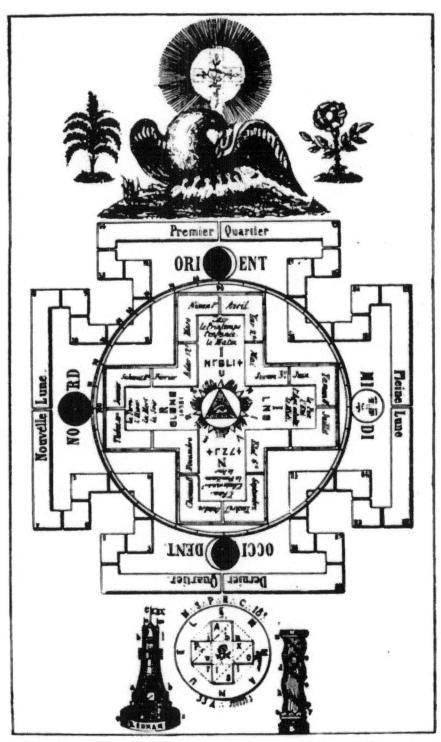

THE PHILOSOPHIC CROSS, OR PLAN OF THE THIRD TEMPLE
PROPHESIED BY EZEKIEL.

THE GREAT HERMETIC ARCANUM.
(After Basil Valentine.)

Arthur Edward Waite - Forgotten Essays: Book Second

Levi supposes the secret tradition to have been embodied in stone monuments, and he summarizes this idea in sketching the Seven Wonders of the World. He believes that the Knights Templar were a heretical sect in conspiracy to rebuild the Temple at Jerusalem and overthrow the papacy. He outlines therefore their plan of a Third Temple, and I have reproduced it here. Personally, I might regard the chivalry as more important than it was, did I think this true in fact. The last plate is the Hermetic Arcanum, one of the Keys of Basil Valentine, and it was used by Levi to illustrate his theory of alchemy.

He believed, like myself, that it had two aspects—one physical, the other symbolical—but this he explained in a moral rather than a spiritual sense. I have given also a portrait of the Magus, which is said to be in the robe of a magician, but it is really a fantastic garment. I should add that the History is divided into seven books, beginning with the traditional foundation of Magic during the period covered by the Book of Genesis and ending practically at the epoch of publication in 1860. The later sections and, speaking generally, the modern aspects of the subject, from the time of the French Revolution, will be found of particular interest. In conclusion, Alphonse Louis Constant was the son of a poor shoemaker in Paris; he was schooled with a view to the priesthood, but did not take final orders. He was always attached to the Latin Church and always insisted on his orthodoxy; but all doctrine was for him a veil and symbol—a view which would have been condemned by the Church, had it been brought to its notice.

A DAUGHTER OF DESIRE

June, 1913

WE are living in an age when "God fulfills Himself in many ways," and if some of them are the old ways, under honored sanctions of the past, it is for us to recognize the fulfillment wherever we meet with it, in a true Catholicism of the heart. Assuredly there are many witnesses to the great truths, and if there were several centuries of this western world of ours when the testimony to the life of life was uttered only from within monastic walls, we should feel no sense of astonishment that there are witnesses still within them. If we have found on our own part that there are many paths which may lead to the center, those which were traveled of yore by innumerable sons and daughters of Divine Doctrine are not for that reason to be held as henceforth of no service in respect of the end proposed. I am speaking, of course, to those who realize—in whatever measure—that there is a life of the soul possible on earth by the following of which it can enter into the experience of God dwelling within the soul. It is more than probable that their understanding of the kind of life is remote from that of asceticism; in the ordinary meaning of the word, I hold no brief for its defense as the best way at the present epoch of the world, much less as the only way; but I have before me the memorial of one whose name is filling at this moment the whole world of Latin Catholicism, the episcopal process of whose beatification was closed in 1911, is now in the hands of the Sacred Congregation of Rites at Rome and will be followed by the Apostolic or Roman Process, the result of which is probably regarded as certain by thousands of devoted hearts. Marie Françoise Thérèse Martin was born on January 2, 1873, and she died of consumption on Thursday, September 30, 1897, in her twenty-fifth year. She is, therefore, in the plenary sense of the term a contemporary instance of that which is represented by her life, the external particulars of which, for the purpose of this brief notice, can be given in a few words.

THÉRÈSE WITH HER MOTHER.

She was a child of profoundly religious parents and bearing from her tenderest years all signs, characters and seals of an uncommon election, she had leave—after much difficulty, involving appeals to the Bishop of Bayeux and Pope Leo XIII himself—to enter the Carmelite Convent of Lisieux at the age of fifteen. This was on April 9, 1889; in conventual language, her "clothing day" was on January 10 of the year following, and she was "professed" on September 8, 1890. It was not long before the charge of the novices passed into her youthful hands. The life and the spirit have naturally evaporated in this bald recital, nor can I say that the book itself conveys more than an intimation of the influence which she exercised within the "Carmel" walls of her dedication. It is rich, however, beyond words in other and more essential respects. It contains in the first place her own "story of my soul," and this memorial is of permanent and living value. It is followed by an account of her death by the Prioress of the Carmel, extracts from her correspondence and certain other writings. Most of the remaining pages are concerned with events after her death which have made her name something like a household word throughout the Romain Catholic world.

Now, it is out of the simple and general matters of fact so far related that the two main points of our concern arise; one is the manner in which Sœur Thérèse appeals to the mystics, while the other is her alleged connection with extraordinary phenomena which are here and now among us. In respect of the first, her rule of life was the perfect and zealous pursuit of the severe regimen prescribed by the Carmelite Order, and she raised it in her own case far beyond the ordinary formal degrees. Whether we like it or not, the lesson which her story conveys is the quality, depth and extent of the graces which remains in the ascetic path for those who are still called to follow it. I speak as a Christian mystic and as an apostle of the other ways, believing that she might have reached her term otherwise, yet recognizing her particular fitness for that state in which the Divine called her. I need not add that such practices are of themselves nothing; it is the motive which makes them aids. Her secret from the beginning was the all-secret of love, and this is why I have called her—in the words of Richard Crashaw—a "daughter of desire." It was in virtue of love that she could say that "days of earth become days of Heaven." She spoke also of "the delicious fruits of perfect love and of complete abandonment to the Divine will." With her, it was loving union in the mode of the purified mind. She was spared for the most part the "visions" and "lovutions." It must be said also that her experience was rather by the way of faith in the childlike spirit than by mystical realization understood in the sense of the mystics, and this notwithstanding that she found high lights in the works of St. John of the Cross. Her first reception of the Eucharist was the great turning-point in her story, and this is why I have chosen her portrait on that day as one of the illustrations to this article. One cannot help feeling that there are many beautiful and sacramental signs which cover the same holy, deep and mysterious things, and yet, amidst all, there is not less the convinced sense that there is no mode practiced in the external religions which so helps towards realization of the Divine inwardly as the Eucharistic rite of the Latin Church. On the day of her First Communion "all the joy of Heaven" came down into the heart of Thérèse and Heaven itself dwelt in her soul.

The beginning thus made was continued to the end with ever-growing frequency and fervor. It was doubtless thereby and therein that she was truly in touch with the infinite and had the gift of being lost therein. So also, her story is one of stages in "the science of love"—an expression of B. Margaret Mary Alacoque. Thérèse reached the fulness of the state of love on June 9, 1895, and so found that her vocation was love simply. But that was a question of consciousness, for this had been her call from the beginning; and hereto was due her valiant chivalry of aspiration, by virtue of which she dared, even as a child, to be a saint in resolve, dared to believe that she was "born for great things," said to herself ever and continually: "I shall be a great saint." Yet the valiance was one of all humility—in virtue of the vesture of Christ. So also, she was catholic in the best sense, in the encompassing sense of love. The whole of the Christian world, that world which she could enfold with love in her consciousness, became to her a garden of the soul and a "living garden" of the Lord. Though she called herself only "a little flower," she reminds one rather of that lady, "the wonder of her kind," who tended "from mom to even" a certain paradise known to the poet Shelley. Thérèse nourished her garden with her love, watered it with her prayers, offered up her many sufferings because of it, filled it with the graces of her days, while those whom she brought to God were the flowers of her tending. And so, at last, God called her by the "death of love." The Prioress of the Carmel says: "Suddenly she raised herself, as though called by a mysterious voice. . . . Thus, she remained for about the space of a Credo, when her blessed soul . . . was borne away" — a victim of Divine Love, as the Prioress says also.

Here is the first point at some length, but of the second I must speak shortly. The desire of Thérèse was to "spend my Heaven in doing good upon earth," to "come down" to her friends, to spread the love of Christ, her Spouse, more fully and more perfectly among men than was possible within the narrow measures of personal life in this world. "After my death I will let fall a shower of roses," and the book says that the graces" attributed to her intercession" are innumerable. They are conversions, physical healings, escape from death, accident averted, even gifts of money. I suppose that the cures of the sick will be most important as evidence to those in search of such things; they include cancer, loss of vision, elephantiasis—among others numberless. I do not adjudicate upon the value of any; that which is given the place of first importance is comparable with certain phenomena of modern spiritualism; an apparition is included, and the transportation of money and notes. The beautiful life of "the little flower of Jesus" is at least becoming known by these means, while, of course, those that are purely spiritual in their compass are of an order which is familiar in the annals of the saints, and they are distinct from psychical happenings.

THE SERVANT OF GOD.

A MASTER OF THE INWARD WAY

November, 1913

STANDING at that point where two strange paths of life and thought and research divide once and for ever, Louis Claude de Saint-Martin said to Martines de Pasqually, his theurgic teacher: "Master, can all this be needed to find God?" The adept in transcendental Masonry and practical occultism answered: "We must even be content with what we have," and I have always regarded this as a memorable maxim, the force and application of which is with us in most of our daily ways and continually in the world of thought. The consequence was that instructor and pupil found that their ways divided. It was a memorable parting, a very memorable talk which led to that parting, and it has a message to us amidst the psychic and mystic activities of the present day. I do not know whether there has been previously a stage of human development on more than a single plane when the distinction thus created was more important in its application to us or when it was illustrating itself more fully, though all unconsciously, in numerous types of minds. Like so many of us here and now, Saint-Martin—then at the beginning of his public career, young, zealous and accomplished—had come already to know quite clearly that which he desired, namely, "the finding of God," but about the way to that goal—also like many of us—he was not in a state of certitude. This was made evident by his question of whether this and that were necessary, and his interlocutor told him virtually that there was no other path. It was a reference to the occult path, and it cast Saint-Martin back upon himself, so that he had to reconsider what is meant by the finding of God.

He did not now question any master outside himself, but began to look into his own nature, his inward being, and there saw—as he could not do otherwise—that the quest did not lie in this direction or in that of the external world, but in his own consciousness. He had heard already that God is within, as we have heard also from time immemorial, but he had to learn that which it means, as we have to learn also. He saw that so long as he postulated—shall I say?—a Deity on a great white throne, facing a crystal sea, and speculated as to whether he could bridge the distance intervening, by the hypothesis, between the earth-bound man living in the light of the material sun, and this paradise of Dante, place of Beatific Vision and heaven of thrones and palaces, he was planning an impossible journey, because consciousness, as here ensphered, does

LOUIS CLAUDE DE SAINT-MARTIN.

not reach other worlds by traveling through an intermediate space. But if the throne of God is in our consciousness, then the journey is in ourselves only and not through stellar distances. It is a travel undertaken in the region of realization—that great of all mystery words. We hear much at this day of unexplored fields within us, under the name of sub-consciousness, but little if anything of that alternative realm which I should call the supra-consciousness—supposing that I were so unwise as to rectify one unphilosophical catchword by another.

There is neither height nor depth, nor are there any other spatial relations, in the conscious self, but there are grades of realization, and the so-called depth and height of the mystery of the knowledge of God are a grade ne plus ultra which we have most of us failed to take because of the multiplicity of trivial and distracting business in which we are immersed by our overweening concern in the external. So far, I have been creating what may be termed a distinction only between two personalities of a period, both of whom were remarkable and both attractive in their way. It was in the great and spacious days of a thousand activities in France prior to the French Revolution. Martines de Pasqually was traveling with a Masonic Rite from a place beyond the Pyrenees, or perhaps further, he being presumably of Spanish origin, though it is not certain. Saint-Martin was a gentleman of Touraine, somewhat over thirty years, when the instructor and pupil met. Let us take from another witness a short account of the one that we may the better be able to judge what it meant to the other when he decided to try a fresh path. The Abbé Fournié was also a follower of Pasqually, and he says of the latter that his daily exhortations were towards unceasing aspiration to God, growth in virtue and zeal for the universal good. Here is the question of fact, because the witness—by all that we know concerning him—spoke with the lip of truth. His inference was that such words of counsel were comparable to those of Christ, though apart from all authority claimed for himself by the speaker. Now, the Rite of Pasqually, though it made pretensions of a kind that were common at the period, not merely in respect of its antiquity—which may be taken in a symbolical sense—but as to its superior position when compared with all other Masonic or pseudo-Masonic Orders and Degrees—the name of which was legion—had nothing whatsoever to do with any art of building symbolized, but was a system of ceremonial magic, the creator of which had conceived a daring project to draw within the circle of communication the great Master of Nazareth, understood as the "Active and Intelligent Cause charged with the conduct of the visible universe."

In the belief of the brotherhood, success attended the project, and long years after Saint-Martin had detached himself from all such ways and processes, he bore testimony to a correspondent that he had been present at communications where "every sign indicative of the 'Repairer' was present." I need only add that for Saint-Martin the Repairer signified Christ. The question which arises is how in the face of such testimony came he who bore it to choose another path, more especially when he put on record the fact that he and his teacher were only" beginning to walk together" when death removed the latter. What must be called an answer to the question is found elsewhere, when he says: (1) "I cannot affirm that the forms which shewed themselves to me may not

MARTINES DE PASQUALLY.

have been assumed forms"; and (2) "I have received by the inward way truths and joys a thousand times higher than those I have received from with certain circumstances of private life caused Pasqually to leave his circle of initiation; he was called into remote places and never returned to France. That he was the vital center of whatever communion was established is shewn by the fact that it all came to an end in his absence; his rite of Masonry vanished or was absorbed; Saint-Martin followed his own course and became not so much the foremost as the only memorable mystic of his country in that day.

COURT DE GÉBELIN.

Arthur Edward Waite - Forgotten Essays: Book Second

The name of Martines de Pasqually remains among a few in France and otherwhere as of interest to the history of occultism, but that of Saint-Martin, I think, has a permanent and high place. At that most un-mystical of all periods, the first half of the nineteenth century, he was recognized by Chateaubriand as a man of extraordinary merits; by Comte Joseph de Maistre as "the most instructive, the wisest and most eloquent of modern theosophists"; by Mme. de Staël as a writer with "sublime gleams." The philosopher Cousin testified that never had mysticism possessed in France "a representative more complete, an interpreter more profound and eloquent, or one who exercised more influence than Saint-Martin." Joubert said that his feet were on earth and his head in heaven, while even the brilliant critic Sainte-Beuve, far as he was from all transcendental interests, admitted that he calls for study.

JACQUES CAZOTTE, THE AUTHOR OF *Le Diable Amoureux.*

Lastly, an open and perhaps unscrupulous enemy of all that savored of mystery and mystic association—the Scottish anti-Mason, Professor Robison—affirmed that Saint-Martin's first book was a Bible or Talmud at least for the French High Grade Masons on the eve of the Revolution. In the most interesting of all literary periods which had ever been seen by France, amidst great awakenings to the messages of instituted mysteries and possibilities of the soul in its manifestation, Saint-Martin stood alone in respect of his dedications and their appeal. Mesmer and the varied tribe of his followers were about him on one hand. There was Court de Gebelin, a distinguished archaeologist for his period, a discoursing of Egypt and its wonders, and discovering vestiges of immemorial antiquity in Tarot cards, found among peasantry by an accident. There was the brilliant littérateur Cazotte, who will be always remembered in his own country as the author of Le Diable Amoureux, a romance with such prodigious intuitions of an occult kind that he is said to have been accused by adepts of betraying those mysteries into which he had not been initiated. There was Cagliostro, whom the mystic distrusted with all his heart; and although that comet of a season, the Comte de St. Germain, had long since vanished from the horizon, the dazzlement of his memory remained. There is reason to believe that Saint-Martin knew all these, and beyond them there were his personal friends, many distinguished in their way. There were Rodolph de Salzmann, a mystic like himself; the Russian prince Galitzin, who confessed that he had not been a man till he knew M. de Saint-Martin; the Comte d'Hauterive, following the occult path, but discerning under his friend's influence a horizon beyond it.

On the side of philosophy Saint-Martin connects with Pasqually, in the sense that the teachings of the latter passed through the alembic of the mystic's mind, issuing under I know not what transmuted forms, but in a way that made them his own after a particular manner. He connects also with Jacob Bohme, whose writings came into his hands in much later life, and there are cer¬tain rare translations, much prized by their possessors, which bear on their titles the name of the "Unknown Philosopher"—that is to say, of Saint-Martin—whose zeal for a "beloved author" had led him to render them into French. The Aurora, Three Principles, Forty Questions, and Threefold Life of Man constitute the series, and one is faintly surprised that they have not been republished in France; but as much might be said of Saint-Martin's own works, so many of which still remain unedited—not to speak of the treasures which are

The Comte de Saint Germain.

held in private hands and have never been printed at all. But it is neither to Pasqually nor Bohme that we owe Saint-Martin as a mystic. The one had little to offer beyond the freedom, to those who could win it, of the region of astral forces; the messages, from however deep a center, of the other came to the French theosophist long after he had found his own way and had placed his experience somewhat fully on record. He had two counsels: (1) To explain material things by man and not man by material things—descending into ourselves for this purpose; and (2) to establish a correspondence between the soul and the Divine by the active part of works. So far as schools are concerned, he was essentially a Christian mystic, though to all intents and purposes he had left the official churches. The life of Christ was for him the history of regeneration in the soul of each individual, and in one of his most important books, he has traced all its stages.

In conclusion, there are two points to be marked regarding this mystic, and one of them—so far as I am aware—has not been expressed previously. The mystics who have been also men or women of vision, seers in the psychic sense, may have been the rule rather than the exception; it was a beginning which somehow; I know how scarcely, may have helped them to open the doors which give entrance to the inward light, into that state where they realize that the soul's eye is not satisfied with this kind of seeing and the soul's ear is not filled with this kind of hearing—that is to say, with the vision and audition so called in the theological science of mysticism. Saint-Martin in the presence of the Repairer recalls such experiences. But the experiences of sanctity in the world of psychic phenomena are one thing, while occult phenomena are another; and Saint-Martin is the sole instance on record of a great mystic who began his career amidst occult and magical practices. This is the first point, and the second is, that albeit he saw the dangers, uncertainties and manifold deceptions of the phenomenal path, and though he left it forever, he always bore testimony to the zeal, the sincerity, the capabilities and high dedications of that master whom he followed therein, when occasion called thereto.

THE WAY OF THE SOIL IN HEALING

January, 1914

IT is possible to attain "a personal and conscious co-ordination with the inscrutable action of the Cosmic Will," and herein lies the way of the soul in the work of physical healing, as there lies also the way of the mystic life. The quotation is from a book which is in several respects remarkable, and may prove epoch-making because of all that is comprised by its intimations of great spiritual laws working in the manifest human order. On account of it, I am about to take a little journey far from my usual paths, the explanation of such an adventure lying obviously in the fact that I have found a vista beyond it, stretching from the known to the unknown. I am not, however, pretending to open a new track nor to discover a horizon which has lain previously under clouds or veils. Had I been questioned two years or more ago as to my opinion of spiritual healing, psycho-therapy, mind cure and the fundamental implicits on which Christian Science may be held to rest, I should have said that it was comparable to my political opinions, being a collection of prejudgments justified by a large ignorance, in which I looked to continue. That is like the city gentleman—quite good and straight of his kind—who, being offered eternal life, replied that he had already too much business on hand. Perhaps I should go further and confess that my sympathies were with the saintly abbot who built his monastery in a marsh, because the practice of interior life was likely to prove unsuccessful if married to rude health in his company of monks. To put it more seriously, I was among those who—

Saw that strong thews and nerves of earth

Win hardly towards the second birth.

There. I have quoted from one of my own poems, contrary to the canons of good taste, but it is only to illustrate my position. Having a leaning towards logic in practice as well as in life, I used my physical instruments as tools of the mind, and disregarded their reasonable needs, hoping that they would serve my purpose, but taking the chance as it stood. The results are a little concern of my own and none of my readers; but interested friends said: "I told you so." Naturally, l could have told them. Meanwhile, the work which it is given me to do was in the course of doing. Now, there are many salvations, and some of them are without desert. I met with Dr. Elizabeth Severn, possibly because she is a daughter of the West and I am a Son in Exile.

DR. ELIZABETH SEVERN.

This was in the early stages of her visit to England. She came with many titles as a practical exponent of physical healing by mind methods, and I found that she was establishing her repute here on a substantial basis of fact. In these things I must confess that I had little concern, but I was arrested by what I must term her philosophical point of view, in which it seemed that "new thought" had entered into a wider field, if it had not experienced transfiguration. I found that her world of practice was related to a world of thought, which, although it was not mine, was somewhere in the same region and was certainly a mystic sphere. In her own terminology, it was essentially idealistic; but the idealism had somehow a freshness, as others will feel when they read the book which she has written. To make an end of my own story, being "an ambitious student in ill health," I accepted her willing proposal to restore my physical balance, as she felt that she could. That is no ordinary power which works in her simple processes, and the result is an almost startling restoration, accompanied by renewed mental freshness. To bear this testimony is a matter of common justice, more especially as I brought with me no living faith, except in her utter sincerity, and my detachment could not have been encouraging.

Dr. Elizabeth Severn's Psycho-Therapy is a remarkable book, as I have said. One point of interest is the course which she has marked out for herself in writing it. In the art of "healing the body through the mind," she saw that the records of the past fall into two divisions: (a) simple tabulations of fact, accompanied by somewhat arid explanatory hypotheses; (b) works of enthusiasm, devoid of scientific method and tolerable scientific explanation. Between these she has sought to hold the balance and "to evolve what might be called a Spiritual Science or a practical doctrine that can be demonstrated as of practical value to humanity." This is an extract from the initial chapter on the Science and Art of Healing, and in discussing thereafter the Psychological Basis of Mind, careful distinction is made between the machinery of the brain and that which works through it. There is, of course, full recognition of all that ordinary usage covers imperfectly enough, by the word sub-conscious, while beyond and behind the mental part of our nature, Dr. Severn postulates Spirit or soul, and here, in treating of this, her work begins to part company with Hudson's Law of Psychic Phenomena and the body general of psycho-therapeutists. I do not suppose that what she tells us concerning the sub-conscious goes further than others have gone, but it is put clearly, and her illustration of the submerged mind is exceedingly taking. The work of the subconscious will is not so usually recognized, and this part of the subject is also an intelligible contribution to the extension of the whole thesis.

I will pass over Dr. Severn's diagnosis of the Mental Causes of Disease, saying only that it is the application of her particular experience to a restatement of what is known hereon, and the chapter on the Rationale of Treatment is beyond my province. In certain Educational Aspects of Healing, she gives valuable counsels of prudence, and some of them have larger issues than may be realized by all her readers. Herein also, as she recognizes, is the key to inward life and the greater consciousness therein. It is used daily by some who scarcely know what they are doing, and they do not dream that it can open the doors which lead into the realm of mystical experience. It is one of those modes of working which are named by the spiritual alchemists, are said to be ready to our hands, but their proper nature is understood only by the wise. In a chapter on the Spiritual Significance of Healing, Dr. Severn comes more especially into her own, and it is here that she presents her apprehension of that larger vista to which I referred at the beginning, and at which I can look with her, though not exactly through the same glasses. She moves far beyond the ordinary range of healing by mind methods into that mystery of our inward nature where God is realized, where the soul passes into the state of silence and has "Consciousness of the All-Life." Her secret of psycho-therapy, psychosophy, or whatever it may be called, is the practice of placing the mind and that which lies beyond it—but is of us and in us—in that condition where it knows itself as a center in the universe, communicating at all its points with the sources of life, power, grace and intelligence. This is Elizabeth Severn's way of health in the physical, her way in mind-cure; but it is the way also of communion between God and the soul—or, as I should put it, of the soul's healing by realization in the Divine. I have no doubt that she is right in things physical, for her method is simple and catholic. I know that she is right in the higher and deeper sense; I see that she has been taught of the spirit; and I think that she has come among us with a saving method of outward practice and inward welfare. The chapter on cases is assuredly a memorable record.

THE PROPHECY OF MALACHI

March, 1915

INDEPENDENTLY of any claims which it may possess from the prophetic standpoint, that list of oracular papal mottoes which has been less or more famous for over three hundred years, under the name of the Prophecy of St. Malachi, has considerable interest from the historical and bibliographical field of view. In the first place, the prelate to whom it is attributed was an important ecclesiastical figure in Ireland of the twelfth century, a man of zeal and activity, a man also of conspicuous personal sanctity. He was successively Abbot of Benchor, now known as Bangor in County Down, Bishop of Connor, now in the county of Antrim, and Archbishop of Armagh, in which capacity he was primate of all Ireland. He was a correspondent of St. Bernard, whom he visited twice at Clairvaux, on his way to Rome, and on the second occasion, the Irish prelate died in the arms of St. Bernard, who preached his funeral sermon. This was in 1148, and in the fifty-fourth year of his age. The discourse is still extant, together with a second sermon on his anniversary festival, certain letters and an extended life of St. Malachi. The last in particular ranks exceedingly high among the works of St. Bernard, that is to say, "among the most methodical and elegant of his writings." Such at least was the opinion of the Jesuit Maffei, who translated it into Italian, and he is said by Alban Butler to have been "a true judge and passionate student of eloquence." Malachi is said to have been one of the first saints who. was canonized in solemn form. The statement is on Latin authority and may mean that the process was recorded in one of the earliest bulls. In any case there was a promulgation of that kind, and it will be found in the great collection of Mabillon.

So far as regards the historical interest in the alleged author of the prophecies, and in the second place there is that of the bibliographical order, which centers largely in the authenticity of the text. Perhaps in part on account of its oracular nature and the repute of its alleged author, but much more because of later explanations designed to exhibit its gradual fulfillment through the centuries, and finally on the ground of expectations concerning possible fulfillments to come, the little work has been curiously popular. The Latin text has been printed many times; there have been various French versions, at least one Italian rendering, and one also in English. The question as to its authorship has been alike of attack and defense, with a predominance on the hostile side, but no special skill on either. The most tolerable adverse criticism is perhaps that of the Rev. M. J. O'Brien, who published an Historical Account of the Prophecy in 1880, while the least satisfactory, being one—as it seems to me—with a touch of insincerity, will be found in Abbé Le Can's Dictionnaire des Prophéties et des Miracles, forming volumes xxiv and xxv of Migne's Nouvelle Encyclopédie Théologique, 1851. The defenses, so far as I am acquainted with them, seem indifferently bad.

The real strength of the case against the prophecies is one of a simple kind and cannot per se be called conclusive, as it is purely negative. The prelate to whom they are attributed died, as we have seen, in 1148, and if they are actually his work, they either preceded the pontificate named first in the list, that of Celestine II, which began in 1143, or they belong at the latest to that of Eugenius III, who was enthroned in 1145. I should certainly prefer the former of these alternatives. So far, however, as research has proceeded on the subject, no reference has been found to the prophecies on the part of contemporary writers or of any historians for a period of 450 years. Their publication for the first time took place under the auspices of Arnold de Wion, in his work called The Tree of Life, which appeared in 1595. He is also the first writer who produced certain explanations of the mottoes, showing how they applied to the succession of pontiffs from Celestine II to his own day. He referred these explanations to R. Alphonsus Ciaconius, who was of the order of Friars Preachers, but they have never been found in his works, and the suspicion is that Arnold invented them. Apart from that writer's good faith, and as to this the materials for judgment are scarcely in our hands, nothing attaches to the question, which is solely the value, if any, of the oracles considered as forecasts and of the explanations considered as evidence in that direction only. Provisionally, therefore, I will grant the contentions on both sides to the most drastic criticism and will assume, not indeed that Arnold de Wion wrote the prophecies and their interpretations out of his own head, but that their antiquity did not much precede the date of his Tree of Life. There will thus remain for our judgment the mottoes or oracles referable, by the hypothesis, to the popes who ascended the throne of St. Peter after 1595 and such explanations as have appeared, from later hands than those of Arnold, in elucidation of these. I am not proposing to furnish a complete list, and the Editor of the Occult Review has given a few notable cases of the way in which recent popes have corresponded to their particular mottoes. I shall select on my own part five examples of interpretation subsequent to Arnold de Wion. They are presumably the work of a French Jesuit, Jean de Brassieres, or they were published at least by him in a work entitled Flosculi Historici, of which there are several editions. I have used that of Oxford, 1663, and the schedule of oracles and meanings will be best presented as follows:

I. Leo XI, 1605.—Motto: Undosus Vir, that is, a man full of waves, or as a French rendering has it, the undulating or flowing man. The meaning is that his life or his activity melted away like a wave. His pontificate lasted 24 days.

II. Paul V, 1605.—Motto: Gens perversa, that is, the perverse race, a reference to the disturbed state of the Church and the Christian world during this pontificate, in part through political causes and for the rest through heresies.

III. Gregory XV, 1621.—Motto: In tribulatione pacis, that is, in the tribulation of peace. The explanation is that this pope was appointed legate to the Duke of Savoy during the pontificate of Paul V, and he brought about a peace between that prince and the Spanish king.

IV. Urban VIII, 1623.—Motto: Lilium et Rosa, that is, the Lily and the Rose. One explanation is that this pontiff had bees in his coat of arms, and bees extract honey from these flowers, which seems childish. Another states that he was a Florentine, and the city of Florence derives its name from a red flower, while its device is a lily. During this pontificate, there was war in France, signified by the lily, and in England, represented by the rose.

V. Innocent X, 1644.—Motto: Jucunditas Crucis, that is, Joy of the Cross. The chief explanation is that he was raised to the pontificate on the Feast of the Exaltation of the Cross. Alternatively, the joy of peace was procured after the crosses and afflictions of many wars. The Peace of Westphalia was concluded in this reign.

Whether the application of these five oracles offers anything which can be called forecast is a question which I am inclined to leave in the hands of my readers, with a simple reminder that the mottoes were in print prior to the pontificates concerned. It is largely a question of personal appeal and judgment. I should call the first interpretation a subtlety. The words undosus vir would be curiously descriptive of a man whose character was conspicuously unstable, but not of the comet of a very brief season. The fifth example seems to me best of all, as a pope who was raised on the Feast of the Exaltation of the Cross had very good cause to take the words Jucunditas Crucis as his motto for the whole period during which he was Vicar of Christ.

Let us glance now at two or three oracles which are referable to earlier reigns, but from the standpoint of hostile criticism were devised after the events. If these are much more to the purpose, there is more to be said for the criticism than appears on the bare surface. Most of them are exceedingly apposite, and there is consequently a wealth of choice, (1) The motto of Celestine II, 1143, is Ex Castro Tiberis, that is, from a Castle on the Tiber, and his name was Guido de Castello, after the town Citta di Castello, situated on the Tiber. (2) The motto of Lucius II, 1144, is Inimicus Expulsus, or the Enemy driven out, and he belonged to the Caccianemici family, a name formed of two Italian words signifying to expel enemies. (3) The motto of Eugenius III, 1145, is Ex Magnitudine Montis, or—according to its free rendering—from a great Mountain, and he was born at Montemagero, near Pisa. (4) The motto of Urban III, 1185, is Sus in Cribo, or the Sow in the Sieve, which device constituted the arms of the House of Crivetti, to which he belonged. (5) The motto of Adrian V is Bonus Comes, the good Count, and he was one of the Counts of Lavagne, while his name was Othobonus, or the good Otho. I might produce almost the whole list with similar results; and it would look therefore that most pontiffs prior to the publication of the prophecies by Arnold de Wion are well characterized by their Malachian oracles, and those who came after vaguely. So far as I am aware, this point has been missed by criticism. There are, however, some items which a forger should have done better. It does not appear, for example, that Honorius III, 1216, was ever a canon of St. John Lateran, but his motto, Canonicus de Latere, carries this meaning.

I have left out of consideration the later oracles, and their application to recent pontificates. It has been shown in these pages that those of Pius IX and Leo X III are exceedingly suggestive. I do not think, in conclusion, that the prophecies are the work of St. Malachi, though he is accredited by his biographer St. Bernard with prophetic gifts, but I should regard the attribution as older than Arnold de Wion. The whole subject is in an unsatisfactory state, and stands over for future research.

MASTER-BUILDING

July, 1915

I HAVE before me a book which is described by its publishers in exceedingly striking terms. It is explained that the work has been written as a commission from the Grand Lodge of Iowa, U.S.A., that it was approved by that Body on June 10, 1914, and that henceforward a copy will be "presented to every man upon whom the degree of Master Mason is conferred in the Grand Jurisdiction of Iowa." The zeal and activity of this American Lodge has been mentioned more than once in the Occult Review, in connection with a National Lodge of Masonic Research, founded recently, and in reviewing its official organ, some issues of which have reached us. That is a collective effort worthy of the highest praise and beginning to deserve it in the best sense of these words.

JOSEPH FORT NEWTON

Under the simple but pregnant title of The Builders, the volume here under notice is, however, an individual effort—though bearing an important imprimatur—and there are two ways in which it marks an epoch. They are the circumstances of its production, as stated, and the value of its contents.

When a man enters Freemasonry, it is customary to present him with the Book of Constitutions and the By-laws of that Lodge by which he has been received into the great community. These things are provided so that he may live in conformity with Masonic rule in things which concern the Brotherhood, and they are therefore put into his hands by an act of necessity, not by an act of grace. During a period of considerably over two hundred years, there may have been rare cases in which other information has been furnished, but they have not come under my notice. The new member has, therefore, very little knowledge of the organization into which he has come, its pretensions or its history. The mystery of speculative building, of temples spiritualized, the Symbols and Rites of the Order, their developments and transformations—of all these things he who would learn must seek—and it might happen that the Master of the Lodge would prove, not only the last person who could guide him, the very last person to instruct, but even the first to feel confused and astonished at direction being sought on such subjects. I am not wishing to suggest that there is no guidance possible. In this as in all things else, a man who wants to learn will not fail to find his teachers, while for the Mason also as for others there is a great cohort of instructors, each at his own value, in books and even in periodicals. There are also a few Lodges which pass as learned and issue transactions that those who wish may see, without very grave difficulty. Of course, in the multitude of counselors there is the confusion to be expected, and the most natural question arises: What have the Masonic headships to say upon the subject of Masonry?

Hereunto there has been so far no answer whatever, and when I come to the real reason, it is likely to be unexpected by some, at least, of my readers. Individual Grand Officers may write of that and this, but only in their private capacity, for—as a matter of fact—any teaching body of the kind implied by the question is not possible in Masonry. It is on the surface a "system of morality, veiled in allegory and illustrated by symbols." The morality is perfectly clear, and »calls for no exposition, while up to a certain point the Rituals exist to explain the allegories and symbols. The essence and spirit of Masonry are not contained, however, within the terms of the definition which I have quoted. Rather, they escape therein. But of that which lies beyond no governing body in Masonry has the power to speak with authority, such bodies being custodians of the surface meaning only and of what is involved thereby. Omnia exeunt in mysterium, and if it should profit little to consult the Master of a Lodge, in the great majority of cases, the profit might be less than nothing to consult the Grand Lodges, which would exceed their province by speaking. If some time or other in the history of Masonry—whether operative, speculative, or both—there grew up or was imported within it that strange ceremonial mystery which constitutes the Third Degree, and if it contains within it as a summary all the instituted Mysteries, the legend of the soul and the doctrine of Christ-Life on earth, the Grand Lodges cannot tell us when and how it was imparted, whence it came, or alternatively how it grew up within the four walls of the Universal Lodge. They cannot unveil the allegories, if this be their inward aspect, nor can they illustrate the symbols. It is their province to maintain landmarks and constitutions without innovations therein.

The result is that every man who becomes a Mason thinks what he pleases to think on all sides of the Masonic subject. He may regard it as a benefit society, a social club, a method of bringing people together, a concern which provides status, or things further from the purpose than one or all of these. He may believe alternatively that it is a great instrument of moral and social amelioration, or an aspect of religion; that it is the wisdom of Egypt projected through the centuries forever and ever; that its first traces are in Aztec or even in Atlantis; that it is Kabalistic theosophy popularized in moving ceremonies; and so forward, without stint or hindrance. It is a perfectly open position, leaving every one rather helpless, but unavoidable in the nature of things.

And now what has happened during these last days? An important Grand Lodge—as we have seen—having otherwise many titles to influence and distinction, has set itself to remedy that portion of the difficulty, which may be called remediable within the best and only measures that it is free to act. It has assumed no seat of authority in teaching; it has sought to arrogate to itself no artificial orthodoxy of opinion on matters of speculation; but it has resolved that the new Mason coming under its obedience shall know what there is to be known, outside controversial regions, on the foundations of Masonry, on general symbolism in its connection with particular forms prevailing in the great Craft, on the region of Masonic legend which goes before Masonic history, on the unquestioned historical data, on the history of the Grand Lodge of England, which is in one sense or another the Mother-Lodge of the whole Masonic world, on the story in brief of her children in other countries, long since grown up and working out their own destiny, and on that which—apart from all dogma—may be thought and held about the deeper meaning of Masonry, its philosophy and its spirit.

To attain this end, the Grand Lodge has chosen Brother Joseph Fort Newton, a doctor of literature, who has prepared the designed memorial; and so it comes about that we have this "story and study of Masonry" which is called The Builders; and I know in my heart that every thinking Mason into whose hands it comes will wish devoutly that it could have been presented to him when he was first made a Mason and will generously envy those who are destined now to receive it under the auspices of the Grand Lodge of Iowa. Dr. Fort Newton is known to us otherwise as author of The Eternal Christ, a series of studies in "the life of vision and service," and as a preacher who on many occasions has proved to have a mouth of gold. In his own words concerning Emerson, he is one of the seers of this day who have "made the Kingdom of the Spirit something more than a visionary scene suspended in the sky." Because of what he is in these respects and, for the rest, because of his Masonic scholarship, he has written a book which is not only the best introduction to the study of Masonry that I have met with in my whole experience—whether in English or another language—but is something also that belongs to the domain of literature. He has gifts, therefore, which have been wanting but too often in the generality of Masonic writers. Finally, he has accomplished a most difficult task without once imperiling the Grand Lodge, of which he is the spokesman by any tincture of extravagance in theory or grave mistake, in fact.

My knowledge of things as they are within Masonic measures is much too wide for me to dream that other Grand Lodges will adopt The Builders as their textbook, but I am not without hope that the high interest and importance which attaches to this little classic will bring it into general demand and that these words may help in that direction.

RELIGION AND SOCIOLOGY

December, 1915

THERE is a science of sociology moving somewhere in the world for the benefit of those who seek instruction in the nature and development of society and the history of social institutions; and as these subjects have attained the dignity which attaches to the word science, I have no doubt that there is a serious and important body of thought ingarnered within the particular circle of research. I do not know whether its exponents have conceived prior to Professor Durkheim the notion that religion is the pre-eminent expression of social life, or that the reality and the universal and eternal objective cause of religion is, in one word, society. I can imagine that some of my readers will conclude out of hand that such a thesis is not worth examination, more especially when it occupies in translation over 450 closely-printed pages and is written in a tedious style, without any relief from the light of literature. They will make a mistake, however, for it is an important work, fortement documenté, and elaborated with exceeding care. Moreover, it is not without moment to hear the last word which has been said on our own subject by a qualified speaker belonging to an opposite camp, while, on the other hand, those who are attracted by myth, custom and rite among so-called primitive people will find a mass of interesting material drawn from authoritative sources and capable, at need, of being considered apart from the thesis which it has been brought together to justify.

Owing to a diffuse method, it takes overlong to get at the idea of religion in the mind of the writer. He calls it "a more or less complex system of myths, dogmas, rites and ceremonies," and more fully "a unified system of beliefs and practices relative to sacred things", that is to say, things "set apart and forbidden"—beliefs and practices which "unite into one single moral community, called a Church, all those who adhere to them." It is to religion thus conceived that scientific sociology is an alleged key; of this kind of faith, it is said that it "has its origin in society"; the "fundamental notions of science" originate therein; the very categories of thought, the processes of the logical understanding have their source in religion when this is reduced to a synonym for society; and society in fine is that one reality which religious thought expresses. It embodies "all that is necessary to arouse the sensation of the divine in minds," and it provides that conviction of "a perpetual dependence" which is produced otherwise by the idea of God, who is a figurative expression of society.

Such is the thesis, and its evidences are drawn from "the most primitive and simple religion," practiced by "very humble societies," for in these Professor Durkheim believes that he has discovered elements out of which "the most fundamental religious notions are made up." It follows that religion is judged throughout on the basis of its most savage characteristics, and by far the larger part of the book is a study of totemism. Why is the appeal made to Australian, American and Melanesian aborigines as most likely to furnish the real elements? The answer is that the whole consideration postulates evolution and the barbarous beginnings of humanity. Having reached this terminus a quo we can look from our own standpoint at this "last thing" which has been set up against all that is called God. We know that the hypothesis of The Vestiges of Creation came and went, that natural selection followed and filled a high throne for a brief period, but it has fallen with its titles. Of evolution, it can be said only that it is on its trial and is not without signs of passing into the melting-pot, with so many other of our explanatory notions of the universe. One has a right to suspect any thesis which takes it for granted unconditionally and depends therefrom. But when such thesis tells us that the reality behind all religions is that which we call society, and when the argument—for all that I know—is tolerable on evolutionary grounds, we who are mystics and we who are even occultists may well set about revising our values in respect of evolution—if we can be said to have declared any. It is as if the House of Prayer had again become a den of thieves.

Professor Durkheim reviews certain defunct explanations of religion without ever conceiving on his own part that which it is in reality. He has forgotten the one thing needful. The Key of religion is God. It arises from Him and in Him attains its end. It manifests with all its processes in man by virtue of a need of nature, and this nature is the soul of man. It is not belief merely but experience, and it has a state of being as its object. The attainment of such a state is a work of love, and the state itself is that union, which is consciousness in God. All this is equivalent to saying that religion at its highest is religion as understood by the mystics, and between it and science, there is none of that conflict to which Professor Durkheim alludes in some luminous and pregnant sentences. Its subject-matter is the eternal, universal, catholic knowledge, wherein are the warrants of all sciences connected with and arising therefrom. If 2

X 2 = 4, this is because of the truth of God and its sovereign reason. Behind us, who cleave hereto, is the testimony of the saints of all ages and all religions—that God is and that He recompenses those who seek Him out. I do not know whether the human race began in pure barbarism. I think that barbarism and civilization have co-existed as far back as there are any vestiges of history. But it does not matter. I know at least that the great thoughts of the great men are found through immemorial time. Before Ruysbroeck and Eckehart there was he who is called Dionysius, before Dionysius Plotinus, and before Plotinus there was Plato, while the East stood behind Plato, and therein are the spiritual giants of the mighty Vedic faith. I know also and therefore that even as alchemical processes are not a criterion for the judgment of modern chemistry, so surviving aboriginal religions, even if we knew that they were primitive and not degraded forms, are no standard by which we can pronounce upon religion—understood in its deepest essence and realized in its highest development. The totem is not the sacrament, nor are certain concomitants of old ritual human sacrifices the root matter of the Eucharist. Finally, the so-called immortality of society—which might be swallowed up in any cataclysm—is no working substitute for the soul which knows no death, nor is Professor Durkheim's clouded doctrine of personality the real side of the life in God. It may be, notwithstanding, that he sees the vestige of a truth and that the concept which he calls society—like the Church, as defined by theology—not apart from individuals and yet, as he tells us, more than the sum of these, is a far-off catching at the integration of souls in God. He may continue to satisfy himself by terming it society rather than the Church militant on earth and triumphant beyond in God's union. I know in any case that it has one formula—and this is "life in God and union there."

STUDIES IN TRANSFORMATION

January, 1916

IN his work on the theory and practice of Transcendental Magic, the chief master of occult interpretation, Eliphas Levi, offers a characteristic theory to explain the recurring stories of werewolves and a multitude of other transformations. Put shortly, all the supposed phenomena of this order are referable to a temporal separation of astral and physical body. "A werewolf is no other than the sidereal body of a man whose savage and sanguinary instincts are typified by the wolf." Such a person is really asleep in his bed, while his phantom—in "that form which corresponds to his evil disposition," and to the dreams with which he is afflicted is wandering through the country-side." Eliphas Levi affirms further that a werewolf may be pursued and wounded, but is never killed on the spot; and that, owing to the correspondence between the physical and psychical body, "hurts inflicted on the werewolf really injure the sleeping person."

If it be asked why the spiritual body of a savage and sanguinary person should assume the guise of a wolf, or should be normally in that form, the answer— of course, within the measures of the theory—is that "animal forms communicate their sympathetic impressions to the astral bodies of humanity." But if it be demanded further, why savagery is represented more typically by the beast in question rather than some other wild creatures, it is unquestionable that Eliphas Levi would have explained—plausibly enough—that the wolf was the commonest of sanguinary animals in those regions where lycanthropy was a supposed recurrent phenomenon in past centuries. The thesis would be simply: no native wolf, no lycanthropy; but in its place Lion and Tiger Men, with other wonders of which there is full and graphic account in that feast of marvels which Miss Frank Hamel has provided in Human Animals. Seeing, however, that—to the credit of our race—it is neither exclusively nor largely composed of the savage and the thirster for blood, there are many other transformations in legend, and as an occult philosopher at large in le monde ensorcele, our French magus had no difficulty in accounting for all and sundry by a single typical example. "A man of intelligent and passive mildness assumes the inert physiognomy and ways of a sheep, but in somnambulism it is a sheep that is seen and not a man merely with a sheepish countenance." On the whole, it is a fantastic interpretation, contradicted on every side by the history of human apparitions. It is quoted by Miss Hamel, but with guarded words of introduction, and I should not think that she regards it seriously. Her book is not otherwise hampered with much explanatory hypothesis—of her own or others—and this is one of its advantages. It is mainly content with simple classification, and does not offer contributions towards a science of folk-lore.

There is something to be said for the science as a thing in process of evolution, but at present it is without any settled canon of judgment or certain landmarks, while it has a confirmed habit of getting on the wrong side and there abiding. On the comparatively rare occasions when Miss Hamel makes brief excursions into speculative regions, it is not to be expected, and does not prove, in fact, that she offers better satisfaction than authoritative comparative mythologists, more especially when they generalize freely. She hazards a hypothesis that belief in animal transformations "originates in the theory that all things are created from one substance, mind or spirit," and that it is "as old as life itself." C. G. Leland is quoted as affirming that "men were as animals and animals as men" at the beginning of things. I do not believe for a moment that primeval savagery possessed a doctrine of pan-psychism, any more than it held the identity of the universe with God. These things are subtleties of a later period, if it be assumed that the human race originated in barbarism and that there was a time when the missing link was somewhere in the world, a combined product of evolution and natural selection. It is the counter-assumption only which, from my standpoint, will give us a true science of folklore. But I speak as a mystic who holds that we have come from the heights or—in the alternative of spiritual symbolism—from a Divine Center of things; that the Garden of Eden is a myth having science behind it, and this is a science of memory, in contra-distinction to the unceasing variations of mythological hypothesis and the scientific folk-lore of the clod. I hold that we are approximating more nearly to the true genesis of man if we believe that our progenitors were manifested in the physical world, not in primeval barbarism, but "trailing clouds of glory," and it was afterwards only that this glory faded into "the light of common day," like the remembrances of that psychic state before man was clothed in skins. The clouds gathered over his sanctuary, and he who had been a priest of the mysteries was licensed no longer to open the Holy of Holies, were it even once a year. But I question whether he was in doubt through any of the past ages as to his paramount position in animate creation, or that he regarded his own status as interchangeable with that of the beasts until man in various places, at one and another epoch, lapsed into savagery. I believe that he possessed always, as he possesses now, a "shaping spirit of imagination," and this spirit was of the light which enlightened his darkness. It gave him also many semblances and many inventions of mind. In the degradation of peoples which brought savagery to pass, the creations of the imaginative mind became superstitious beliefs, and the beliefs produced practices. The practices in their turn opened many doors to deception and self-deception, and man entered the world of hallucination. It is to such periods and conditions that animal transformations belong, and in so far as there is colorable evidence of wer-wolves et hoc genus omne, the explanatory theory is not one of astral imitation, or Lamb's assertion of "metaphor," but of imagination in the vortex of disease. On the other hand, the explanatory theory of mythological transformations, like those of Egyptian religions, is one of pure allegory, which had a "shaping spirit of its own."

I am conscious, however, that I have passed far into the debatable region which I have praised Miss Hamel for having forborne to enter. In conclusion, therefore, I will mention her titles of excellence, which are titles of wonder-stories. You can forget Frazer and his Golden Bough, Grimm and his Teutonic Mythology, all the Demonomania of Sorcerers, not excepting my own contribution as a counterblast to the "science of folklore"; and in the successive chapters of Human Animals, you can read about Were-Foxes and Were-Vixens, beautiful Bird-Women, Cockatrices and Lamias, and the very curious Mouse-Maiden. Whether you believe or not that re-embodiments are universal in nature, you will find that transformations are universal in the mind's imaginings, all the wide world over; and many, as I think, will be grateful that I have brought them to the covers of this pleasant book concerning Human Animals.

SOCIAL DESTINY OF MAN

May, 1916

THERE are certain names which stand out in occult literature, being of universal knowledge among students and repute among informed readers, but—at least, in this country—few are acquainted at first hand with their personalities, much less with their writings. Some of these names are on the fringe of esoteric subjects, symbols of erudition thereon but not belonging to the golden chain of tradition, which—according to Eliphas Lévi—began with Hermes and will end only with the world. There is, for example, Athanasius Kircher, a Jesuit of the seventeenth century, whose contributions to Kabalism, early Egyptology, Divination, Alchemy, Astral Travelling's, exceed thirty folio volumes. He is quoted from mouth to mouth by many writers; but—albeit his scholastic Latin is of unusual simplicity—how many outside experts have consulted his vast treatises, or have even examined their curious folding plates? It is the same with certain writers whose names are hung up like lamps in the occult sanctuary itself. Notwithstanding one illuminating monograph of Archdeacon Craven on the Kentish mystic, Robert Fludd, who knows his theosophical cosmogony, his infoldings and unfolding of the microcosm, his works on medecina catholica and occult anatomy? Through whose hands have passed the treatises on esoteric theology, attributed to Raymund Lully? These names and some others are like noticeable beacons pointing to tropical regions of research which few have visited. Much nearer to our period, and yet in the same category, is the French scholar and utopian philosopher Fabre d'Olivet. But I conceive that we are destined to know more in the time to come about these and other immortals, and the occasion of the present notice is a sign pointing in this direction.

It is perilous to pronounce on any adventure in literature as antecedently improbable, but one might have thought that the translation of a work by Fabre d'Olivet was, to say the least, unlikely, while most unexpected of all was a rendering of his Philosophical History of the Human Race, as it is called in the original French. Thereafter, one need not despair of Raymund Lully on several untraversed fields of metaphysics and theology or Paracelsus De Cæna Domini. Antecedent probabilities melt under the dissolvent of our period, and we have not only this work made available in a handsome form, and passably rendered, but—to my certain knowledge—a disciple of Dr. Rudolf Steiner was seeking some three years ago to secure publication in English of The Hebrew Language Restored, by the same author, in the belief that it would be of service in the work of presenting German Christo-Theosophy to the notice of English students. This attempt proved a failure, but it may be made again, and then it may not fail.

The works of Fabre d'Olivet are appreciated at the present day in France by the school of Martinists. Dr. Gérard Encausse, who—under the pen-name of Papus—is president of the Martinist Order and the most prolific of Parisian occultists, regards d 'Olivet in the light of a master and says: "It is to him that we owe an almost complete reconstruction of sciences taught in the sanctuaries of India and Egypt." This is decisive as to the point of view, and is quoted in this sense. For Stanislas de Guaita, Saint-Martin was a precursor of Fabre d'Olivet, or at least a source of inspiration—about which I am more than doubtful, but again it is a point of view. It is at least certain that in the line of succession stands one of our contemporaries, Saint Yves d'Alvedre, with a political doctrine of synarchy, as his work on The Mission of the Jews proves from cover to cover. Finally, Miss Redfield, the American translator of Fabre d'Olivet, has approached him as an occultist and, reflecting the panegyric of Papus, describes her author as one "who penetrated to the tabernacle of the most mysterious arcana." She believes that France will be honored in his honoring when esoteric science has come once more into its own and has been restored upon its own foundation.

I think personally that for that branch of occultism which Miss Redfield would term Hermeneutics, the attempted restoration of the Hebrew language is of more considerable appeal than an history of the human race conceived philosophically, for the latter is a political work, though with a distinct basis of religion. My suggestion on the surface may sound much as if I recommended a reconsideration of Bridgewater Treatises or Mr. PyeSmith as an authoritative writer on geology. But I am speaking of that which may appeal at its value to one section of the reading and thinking public. The work in question is a speculation on the origin of human speech, and the real meaning imbedded in Hebrew words. It claims to re-establish a lost language according to its original principles, throwing over the yoke of the Hellenists and exhibiting behind the cortex of Genesis a hidden doctrine containing "treasures amassed by the wisdom of Egypt." Whether this interpretation is in the last resource a fantasy—like other occult hermeneutics—and whether the reconstruction of Hebrew is beneath attention by scholarship are of course extrinsic questions. But among the works of Fabre d'Olivet it is here that the interest lies from the occult standpoint, and I have very little doubt that a translation of his "cosmogony of Moses," with annotations simplified and some of the excursuses removed, would be of value to those circles.

As regards the "philosophical history of the human race," I have said that our author was a scholar and a utopian. There is no doubt of the scholarship: it was encyclopedic in the matter of languages, like that of Athanasius Kircher. In addition to Hebrew and the classical tongues, it included Chinese, Sanskrit and Arabic. Born at the end of 1768, d'Olivet led the life of a student, and the chief event in his history, being an exile to Africa by Napoleon on account of his opinions, only provided him with a refuge where he was immersed more deeply in research—as he himself tells us. But he was also a utopian philosopher, and this work on the social state of man offers full proof. It is extensive enough as a treatise, but the ground which it covers is vast, and it is really an example of compression. In addition to comprehensiveness, it has breadth of outlook and a certain ability of expression, notwithstanding eccentricities of construction to which the translator alludes. For those who can tolerate its outcome, there is food for thought in its pages, which might last some earnest people a lifetime. Man is presented as one of three great powers in the universe, because he is endowed with will, which implies liberty. The other powers—between which he finds himself placed—are destiny, which is the old natura naturata, and Providence, the natura naturans, exhibiting in manifested things the free will of God, Who is above this triad, envelopes them in His unfathomable unity and forms with them "the Sacred Tetrad of the ancients, which constitutes the All in All." If the root of this thesis, apart from certain developments, is not of universal agreement, it will command concurrence on the part of occultists at large and my own, writing as a mystic. Let us see how it unfolds. The work being confined to the social state of the White or Borean Race, to which we belong, Book I offers a purely hypothetical history of its development and brings us to the threshold of what is called the social edifice, with a college of women regulating cult, law and government. It illustrates the struggle of human will with destiny. The second book sketches the rise of monarchy and empire, mainly on hypothetical lines. It affirms that destiny, apart from the other principles, leads to conquests more or less rapid and disastrous; will institutes republics less or more stormy and transitory, "while it is only with the intervention of

Providence that regular states are founded." Book III brings human intelligence to its highest development in Greece and affirms that the universal empire must be theocratic in government. Later divisions sketch the continual struggle between liberty and necessity, with the work of Providence between these opposing forces, succoring the weakest side and bringing the greatest efforts to nothing when the aim is absolutism. The effect is really striking, like the continuous unrolling of a canvas on which everything is depicted in bold outline. But we come in fine to the matter of the seventh book, which surveys the world after that Revolution in France when absolute victory appeared to remain with the will, but when the will was seized in a snare "as adroitly, as vigorously set" and another struggle was to begin, which "Providence alone can terminate." It lays down that theocratic government is providential and intellectual, republican is animistic and volitive, while monarchical is prophetic and intuitive. The last belongs to natura naturaia, the first to natura naturans, and hereunto the whole social state aspires. The salvation of Europe can come only from providence and theocracy. The last chapter is therefore a vision of empire under a Supreme Pontiff recognized by all Europe; organ of Providence and channel of that life which is now lacked by Government. It is to this that the work leads up, and hence I call it utopian. Apparently, this "highest person of the world" would be the nominee of political powers; and as the essence alone of religion is providential, while its forms belong to destiny and will, it is idle to speculate what old or new cult would be represented by such a pontiff, what Christ or anti-Christ might reign on earth. Finally, as neither in nor out of occult or mystic schools is any one expecting or desiring a purely mechanical theocracy, it is difficult to see where this translation will find its public. But as we have it, one is glad to recognize that, apart from the main thesis, it has several marks of excellence and some indeed that are high.

THE EASTERN RELIGIONS

September, 1916

AS the record which I am about to review will take its place, in my opinion, among standard works on its subject, I shall introduce it to my readers after the simplest possible manner, with a foreword concerning its writer and the circumstances which have brought it into being, and with a summary account of its contents. Dr. Pratt is Professor of Philosophy in Williams College, Massachusetts, U.S.A., and is the author of certain studies on Pragmatism and the Psychology of Religious Belief. From the claims of his present undertaking, and from his position otherwise, I have no doubt that they are of consequence, each in its own degree, and are probably well known; but they have not come into my hands. His latest volume, which is of considerable dimensions, describes itself in the sub-title as a traveler's record, and is therefore put forward with all the modesty and restraint which characterize the work as a whole. The description is justified on the surface by a suggestion here and there of places visited in the course of that philosophical investigation, the results of which have assumed their permanent form herein. Such a suggestion is not unimportant to the general purpose in view, for personal impressions of scenes, people and objects are communicated to the reader wherever they may prove helpful, but not otherwise. It is desirable to mention this and establish, once and for all, that while the work is a traveler's record, it is in no sense a volume of travels. It is a study at first hand on the spot and would have been impossible to a book student—however far he had journeyed through highways and by-ways of research. This is why it differs generally from a number of good treatises which offer synoptic accounts of the chief eastern religions. The statement leads naturally to my next point. This is not in the conventional sense of scholarship an exceptionally learned work. There is not only no textual equipment of the kind which makes a lay reader afraid to dissent from, or even question, certain authoritative judgments, whether they satisfy or not, but Dr. Pratt makes it clear from the beginning that he is not, e.g., a Sanskrit expert. The result is that though there is everything in his pages to show that he is a safe guide, there is nothing to overburden the reader, while there is throughout a very sparing use of eastern technical terms. Moreover, on starting for India, Dr. Pratt had no thought of writing a book, whether of travels or otherwise. His object was a fresh light on the psychology of religion.

The book itself, as we have it, has grown up "from observation and conversation with ah sorts of people"—learned natives, monks, ascetics and saints, converts to Indian religions, active missionaries, even the typical Anglo-Indian. All these came in his way and all were drawn into a net which he had spread widely. A psychologist and writer on psychology, there is no need to add that the foundations had been laid long since: he did not go to discover that there is a psychology of religion in India, but to extend his knowledge. To all this must be added the live interest of a particularly alert observer, and it will then begin to be seen not only how the record came into being, but why I am likely to prove right in my feeling as to the place which it will take. I have sought to judge it by all standards at my disposition, and I do not know whether I am more impressed by its catholic sympathies or its distinguished impartiality, by its thoroughness or freedom from the vanity of dogmatism, by its simplicity of presentation or the mass of well-ordered knowledge which it places at the disposition of those who know little but are concerned in learning generally about religions in India.

I am putting forward Dr. Pratt's undertaking as the most comprehensive living account of Indian faiths which I have met with, and I believe it to be the best general survey so far attempted. I am not offering it as final in respect of views, either generally or particularly. He would be the first to dissuade me. Furthermore, that I may be frank in regard to myself, there are many matters of detail on which he might well err and I be unaware of the fact. Let me add only hereto that by the grace of a life of study I can recognize out of hand a first-class methodical summary when it lies before me. There is but one thing more on this part of my subject: I have said that this is a living book, showing things as they were and are, and it does not contain a single dull page or one page that can be termed heavy by any suitably prepared reader.

And now as to the content itself. Roughly speaking, there is nearly one half devoted to Hindu religion, its gods and doctrines, its ecclesiastical hierarchy and the chief reform movements which have arisen from time to time within it, more especially the Brahmo Samaj and the Arya Samaj, the names of which at least are familiar to every person who knows anything of Indian thought and movements at this day. In the second half there is an excellent account of the Sikh religion, the Jaina, Mohammedans, Parsees, and the Buddhists of Burma and Ceylon, including doctrines of modem Buddhism and a monograph—admirably done—on its value and springs of power. A considerable space is devoted, as we approach the end of the record, to Christian missions in India, and this—as it seems to me—is written with good taste and discretion, nor so only, but with large-hearted philosophical insight. Finally, there is a chapter on things which the West might learn from the East—e.g., something of the inward root from which issue the Indian's temperance and his sense of public decorum; his sacred feeling towards all forms of life; his vision of the eternal; and the object of his supreme desire, which is the culture of the soul.

It might be thought, and not unreasonably, that having reached this point a reviewer's task is ended, for Dr. Pratt's impressions and conclusions on the several religions which he has passed under consideration would call for a lengthy notice, while their criticism would make for a volume. But having said so much in favor of what I have found so excellent, it is fitting to put on record the conclusion in chief which is brought away from this new presentation of the great experiment of religion in that great division of the eastern world which is India. I came to the book as a mystic; I can judge it as a mystic only. Dr. Pratt is a cultured Christian gentleman who knows, as I do, that the time is long dead and gone when we can class the Christianity which we love, and in which we are rooted, as other than one of several great faiths that rule in this world of ours. Without mystical sympathies and a certain insight into that science of attainment which we have agreed to call mysticism, he could not have written as he has, nor could he have brought to any mystic the satisfaction that he has brought to me; but he is not himself a mystic. I have no occasion therefore to pronounce on him and his work from that standpoint. He knows, I am certain, that there is one thing only needful for him as for me, and that this is God; but if he were asked whether there is a way of realization in God which is open here and now to those who can walk therein, I question how he would answer and whether he would answer at all. In any case, the point for myself is what I take away from this volume as to the unity of doctrine and experience on the highest subject of research. I am not concerned with official religions, however denominated, save in respect of their essence, understood as the heart of this subject. I did not approach Dr. Pratt's book with an idea that I should learn further as to the essence itself, or that I might become more assured as to the truth of the way and the end that is attained therein. But as Dr. Pratt sought to gain fresh light on the psychology of religion by proceeding to India, so in going over his record with something like loving care, I sought to gain light on the certitude and unanimity of the world-wide chain of witnesses. I derived recently from my own new study of the Christian testimonies a plenary conviction that there is only one doctrine which matters to the mystical experiment, and it is this—that God is, and that He recompenses those who seek Him out. Here is the root-matter, but after what manner God is and what is the precise nature of the mystic's relation to God beyond that of a seeker to object, so long as the search lasts, are other questions. I came to see that these are points of debate on which the schools have originated, that the quest goes on and the end is reached, out of the schools and in, whatever the findings thereon. The fact that you are a Latin of your period, subscribing to all the councils and the last dogmas issued by the Vatican, does not prevent you from becoming a mystic citizen of the Eternal Kingdom. The fact that you are Hindu or Buddhist, holding to the law of Karma and the age-long cycle of rebirths, does not prevent you either. And hence, as I have endeavored to show on various occasions previously, the time has gone by also when we can deny the fact of attainment except within a single circle of official religion. The memorials of it are everywhere in this book, and it is summed up by Dr. Pratt as a belief that "the human soul may enter into, or is already and forever in, immediate communion with the Divine." Here is the root-matter of the chief faiths of India; here is the Indian quest and here also its end. However well I may have known these things previously, I have learned them more fully and realistically with the help of this record, and hence it has served me well.

One word in conclusion, in this English edition of an American book, the illustrations mentioned in the preface have been unaccountably omitted.

SAINTE ODILE: THE GROWTH OF A LEGEND

October, 1916

A CRITICAL study of the prophecies which have either come into being or have taken up a new lease of interest and importance owing to the Great War is no improbable undertaking when the war itself shall be over, and it might provide a curious kind of instruction as well as some entertainment. The latest contribution to the subject and no unfruitful opportunity for a freeman of byways in historical research are furnished by the Prophecy of Sainte Odile, about which it has been affirmed (1) that it is well known to the Kaiser, (2) that he has taken steps to prevent its publication in Germany, but (3) that on the other side of the Rhine it was a subject of gossip prior to August, 1914, more especially in Alsace and Lorraine. About these points, we shall be able to judge at the end; but whether or not "the vision of the Maid of Hohenbourg" was in Alsatian minds prior to the epoch mentioned, there is considerable interest just now, both here and in France, about her and her prophecy. My first knowledge of the latter is due to our contemporary Light, in its recent article on The Prophets and the War The subject was followed up by Mr. Ralph Shirley, who obtained the Latin text of the document from Paris and collected other papers, which have enabled me to pursue my inquiries with rather remarkable results. Apart from summary reductions and reports at second hand, the French literature of the subject is contained in the following monographs, of which one is a sequel to the other:

1. La Prophétie de Sainte Odile et la Fin de la Guerre, avec notes et commentaires de Georges Stoffler. 8vo, pp. 64. This has reached a second edition,

2. La Prophétie de Sainte Odile, Texte et Traduction: pages complementaires, donnant le Texte Latin, la Traduction Française et quelques preuves d'Authenticité. 8vo, 12 pp. The heads of the Prophecy are as follows:—1. A time cometh when there shall arise in the heart of Germany a terrible warrior who will carry on the war of the world, and whom belligerents will call Antichrist. 2. He will come from the banks of the Danube, a ruler notable among all. 3. It will prove the most frightful war ever experienced by mankind. 4. His victories will be obtained on earth, by sea and in heaven itself, for his winged warriors will rise in raucous progress, even to the clouds, to seize the stars and cast them down upon the cities—that they may be burned with most fierce fire. 5. The earth

will tremble with the shock of combat, and the war will be of long duration. 6. The height of the leader's triumph will be reached about the middle of the sixth month in the second year, and this will close the first epoch of the war. 7. The second part will be half the length of the first; in the midst of it, the people under his yoke will cry for peace; but there shall be no peace. 8. It will be, however, the beginning of the end when there shall be a hand-to-hand struggle in the city of cities. 9. The third epoch will be shorter than the two others, and then the conqueror's realm will be invaded on all sides and devastated. 10. Torrents of blood will flow about a high mountain in the last battle, and thereafter the nations will chant hymns of gratitude in the Temples of the Lord, while the prince of princes shall appear, by whom they shall conquer the conquerors from whose hands the scepter shall pass. 11. Paris shall be saved because of the blessed mountains and the devoted women. 12. Thereafter cometh the time when men shall rejoice in peace, obtained at the sword's point, and shall behold the two horns of the moon fixed to the cross. Many shall worship God truly, and the sun shall shine with new splendor. Such is the prophecy in brief, and our next step is to learn something concerning its allegoral author. While on one side the burden of a severe tradition was taken over by Christendom from Jewry, it wore on the other many garlands of a lighter yoke brought over from the pagan world, represented by Greece and Rome. It has been suggested that the legend of S. Odile may illustrate the latter point, but there is nothing especially in favor of such a hypothesis, for its elements are purely Christian. In the root, it is very simple; in the development, it became a monastic tale of Faerie, with a mise-en-scène of sanctity. The scene is Mount Hohenbourg in Alsace, said to have been a retreat of Alsatian Celts, who protected it by a wall. Afterwards it was a Roman camp, and in the second half of the seventh century a castle erected on the site was in possession of Adalric, Duke of Alsace, a reputed descendant of Archinould, Duke of Normandy and a near kinsman of Dagobert the Great. He was a turbulent noble of his period, under King Childeric II, and was married to Bereshinde or Berswinde, a relative of S. Leodégar. The first child of this union—circa 660—was a daughter who was born blind and was promptly condemned to death by the enraged father. Her mother, however, placed her secretly in charge of an old servant, subsequently to which she obtained her sight, was reconciled to her father, became a nun and the abbess of a convent—which was actually the Castle of Hohenbourg. There she lived for a long period, and there she died in sanctity.

This is the root of the story, and the romance follows. From the care of the servant, she was transferred to the Convent of Baume or Palma in Burgundy, the superior of which was an aunt of Bereshinde. She became a pattern of intelligence and piety, her blindness notwithstanding, but she had never been baptized. J When she was somewhere between the ages of six and twelve years, S. Everard, Bishop of Ratisbon, fell into an ecstasy and received orders to christen a blind girl at Baume, who was to be named Odile and would receive sight with the sacrament. He undertook the necessary journey, the promised miracle followed, and when Everard saw her eyes open, he said: "So, my child, may you look at me in the Kingdom of Heaven." The news of this wonder reached the father, and his daughter ultimately returned home. A few years passed away, and he decided to arrange for her marriage, as an escape from which she fled across the Rhine in a beggar's clothes. The Duke followed and was overtaking her near Friburg, when she hid under a rock, which opened at her prayer and gave her refuge. It opened again to liberate her, and a healing spring issued from the fissure. This new miracle decided the father to permit her return in complete freedom. She opened her heart to him, recounting her desire to establish a community of nuns, practicing the principles of the Gospel literally. From his various possessions, he gave her the Castle of Hohenbourg, which was altered to suit her purpose, and she added a great church. There she established a rule of life, possibly on principles of her own. When their time came, her father and mother died in this convent. She rescued the former from purgatory, performed various miracles and attained the age of 103 years. On her deathbed, a radiant angel descended and in the sight of her nuns presented her with a chalice containing both elements of the Eucharist. She received it in her hands; it remained with her after communion and was preserved at Hohenbourg till 1546.

I have introduced here but a part of the miraculous events which fill the pages of the legend. The cultus of S. Odile grew. She became the patron saint of Alsace; and Hohenbourg, with the relics of its first abbess, was a great place of pilgrimage. She was invoked for ocular affections, and her symbol is two eyes lying on a book carried in her hands. A Besançon Breviary of 1761 has her commemoration with its proper lesson, and a prayer as follows. "O God, Who in Holy Baptism didst not only illuminate the mind, but the bodily eyes of Holy Othilia, enlighten the eyes of our heart that we may walk always in the light of Thy truth." There is also a Litany of S. Odile which ascribes to her several titles of the Blessed Virgin Mary. She is hailed as Child of Light, Glory of Kings and Princes, Ornament of Nobility, Hill of Perfection, Fount of Living Waters, Shining Star, Eyes of the Blind, Consolation of the Afflicted, Help of souls in purgatory, thus embodying the chief features of her legend.

No variant or development of that legend represents her as a prophetess, or a habitual seer of visions. One of her biographers mentions that a certain testament and some exhortations have been regarded as unquestionably fraudulent. She is credited also with having written letters to her brother Hugh, but no one claims that they have been preserved. The Latin text of her alleged prophecy has been published by no one but M. Georges Stoffler, and the next question is how it came into his possession. Now, he tells us only that it has been "drawn from a good source, as those who know the history of S. Odile and the legends connected therewith can easily satisfy themselves." This is precisely the kind of mystery which usually covers a deceit; but certain authorities are named "on the subject of authenticity," with the proviso that "it seems useless to refer the reader" thereto—ostensibly because he will take no pains to verify, but as to whether his is the true reason the reader may draw his own conclusions from the following facts. The references are mere mockery. I will take some of them seriatim. If anyone wishes to appreciate the derisive suggestion that Roger Bacon's Opus Tertium alludes to the Prophecy of S. Odile, let him consult that work in Chronicles and Memorials of Great Britain and Ireland. It is an introduction and complement to his previous writings, especially Opus Majus and Opus Minus, and has no concern in saints or their previsions. On the other hand, some references belong to S. Odile's bibliography, among which is Repertoire des Sources Historiques du Moyen Age, by Chevalier. It gives a list of books regarding the Saint, but no indication of prophecies. Jerome Vignier, another alleged witness, furnishes a genealogical list of Duke Adalric's family, with extracts from a MS. biography of his daughter in the Jesuit College at Clermont, which document now appears to be lost. The prophecy is again absent. Grandidier, also cited, is an authority for the Abbey of Hohenbourg, but not for the prophetic document. The same may be said of Mabillon, the first person who printed the life of St. Odile. Julien Havet is also mentioned, but his Questions Mérovingiennes are again outside our subject. I have consulted other sources not furnished by M. Stoffler, and as a result, it seems certain that prior to the present year there are no records of the Prophecy of Sainte

Odile. It does not strictly follow that it has been invented by its editor, yet if it had a source outside himself, it is difficult to understand why he should conceal its whereabouts, while the catalogue of witnesses to the document who are found not to mention it is inevitably calculated to arouse suspicion. The text, in any case is undoubtedly another contribution to the growing budget of mystical prophecies connected with the Great War.

PAPUS: A BIOGRAPHICAL NOTE

January, 1917

THE War has removed one of the most interesting and notable personalities from the occult circles of Paris. Dr. Gérard Encausse, more familiarly and indeed universally known as "M. le docteur Papus," this being his pen-name, has died in Paris from a contagious disease contracted in hospital, where he was serving as a military surgeon. For more ample biographical particulars we may have to wait a considerable time, owing to the suspension of practically all the French periodicals which represented his particular field of activity. So far as it extends, much of our present knowledge is referable to M. Henri Durville's Psychic Magazine, which, in one of its recent issues, has a sketch of le maître occultiste. Meanwhile, it is satisfactory to know, as we can no longer count him among us, that the indefatigable occultist has passed away in the service of humanity and in the sacred cause of his country. Biographical facts concerning him have always been curiously scarce, considering his general repute, and the few words which can be hazarded upon this side of the subject may call for correction later on. He was born at La Corogne in Spain on July 13, 1865, his father being a French chemist—Louis Encausse—and his mother a Spanish lady. After graduating in medicine and surgery, his attraction to the psychical and occult side of things was shown by a passing connexion with the Theosophical Society in Paris. In a brief note—autobiographical in respect of ideas—appended to the fifth edition of his Traité Elémentaire de Science Occulte, he tells us that under the materialistic influence of the medical Ecole de Paris he became an ardent evolutionist, but discovered very soon the incompleteness of this doctrine, which preached the law of struggle for existence but knew nothing of a law of sacrifice. In the opinion of Papus, this latter dominates all phenomena. The idea concerning it seems to have reached him independently, but he found it subsequently in the writings of Louis Lucas, in old Hermetic texts, the religious traditions of India, and in the Hebrew Kabalah. He found also the doctrine of correspondences, which became for him—as for many others like him—a general key, not only to the mysteries of philosophy and religion but to those of science, and to the inter-relation of all sciences by means of a common synthesis. Very curiously also, as it will seem to many, he found much to his purpose in the rituals of old grimoires, and this led him to the general literature of magic, as well as to a sympathy with its claims and practices. He left the Theosophical Society for reasons which he explains in his Traité Méthodique de Science Occulte and which do not concern us, especially at this date. It was not long before he began to establish independent groups, in collaboration with others whose names are also well known. They represented what he calls the Resurrection of Occult Science. There was a Groupe Indépendant d'Etudes Esotériques, and above all there was the Ordre Martiniste, which made use of a simple ritual, arranged in three degrees, modestly conceived and well arranged. Out of these there grew ultimately a Faculté des Sciences Hermétiques, which issued diplomas to students, and occasionally causa honoris, to persons who had attained distinction as mystic or occult writers in France and some foreign countries.

The Martinist Order was extremely successful and the Supreme Council of France, with Papus as its president, had branches over the whole world—in Italy, Sweden, Germany, Switzerland, England, Belgium, Spain, Denmark, Holland, Austria, even in Russia and Rumania, Egypt and Indo-China. There was also a vast membership in America, both North and South, but the Lodges of the Northern Jurisdiction broke away from the Paris Supreme Council, partly over questions of Masonic procedure and partly on other grounds which are too complex and controversial for enumeration here. It is desirable to mention one point, at least, in favor of the Martinist Order. Unlike so many organizations which assume in modem days a Masonic or kindred origin, it did not make false and fantastic claims regarding its sources. Papus never concealed the fact that he and no other was the author and fount of its rituals. He connected it indeed with the name of L.C. de Saint-Martin as a sort of traditional founder, but not—so far as can be seen—in a direct way. It was rather an attempt to carry on in an incorporated form the work which the French mystic was supposed to have done individually among his admirers and disciples.

The foundation of this group, moreover, represented what must have been not only an early interest but also a dedication of Papus to the saintly personality, wide influence and philosophical illumination of Saint-Martin. His understanding of the philosophy in particular differs from our own in England, and—in accordance with French romantic tradition, which has no base in history—he regarded Saint-Martin as a reformer of High Grades in Masonry, and the inventor of a Rite of his own. But these things are accidents, comparatively speaking at least. One important result was that the interest led to personal research, and that this brought Papus into relation with persons and things belonging to Martinist tradition. Valuable documents came into his hands, so that he was able to throw great light, in a work devoted to Martinism, on the mystical and occult schools of Lyons, on the life of Martines de Pasqually, the first master of Saint-Martin, and to some extent on the mystic himself. In this manner, the Order of Martinism justifies itself by the subsequent work of its founder, whose literary history, were it only in this connexion, is honorable to himself and of lasting value to students.

Papus was also a friend and perhaps at first a guide of the Marquis Stanislas de Guaita, another light of occultism in Paris at the end of the nineteenth century. De Guaita founded a Kabalistic Order of the Rosy Cross, which was carried on in great secrecy, and when he died at an early age, it is said that its direction passed over to Papus. It neither had nor claimed any connexions with the old mysterious Fraternity, but seems to have been quite sincere in its motives. Some valuable texts have been published from time to time under its auspices. Outside these activities, Papus took a hand in exposing the Leo Taxil conspiracy against Masonry and the Latin Church. When the star of peace again shines over the life of France, and when the occult circles reassemble, the pleasant personality of Papus is certain to be missed, and it is difficult to say precisely how his vacant place will be filled at the head of the various groups.

Though he appears to have broken away alike from the tradition and practice of the orthodox medical school, earning the usual consequences in its open and secret hostility, he was a successful and popular physician, and his clinic in the Rue Rodier is said to have been crowded. The little monograph in the Psychic Magazine affirms that he died for his country, literally worn out by his exertions on behalf of the wounded. The claim is therefore true, and of him it may be said that death crowned his life. Personally, I shall always remember our pleasant communications during his two brief visits to London, now many years ago.

As it is customary for French occultists to acknowledge masters, it may be desirable to mention those to whom Papus more especially deferred. They were Eliphas Levi in the philosophy of magic, Lacuria in the mystery of numbers, and Hoene Wronski in the doctrine of synthesis, applied to a projected "reform of all the sciences."

THE DORIS CASE:
A STUDY IN MULTIPLE PERSONALITIES

April, 1917

MY office on the present occasion is chiefly that of a recorder in the simplest and most summary form, and I shall postpone to the end a brief intimation of the reason which has led me to assume the role. Apart from any personal motive, the subject will testify sufficiently to its own importance. If I make the bare facts intelligible to readers of the Occult Review, that they may judge of them on their own part, I shall have served one good purpose; that which is over and above is necessarily for a few only. The material before me, which contains the facts set out and certain tentative conclusions drawn therefrom, considerably exceeds two thousand octavo pages and forms as such three of the largest volumes ever issued as Proceedings of the American Society for Psychical Research. It is called therein The Doris Case of Multiple Personality, and a sub-title of admirable lucidity explains that it is "a biography of five personalities in connection with one body and a daily record of a therapeutic process ending in the restoration of the primary member to integrity and continuity of consciousness." Setting aside certain prefatory matter and occasional annotation, two out of the three volumes contain the digest and record at large of Dr. Walter Franklin Prince, a clergyman of the Episcopal Church in America, who had the case under his charge at his own home for a period of five years, ending in the cure of the subject. The third volume comprises mediumistic investigations and conclusions based thereon—for the most part rigidly tentative—of Prof. James Henry Hyslop, who is known to us all as the untiring secretary of the society, and who in this volume has done singular honor to himself and will receive honor on account of it, from those who know the difficulties of psychical research and the extreme difficulty of dealing adequately with the hypotheses and counter-hypotheses to which it gives rise. Among the important features of the case are (1) the number of personalities using the same vehicle and (2) the appearance of a secondary personality "as early as the third year of the subject's life." But as a fact there is no case, within my knowledge, being that of a literate student only, which can compare with the case of Doris, for the protean interest of its elements or for the rich minutiae of its details in the record concerning it. I shall count it henceforward among my treasures of psychical literature, and I wish only that it were possible to give something more than this poor analysis of contents. May it lead many to obtain the volumes for themselves: their study at length will do more than justify the present encomium.

Doris Fischer was born on March 31, 1889, of Geripan parents, "without known neurotic tendencies on either side." But the father was a man of violent temper and given to gross intemperance for many years prior to her birth, while the mother was exceedingly imaginative and had a "thwarted craving for affection and refined surroundings." A bad man apparently in every relation of life, the father—his excesses notwithstanding—had an iron constitution, while the health of the mother was magnificent. At the age of three years, the child was taken from bed and thrown brutally on the floor by her drunken father, and it was concurrently with this event that two of the secondary personalities "came into being," or alternatively into communication with Doris. They are known respectively as Margaret and Sleeping Margaret. Of the event itself, Doris as Doris remembers nothing: it constitutes what is called in the record the First Dissociating Shock. The second was consequent upon painful and indeed appalling circumstances connected with the death of the girl's much-loved mother—when Doris was seventeen—and a new personality was born or intervened, being "the so-called sick Doris." This was the Second Dissociating Shock, and the Third, brought about by a sufficiently ordinary accident, in which the head was bruised and the back is said to have been injured slightly, led to the first manifestation of Sleeping Real Doris.

Two points call for notification at this stage, (1) The Real Doris, who "is absolutely veracious," testifies that there was hardly a day within her recollection when she did not have lapses from consciousness, signifying that one or more than one of the alternating personalities intervened, and she herself passed consequently into abeyance. In particular, she was never aware of going to bed or of sleeping, prior to 1911. "In early childhood, she had exactly the same types of evidence of the existence of another consciousness in connection with her organism that she had in later years." (2) The sum total of all the five personalities, who is termed Doris pure and simple in the records, notwithstanding the interventions, their distinctions and suddenness, was about the business of her life in and through all the phases—at school and quick in her learning, till the days of schooling ended; at work from a very early period, in the business of humble wage-earning for a family which had been ruined by its head.

The next matter for our consideration is the characteristics of the intervening personalities and their history. (1) Margaret was "mentally and emotionally" a child of ten years old, but she had even a string of notions which are abandoned commonly by children about five or six. She was mischievous, roguish, witty, a mimic, inventive, given to romancing—which frequently betrayed itself—and was lovable as a rule. The subject was transformed along these lines when she was in power. The Real Doris was religiously disposed, while Margaret was little better than a pagan. Her conceptions of wickedness were infantile, but she was naturally jealous and acquisitive. She was childishly fond of eating, whereas Real Doris was rather poor in her appetite. A time came when her intelligence, such as it was, seemed to grow backward, and at the date of her departure she was intellectually some five years old. (2) Sleeping Margaret, who was neither Margaret nor another asleep, professing indeed to be a stranger to this condition, must be said to have adopted a purely emblematical name, and attempts to account for it carry no conviction. She is called the riddle of the case. It is explained that she talked only with eyes closed, meaning the eyes of the subject, and never wandered in her speech or oscillated in the clearness of her understanding. She underwent, through all the years of her presence, very little mental alteration, being thus in marked contrast to her namesake. (3) Sick Doris came into manifestation with "mind as void of factual and verbal content as a new-born infants," but she is said to have developed under the tuition of Margaret with, amazing rapidity. Her expression—as presented by the subject—was wooden, her eye dull, her voice hard. She was destitute of affection, though capable of a "dog-like friendship," and was a slave to certain narrow conceptions of duty. She also was religiously disposed. Her name arose from her general state of health, as manifested, of course, through the subject. (4) Sleeping Real Doris was a "somnambulic personality" who appeared now and then only, after Real Doris fell asleep. I give the statement as made by Dr. Prince in his Cursory Description of the Five Personalities, but this abnormal "personality" first appeared in 1907, and it is on record—as we have seen—that Doris in propria persona as Real Doris knew nothing of sleep until 1911. Sleeping Real Doris was not Real Doris asleep, and in what sense the latter is said to be asleep in 1907, and thus to make room for the former, remains doubtful. It is, however, a minor question. For the rest, this new manifestation is described as a mere evocation of past memories, mainly of Real and Sick Doris, but occasionally of her own. It is questioned whether she was possessed of self-consciousness and also whether she ever "rose fully above the threshold or Real Doris ever sank completely below it during her manifestations." It should be added that, broadly speaking, the history of the secondary personalities was elicited by Dr. Prince during his long study of the case, and as regards the past is that which they told of themselves and one another.

What was the relation of these secondary personalities to the personality which was primary and to each other? (1) It is said that Real Doris had no direct knowledge of the thoughts or acts of any of those forms of consciousness which—outside herself or otherwise—took possession of her vehicle and operated through long years therein. "She could not see into their minds or remember anything that had occurred during their supraliminal periods." One of them in the subliminal state communicated with her verbally, both in childhood and occasionally after, "using the same mouth without her volition." Two of them wrote her notes, using her hand, when their consciousness was in activity and her own in abeyance. In these ways and in others less direct but far more continuous, she knew concerning them, or more correctly concerning Margaret and Sick Doris. Of Sleeping Margaret, who—According to her own claim—was the earliest of the secondary group, Real Doris knew nothing until an accident enlightened her—when she was already on the path of cure. This is explicable by the fact that Sleeping Margaret manifested only when Margaret was supraliminal, though asleep, and Real Doris must have been therefore in very deep abeyance. It is, I presume, mainly for this reason, that Sleeping Margaret is termed the riddle of the case. She was unknown also to the rest of the secondary personalities, a point which deserves observation, having regard to her knowledge of them. As by the hypothesis concerning her Sleeping Real Doris could manifest only when Real Doris was asleep, it will be understood that the latter in her waking state knew nothing concerning her namesake.

For the primary personality, therefore, two of the secondary personalities were in evidence and two out of sight, but so far as her own insight was concerned, "every secondary personality" was separated from Real Doris by "an opaque wall." Now, for something like twenty years prior to 1911, the conscious life of the latter is stated to have averaged less than five minutes per diem. It would appear, therefore, that the growth of her personality took place in and with and through the coadjutors who made use of her vehicle; but the sense in which this statement is understood on my own part will be seen later. (2) So much concerning the relation of Real Doris to the personalities which shared her vehicle. Dr. Prince in his Summary Statement registers (a) that Margaret knew or had capacity for knowing all the experiences and thoughts of Real and Sick Doris; (b) that Sick Doris knew or had capacity for knowing all that the primary personality "did, said, experienced and thought"; (c) that Sleeping Real Doris "had no knowledge, properly speaking, of any of the others," the primary personality included; (d) that Sleeping Margaret "had insight into all the content of the consciousness of Real Doris, Sick Doris and Margaret," which insight—subject to fluctuations of attention—appeared potentially perfect. As regards Sleeping Real Doris, she was better known by Margaret than by Sleeping Margaret, the first seeing things directly, and the second by reflection from the first.

My brief account of relations between the five personalities has been so far apart from any idea of purpose actuating the secondary personalities in respect of the primary member; but such a purpose existed in the case of the two Margarets, though it was not the same in kind. Margaret, by her own testimony, came in the infancy of Real Doris to take care of the latter. Those who read the record for themselves will see that it was a mixed influence and an exceedingly flexible purpose, that it admitted a good deal of tyranny, teasing, mischief, with an occasional spice of more direct and real cruelty; but after every allowance for the fact of these elements, the intention to help remains, and I believe it to have been always present, even when it was most veiled. The statement of Margaret recurs: "I came because Doris didn't have anyone to care for her." At the same time, the purpose was deficient, if not entirely wanting, in ethical life. Margaret, as a moral and responsible personality, could be scarcely said to exist. On the other hand, whatsoever mode of consciousness and self-knowing being is veiled by the denomination of Sleeping Margaret, it was that of a moral and responsible nature, in mentality alert and vigilant, and my impression of the record at length concurs with her own claim that she was "always conscious somewhere, without distinctions of degree." I am reminded of the epithets applied to the poet Chatterton, for hers—like his—seems to have been a marvelous and sleepless soul. Dr. Prince affirms that she was his coadjutor in chief in the cure of Real Doris—though Margaret also was" generally anxious to help." Her position towards Real Doris, as described by herself, was that of a guardian.

I have now placed my readers in touch with the five personalities as fully as it is possible to do within the limits of a magazine article. About the imperfections and deficiencies of such a summary, there is no need to say that I am painfully conscious. The cure of the subject is the next point before us, and the bare facts can be stated in a few words. The cure was inaugurated when Doris, who had become acquainted with Mrs. Prince, began to visit at the house of the clergyman, of which she was afterwards persuaded to be an inmate, becoming finally and still being their beloved adopted daughter. There is nothing more admirable in the vast body of the record than the simple narrative which contains the fact of the girl's rescue from those infamous surroundings created by the unhappy father. The physical basis of the cure was good food and increased natural sleep; but this is the testimony of Dr. Prince, and it is for us to do justice to the spiritual factor of a refined, happy, intellectual home, full of kindness and care, full above all of sympathy, developing into a high degree of understanding. Finally, on the part of Dr. Prince, there was "scientific observation daily and almost hourly," assisted for a period by a university professor of psychiatry. Between them there was therefore ordered and enlightened psychical treatment, into the particulars of which it is impossible to enter here. The end of the matter was the establishment and maintenance of continuity of uni-consciousness, in which the Real Doris is now—and as it would seem henceforward—the only Doris, that is to say, herself and no other, continuing to "improve in physical health and mental tone." And this after "nineteen years of psychical dissociation." Perhaps I should add that Sleeping Margaret, in her capacity as guardian, still comes in the sleep of the subject for a few minutes of an evening, and it is said that this will continue until she has given proof as to her own nature, unless indeed Dr. Prince should wish otherwise.

A word must be said now as to the circumstances which characterized the departures of the several secondary personalities. The order in which I shall take them can be held to indicate the chronology of their exodus, (1) At a comparatively early stage of the cure, Sick Doris began to lose her memories and a tie which had previously subsisted between her and Margaret was broken, so that thenceforward they never communicated with one another. As a fact, Sick Doris could no longer hear her, and the fading memories emerged in the primary personality. The next stage was one of failure to manifest for several days together. Bodily anesthesia supervened and before long, taste and smell were practically dead. She became childish, apathetic, had forgotten how to read, and even her own name. All evidence of will, vanished, sight failed, and during a visit with the Prince family to Massachusetts she came and went for the last time. (2) It is thought that the departure of Sick Doris liberated "a transient breeze of energy" in the "flickering consciousness" of Sleeping Real Doris, but it faded soon and "suddenly went out altogether," the joy of Real Doris at the prospect of going to California being regarded as a factor in her extinction. (3) The declension of Margaret is a very long story in the record of Dr. Prince, and as I can do no manner of justice to his priceless wealth of detail, it will be better to adopt a few lines from his summary. The declension was much slower than that of Sick Doris; her taste and smell became increasingly dull; there was tactile and muscular anesthesia; her field of vision was narrowed and shortened, till in the end she was reduced to blindness. She diminished also in mentality, so that she seemed to grow backward, and she was intellectually about five years old at the date of her disappearance, which occurred "without particular warning." (4) Sleeping Margaret was always herself, without increase or diminution, and it has been shown already that she did not disappear at all; but as her office of guardian became more and more a sinecure, with the progress of the subject towards health, she transferred most of her attention to what she called her own affairs.

Such is the Doris case of multiple personality in a bare summary of the facts, from which life and essence are almost of necessity excluded. The next question is as to the identity of the intervening personalities. Are they to be regarded as "split off groups of mental states, memories and ideas, of the same subject as the normal states, except that they are not adjusted" to the life of the normal states? In other words, are they "merely phenomena of the same mind or organism as the normal states"? In Professor Hyslop's opinion, there is no evidence on the surface that obsession or foreign invasion is the correct diagnosis. I suspect that no commonly careful and instructed reader of the record at large would demur in the case of such personalities as Sick Doris and Sleeping Real Doris. To myself, it must be owned that I experience considerable difficulty in respect of Margaret, while Sleeping Margaret looks like a difficulty raised to the insuperable degree. I suppose that this is due to her set and independent purpose, her maturity in respect of the other personalities—Real Doris included—her extraordinary analytical skill, in a word, her great individuality. I am not pitting my lay impression against an opinion, so wisely guarded, of an observer so acute and experienced as Professor Hyslop, but I must add that notwithstanding some initial denials on her part—and these were explained subsequently—the reiterated claim of Sleeping Margaret that she is "some species of a spirit" and was "sent by someone higher to guard Doris" carries a certain weight, to my own mind, when taken in connection with her persistent determination to "come" until she can furnish a proof respecting her own nature. The facts that she has no recollection of an incarnate life on earth and no particular views as to whether she ever inhabited an earthly body are of course, for what they are worth, on the other side of the scale, and I agree fully with Professor Hyslop that "the first test of a discarnate spirit must be its ability to prove its terrestrial identity." But there is plenty of room in the universe for spirits that have been always "discarnate," so far as this earth is concerned; there is probably plenty of room for their occasional intervention in human affairs; while as regards those who have "passed over" from this life, if we grant that they may and do communicate, it is obviously—in the great majority of cases—under the very opposite of test conditions. Moreover, there may be numberless people on "the other side" whose memories are in a state of arrestation respecting their life on earth. These considerations are not put forward as arguments that Sleeping Margaret should be regarded as "some species of a spirit" but as offering justification for the fact that in view of her resolute will and unchanging purpose I am able to understand her as such and not at all as "a split off group of mental states." On the contrary side must be placed the definite view of Professor Hyslop that "Margaret, Sleeping Margaret and Sick Doris. . . showed not the slightest scientific evidence of being transcendental agents." But for reasons fully set forth, though they cannot be cited here, he had recourse to experiments with a "trained psychic who knew nothing about the case," to ascertain whether the various personalities would communicate, on the hypothesis that "if they were really spirits . . . they would. . . either prove their identity or show that they were the same personalities that affected Doris." The results may be tabulated thus, (1) Margaret did communicate and Sleeping Margaret did not. (2) Sick Doris "did not communicate in any way to prove identity", that is to say, "as verifiable by the living"—an explanation given elsewhere; but in yet another place, the identity of Margaret is regarded as in the same position. (3) The experiments brought another and previously unknown personality who told much about the life of Doris and claimed connection with her, which claim, according to Professor Hyslop, is assured, "if there is any evidence at all for foreign presences." (4) After revealing the main personalities connected with the case, "the controls made it still more complex by bringing personality after personality said to be influences" thereupon. (5) One of the communicators maintained that Sleeping Margaret was the spirit of Doris herself when "half-way in and half-way out," i.e., between subliminal and supraliminal. (6) The Doris phenomena were affirmed otherwise to be those of demoniacal possession. (7) The more general term "obsession" was, however, in more general use, apparently to distinguish between the constant occupation characteristic of the Doris case and the occasional occupation of mediums under control of spirits. To all these complexities must be added the fact that, concurrently with the experimental work here under notice, the recovered Doris Fischer was developing as a psychic and automatic writer, under the influence of that Imperator group made famous originally by the mediumship of the Rev. Stainton Moses and afterwards by that of Mrs. Piper. The evidence of identity as regards this group is satisfactory in Professor Hyslop's view; and on the whole question he appears to conclude that albeit on the surface the Doris case offers no proof of obsession, "some sort of influence of a foreign type" is evident as-a result of the psychic experiments, whatever the sort may be. He goes on to explain that secondary or multiple personality is a descriptive conception, whereas obsession is explanatory, so that they are not rival hypotheses. Therefore Margaret, Sleeping Margaret and Sick Doris, "as phenomenal manifestations in Doris," can be regarded as "sub-conscious effects of spirits with interfusion of their own influences," instead of as being actually spirits themselves. In this case they represent instigated and not transmitted states. I think that this is actually Professor Hyslop's view, though he uses guarded language, and as such I shall leave my readers to choose between it and what may be called a spiritistic explanation.

Now, I have suggested that the growth of the prime personality throughout the whole case went on amidst all the interventions and all the substitutions. The personality of Real Doris invariably emerged, no other than Real Doris, notwithstanding obsessions, dissociations, or whatever the terms should be. It was always she and no other when the waking life was but one of a few minutes per diem. It is she and no other in the continuity of consciousness now. The secondary personalities acknowledged her priority and that the vehicle was hers. It is this fact that has quickened and sustained my interest in going through the vast memorial. It is to me and will be surely to others the most remarkable record we have of the persistence of personality—though if there be others not less salient outside my knowledge; it is only so much the better. It is, for me, a signal witness to the simplicity and unity of the abiding personality of our nature. I have no doubt that it will be not less important as such to instructed spiritists, and it should be vital also to persons of every religious denomination who are open to consider the evidence of psychical research. To myself, as a Christian mystic, that which emerges from the case is beyond all price, not that I am personally in need of the evidence but because of the way in which it has arisen and the light which it casts so silently, firstly, on modern philosophical speculations about the impermanence of personality and, secondly, on old dreams and current renderings of old dreams upon the multiple constitution of inward man. With the whole of the Thomist school, I believe in the simplicity of our spiritual nature, to which Christian mystical experience has always testified unconsciously and which here receives new illustration in a very different category of experience. It may be that in twenty years' time our current talk of "split off groups of mental states" will occupy the same position towards more developed knowledge of mind and soul that the Belfast address now bears to scientific theory as it is. But however, the groups split off, there remains a Real Doris, her noumenal part of being. It is this which, according to spiritism, goes into Summer Lands and progresses from sphere to sphere; it is this which in mystical experience, by virtue of analogy of nature, has a capacity for union with the Divine in the universe and does, or may ultimately return, a self-knowing being, to God.

THE EVERLASTING FUTURE:
A MYSTIC AND PSYCHIC CONTRAST

July, 1917

THE standpoint regarding our everlasting future from which mystics look is in notable contrast with that of equally earnest thinkers in other schools of spiritual thought. I speak of the present day and modern minds therein. I speak also of what is based on experience rather than on official belief in doctrinal sources of teaching, important as these are in the history of universal religion. Moreover, most mystics themselves have authority and history as their basis, in the sense that these have taught them the possibility of an experiment within their own nature. From such ground, the mystic proceeds to the experiment itself, being the attempted realization of a union—usually much qualified and yet expansible—between his knowing, self-knowing part and that universal mode of being called God. In virtue of whatever quality of correspondence between knower and known this realization is possible, there is something on the knower's side which must pass away or be suspended for a time, in order to success in the experiment: he must cease from self-knowing and attain knowing in God; he must realize pure being outside thought-processes. All that is commonly understood as meditation, contemplation, concentration must go utterly; he is not dealing with a thing conceived intellectually, or following out a process in the mind. I am not proposing to speak of the work itself, nor am I concerned now, even with its validity or with the veridic nature of what may be reached therein. With the cloud of witnesses who stand behind my thesis, there is warrant, however, to conclude that I am dealing in no mere dreams and am justified in postulating attainment—provisionally at least and at least in certain cases—so that we may consider the position in which a mystic is left after such an experience. An Apologia pro vita mystica, much larger than the Apologia sua of Newman, would arise from an answer in full, but I am concerned here with the standpoint from which any mystic who has reached the proposed term must regard the everlasting future and the part of his being therein. There is no need to say that immortality for him is found; but it is set apart by a gulf from all the picture-heavens of old theologies, for even the Thomist doctrine of Beatific Vision is as far apart from the state mystic as subject is apart from object in a dualistic understanding of being. Not only do the past pantheons fold up their tents of dream but also old legends of the soul, its travels and metamorphoses, its transmigrations, metempsy-choses and incarnations. It is not that they have been put out of court as provisional hypotheses, but that the past has ceased to signify. So also, as regards the future, there is a manner in which the end of things is known; and, with the pictured heavens, Summer Lands and Blessed Vi-sion, there goes also—once and for all—the human anxiety for reunion with those loved on earth. The experiment which is possible to one is impossible to no other of the human race, and the law which secures it to one must be law for all—to-morrow if not to-day, in a year or an age to come. Does this make it clear why the mystic as such is never an occultist, is not a psychical researcher, and is not concerned with the question whether the dead return? He may recognize in these explora-tions an accumulated body of discovered facts, out of which at the very least provisional hypotheses can be constructed. He will infer on his own part the existence of intermediate states between earthly life and Divine Union attained. Curiously enough, he will have the chief seer of modem spiritism on his side. Though Andrew Jackson Davis had no means of construing rightly the Divine End of being, his concentric se-ries of Summer Lands brings pilgrim souls gradually to a state of Deific Vision, after the manner of Thomists and of Dante—their spokesman in immortal verse.

Having looked on one aspect of the everlasting future, let us look also on another, being the standpoint of innumerable earnest persons, whose way of progression towards certitude is through paths of psy-chical research or paths of spiritism. We have to recognize that the two aspects do not exclude one another, though for want of mystical experi-ence, the psychic school knows little of the end of things. How earnest this school is may be learned from the lives and work of its chief apostles and exponents, from Hodgson, Myers and James, each fully qualified to speak on the deep things of their subject and the vistas opening there-from. Of the reaction of their research on character, James has testified eloquently in the case of his friends. If ever a man died with his face towards the Higher Salem in these our modem days, that man was Fred-eric Myers. There is another who also testifies. An old hand at research, an old friend of them all, Mr. Henry Holt, of Vermont, U.S.A., has come recently among us with two strange volumes. Much as the result may surprise him, they have brought to my mind the distinction with which I am here dealing and have led me to conceive the eirenicon which is passing, also here, into a rough form of expression. They are full of curious and sometimes suggestive speculation—"candid guesswork," as he says—regarding ingarnered facts. Some of this guesswork is paradoxical enough and some at issue with itself, as he admits bravely. The most valuable part is the record in summary form drawn from Proceedings of Societies of Psychical Research and other sources, here and in America, and presenting vivid aspects of Telekinesis, Autokinesis, Psychokinesis, and so forth. Here is important material put into the hands of those who would think for themselves on these phenomenal issues. It matters little if they do not even thinly chaperone the writer's views on Cosmic Relations, Cosmic Inflow and the Divine Being—conceived somewhat vaguely as a Cosmic Soul, which pours itself into our human nature or from which our nature draws. He is much more vitally concerned with the evidences for an "unknown universe" in the relations between tele-kinetic forces and better-known modes of force, in the psychic relations termed telepathic, and in those classed broadly as spiritistic. Their consideration leads up to a conception of the immediate future spirit-world on the basis of the records, and hence comes my final point.

We have seen that the theological heaven has dissolved for the mystic; so far as records go, it has dissolved also from the life beyond the grave of spiritism and its adjuncts. We are vis a vis with a post mortem state, which is "simply this life with all its healthy interests expanded and relieved of many limitations and pains." So testifies Mr. Holt, and so agrees A. J. Davis. For both also it is a place of progress, a place of satisfied longings. But these things granted on the warrant of the records, their message to me as a mystic is in their delineation of a training state, leading up to our end in God, as an infinite fullness of being. We may miss that end in life, but we do not fail in fine; we may gain in part here, but there we shall win through utterly; we may arrive here intellectually, not essentially, but there with very life in all-embracing experience. It comes about in this manner that there is possible a real peace in understanding between convinced exponents of psychical, spiritistic research and followers of the inward path.

THE HERMETIC TRADITION

July, 1918

THOSE who appreciate the publication of important books in a distinguished and worthy manner, owe no small debt of gratitude to Mr. Tait for the care and excellence with which he has produced his reprint of Mrs. Atwood's remarkable work. It is admirably printed, in a sharp and clear type, on paper which shows that a publisher in Belfast is by no means at the end of his resources in this respect, notwithstanding the scarcity of supplies and their fourfold cost. There is, moreover, a good plain binding, eminently suitable to the volume; altogether the result compares well with that which was attained in the year 1850 by those who had charge of the first edition. There is another debt, but it is due more especially from persons who have been waiting and hoping for the text to be made available. At this day one has scarcely any need to inform occult readers, or indeed many who would not subscribe to this designation, that very soon after its appearance Mrs. Atwood called in the original impression, destroyed the sheets and for some years subsequently secured—with the same intention—every copy which she heard of in the book market. In this manner, it became very rare, and on those occasions when it was available, a purchaser did well if he obtained it for four or five pounds. I have seen it at much higher prices. Gratitude is due therefore to Mr. Tait for taking the risk of reproduction and for offering it at what is—under all the circumstances—a moderate price.

From whatever point of view, it be regarded, the Suggestive Inquiry—as I have indicated—is a remarkable performance, and among modem books it was one of my enthusiasms at the beginning of literary life. It continues to impress me as the production of a comparatively young woman and, beyond a certain extravagance of expression, I have nothing to reduce in the notice which I wrote so far back as 1887. But I stood then only at the threshold of the Secret Tradition in Hermetic literature and in other literatures and movements of Christian times. The years have elapsed, and without alluding to the natural and ordinary growth of a student's mind, I have had the opportunity as it happened—besides other activities—to make a special research into alchemical texts and into the history of alchemy. The criticism which was put forward in the year mentioned would no doubt be extended further, did occasion arise seriously, but I question whether it will do so beyond the scope of these brief paragraphs, which are primarily a thank-offering to a deserving publisher. In the year 1887 a great opportunity was given to research by M. Berthelot's publication of the Byzantine texts of alchemy, followed at no distant date by the Arabian and Syriac alchemists. In this manner and in others, one came to know, at first hand, the memorials and remains of personalities who had been almost mythical names in the long story of alchemy. Such were Zosimus the Panopolite, Ostanes and Democritus. One came also to know that the Latin Geber bears practically no relation to the original Djaber and that the collection which passes under the former variant of the true name is what is called a forgery in the sense of literature. No such additions to equipment were needed to discover that the first part of Mrs. Atwood's work is—to say the least—uncritical. She accepted every ascription in a literature which abounds in false references and accounted for any counter-views as "unscrupulous private prejudices." She did not distinguish Raymund Lully, the propagator of Latin Christianity among the Moslems and the author of Ars Magna, from the pseudonymous adept who adopted that name and wrote the alchemical texts. She received such testimony concerning the latter personality as is borne by a so-called Abbot of Westminster, named John Cremer, who is not in the historical list of persons bearing that title. In one place, she refers the Open Entrance to Alexander Sethon and contradicts it in another; her great debt to Thomas Vaughan notwithstanding, she seems unacquainted with Aula Lucis; while she ascribes to Vaughan the translation of Fama et Confessio R.C., notwithstanding his express denial. Finally, she speaks of the exceedingly late Tractatus Aureus as a most ancient text. It does not follow that her general understanding of alchemy is wrong because she is not a guide in criticism or a textual or historical scholar, though the free use of exceedingly doubtful documents is discouraging from any standpoint. The grounds of her interpretation are in Vaughan and there is no one whom she quotes more often, but it is only the simple grounds. She carried her developments to such a point that the debt—which is of little or indeed no consequence in any case—almost ceases to exist, and her book is her own and no other's. She failed, however, to recognize that there are two sides to alchemical literature, by which I mean that some writers who pass as adepts had no special concern outside the transmutation of metals, while others dealt only with a spiritual experiment under the same veils. So far as there is evidence—good or bad—of metallic transmutation in the past—as, e.g., that of Helvetius—it does not tolerate her view as to how ex hypothesi it was accomplished.

But when she passes to another ground, to the consideration of Greek Mysteries and that which lay behind them—whether we can accept her explanation or not in the later light of researches by German and English scholars—her thesis is profound and original. As a lover of good and beautiful things in the world of imagining, I prefer them to all the learning of those who find dry bones only in the sanctuaries of old. She offers an elaborate and enlightening commentary on Plato's direct "contact with the object of rational inquiry" and on the classical notion of "participation in Deity." I cannot help thinking that had she known to what extent Eckehart and Ruysbroeck were concerned with the same experiment and how they explored the same ground, attaining a deep realization in an identical end, she might have reconsidered the efficacy or likelihood of that "key" which she offers to unlock the mystery. This is Animal Magnetism carried to a grade of which that art or science has not dreamed in these days.

The text is now available, for all and any who are concerned to take as they can. It reminds us in any case of that great experiment which has been always in the world, however much it may misconstrue the modus operandi. For myself as a mystic, I know no "mesmerist" but God, no odic force but the work of His grace in the heart of love. If the experiment of alchemy and that shadowed forth in the Mysteries attained the end in God, it was by no other way than this. If they carried any disciple or master to the end more deeply, it was by this Divine Operation extended more fully and this Divine Force more utterly received within. Mr. Wilmshurst has had the advantage of two revised copies of the original edition—one of them made by Mrs. Atwood—and we are therefore in possession of a sound and correct text. He has furnished also a sketch of the writer's life and a general introduction.

THE TAROT AND SECRET TRADITION

March, 1919

THE Tarot is a puzzle for archaeology and it is also an intellectual puzzle. When the bare fact of its existence first became public in Europe, the seventy-eight cards were in use as a game and also as a method of divination and may have served these purposes for generations. Yet from the first to the last everyone who has taken up their study at all seriously has felt that the Trumps Major at least belonged originally neither to a game of chance nor to that other kind of chance which is called fortunetelling. They have been regarded as (i) allegorical designs containing religious and philosophical doctrine; (2) a veiled treatise on theosophy; (3) the science of the universe in hieroglyphics; (4) a keystone of occult science; (5) a summary of Kabalistic teaching; (6) the key of alchemy; and (7) the most ancient book in the world. But as these impressions have not been put forward, accompanied by any tolerable evidence, it has been thought to follow in logic that Tarot cards belong to those arts in which they appear to have been used and to nothing else. In a little study of the Tarot, accompanied by the striking designs of Miss Pamela Colman Smith, and in its enlarged form as The Pictorial Key to the Tarot I have intimated that a secret tradition exists regarding the cards. The statement is open to every kind of misjudgment, and it is time to correct a few exaggerated inferences which have arisen out of it. An opportunity seems given by the very interesting article of Mr. J.W. Brodie-Innes, in the last issue of the Occult Review. He has reminded me of the whole subject and has mentioned one collection of cards, which is a name only to myself. I will add to my remarks certain points of fact which are not mentioned in my books.

There are in reality two Tarot traditions, or—shall I say?—unpublished sources of knowledge: one is of the occult order, and one is purely mystical. Each of the occult sciences has a golden side of its particular shield, and this is a mystical side, alchemy being a ready case in point. The art of transmuting metals was pursued secretly, and a long line of physical adepts claim to have attained its end, their procedure being recorded in books which ex hypothesi are clear to initiates, and to no one else. But there was another school or order of research speaking the same language of symbolisms, by means of which they delineated a different quest and a distinct attainment—both of the spiritual kind. I am led to infer that this spiritual or mystical school was later, though the peculiar veil of emblems used by Zosimus the Panopolite makes one inclined to suspend judgment. After the same manner there was Operative Masonry, but there came a period—placed usually towards the end of the seventeenth century—when there arose out of it that Emblematical Art which is so familiar now among us. In this case also there are vestiges of a figurative school at an earlier period, so again, it is prudent to keep an open mind. Masonry is of course occult only in an attributed sense but—as a last example—there remains Ceremonial Magic and its connexions, an occult art above all and in respect both of object and procedure about the last which might be supposed to have an alternative mystical aspect; but the fact remains. The occult tradition of the Tarot is concerned with cartomancy in so far as it belongs to the manipulation and play of the cards for fortune-telling, but it has also a curious astrological side. The mystical tradition is confined to the Trumps Major, which I have termed the Greater Arcana in my two handbooks. The occult tradition leads no one anywhere, and its mode of practice in respect of the cards is—I am told—little, if anything, better than the published kinds—so far as results are concerned. I am not, of course, adjudicating on this question: as a mystic, I should regard all such results as worthless. A prognostication which turns out amazingly correct is of no more consequence to the soul of man than another which proves far from the mark. The occult astrology of the Tarot has naturally its divinatory side, but it is not without traces of another and deeper intention. I should think it likely that the occult tradition will "leak out," as the saying is, one of these days, for it has passed through various hands which do not seem to respect it. The mystical aspect may be explained most readily as belonging to Kabalistic theosophy, and has proved illuminating to many on the mystic quest, provided that they happen to find help in symbolism. It is precisely the same here as it is in the Churches and secret societies like Masonry. Certain are aided by its pageants of ritual, while to others they are little better than a rock of offence. The Eighteenth Degree of Rose-Croix is a hopeless adventure for those to whom ritual speaks no language, but so also is a Pontifical High Mass. Moreover, such good people would probably be well advised not to concern themselves about the mystical tradition of Tarot cards. They are not for such reason to be relegated to a lower scale and those of an opposite temperament have no warrant for assuming superiority. No one is further from God because the Ode Written in Dejection by Coleridge carries no message to his heart. There is no off or near side of the Kingdom of Heaven by these alternatives of inward character.

Such being the nature of the Tarot tradition in its two aspects there remains to be said that it has no information to offer on the time, place or circumstances of Tarot origins, nor on the question of its importation into Europe, supposing that it came from the East. There are, of course, expressions of opinion on the part of people who know the occult tradition, but I have not found that they are of more consequence than those of outside speculation. Speaking generally, my experience of all such traditions, when they happen to make a claim on history, is that they present mere figments of invention. The great mass of Masonic Rites and Orders have fraudulent traditional claims, and those of most Rosicrucian Societies are equally mendacious myths. Among notable exceptions are the Régime Eccosais et Rectifié—which includes the important Grades of Novice and Knight Beneficent of the Holy City—the Military and Religious Order of the Temple, the Order of Rose-Croix of Hendover, and one mystical society which is referable in the last resort to the third quarter of the eighteenth century. As regards Craft Masonry, it has worked out its own redemption by emerging from the Anderson period and its foolish fictions. If it be worthwhile to say so, by way of conclusion to this part of my subject, the Tarot tradition—whether mystical or occult—bears no marks of antiquity. It would not signify how old they were if they had no other claim or value, while if they offer light on any questions of the soul, it matters nothing if they are of yesterday.

On their mystical side the Trumps Major offers most notable differences from any of the known recensions, including those of Miss Colman Smith. It will be obvious then I can offer no details; but Death, the Hanged Man, the Sun and Fool are among notable cases in point. I have said, now long ago, (1) that there are vague rumors concerning a higher meaning in the minor cards, but (2) they have never yet been translated into another language than that of fortune-telling. Yet one knows not all that is doing nor always that which has been done, so it is well to add that I spoke within the measures of my own acquaintance—though I have had more than usual opportunities. In any case, the four suits of Wands, Cups, Swords and Pentacles have two strange connexions in folk-lore, to one of which I drew attention briefly in The Hidden Church of the Holy Graal. So far as my recollection goes, I have not mentioned the other in any published work.

The four Hallows of the Holy Graal are (1) the Graal itself, understood as a Cup or Chalice, being the first Cup of the Eucharist; (2) the Spear, traditionally that of Longinus; (3) the Sword, which was made and broken under strange circumstances of allegory; and (4) the Dish of Plenty, about which the Graal tradition is composed, but it is understood generally as the Paschal Dish. The correspondence of these Hallows or Tokens with the Tarot suits will be noted, and the point is that albeit three out of the four belong to the Christian history of relics, they have an antecedent folk-lore history belonging to the world of Celtic myth. This is a subject which I shall hope to carry farther one of these days. There are also the four treasures of the Tuatha de Danaan: these were the Sword of the Dogda, the Spear of Lug, the Cauldron of Plenty and Lia Fail, the Stone of Destiny which indicated the rightful King. I remember one of our folk-lore scholars, and a recognized authority on the texts of Graal literature, suggesting to me that something might be done to link these pagan talismans with the Tarot suits, but I know as yet of no means by which the gulf of centuries can be bridged over. For the Tuatha de Danaan are of pre-Christian myth, but no one has traced Tarot cards earlier than the fourteenth century. The Tuatha de Danaan were mysterious beings of Ireland and divinities of Wales: some information concerning them will be found in Alfred Nutt's Voyage of Bran. They are said to be (1) earth-gods, (2) gods of growth and vegetation, (3) lords of the essence of life. They are connected with the idea of rebirth, usually of a god or hero. I assume that an adequate survey of the vast field of folk-lore would produce other analogies, without appealing—like excellent old Court de Gebelin—to Chinese inscriptions or the avatars of Vishnu. It follows that the archaeology of the Tarot has made a beginning only and we know not whither it may lead us. Much yet remains to be done with antique packs, and I should be glad to follow up the reference of Mr. Brodie-Innes to the Clulow collection—now, as he mentions, in America.

Whether it is in a public museum and whether there is a descriptive catalogue are among the first questions concerning it. One is continually coming across the titles of foreign books on Tarot and Playing Cards which might be followed up, not without profit, if we could get at the works themselves; but they are not in our public libraries. Were it otherwise, my bibliography of works dealing with the Tarot and its connexions might be much extended. As regards packs, since the appearance of The Pictorial Key I have inspected a Jewish Tarot which has not, I think, been printed. It represents the black magic of divination—a most extraordinary series of designs, carrying messages of evil in every sign and symbol. It is, so to speak, a Grimoire Tarot, and if it is not of French

THE TAROT AND SECRET TRADITION 137

origin, the inscriptions and readings are in the French language. I have seen only the Trumps Major and two or three of the lesser Court Cards, but I understood that there is at least one complete pack in existence.

Mr. Brodie-Innes speculates as to the authority for my allocation of Tarot suits to those of ordinary playing-cards. Its source is similar to that from which Florence Emery—one of my old friends and of whom I am glad to be reminded—derived her divinatory meanings mentioned by Mr. Brodie-Innes. The source to which I refer knew well of the alternative attribution and had come to the conclusion that it was wrong. In adopting it, I was careful that no allocation should be of consequence to "the outer method of the oracles" and the meanings of the Lesser Cards. Nothing follows therefore from the attribution of Swords to Clubs and Pentacles to Spades. In my book on the Graal I had already taken the other allocation of Swords to Spades and Pentacles to Clubs. I cannot say that I am especially satisfied by either mode of comparison. There is no connexion in symbolism between a sword and spade, at least until the League of Nations turns all our weapons of offence into plowshares and reaping-hooks. A little correspondence appears between so-called pentacles and clubs, but it is Hobson's choice. In the absence of a canon of criticism, I should prefer to say nothing as to the mystic virtues of numbers in this connexion.

MYSTICAL REALISATION

September, 1919

T HE testimony to mystical experience has been borne in the modern world, in the main on the faith of the records, and under the Christian aegis—through all the Christian centuries—it has been borne at first hand by those who have attained therein some part at least of that which awaits the souls of men in the fruition of Divine Union. The annals of old sanctity and the commentaries of expert theology constitute together an exceedingly large literature, over and above which there is a yet larger testimony going back into remote ages and concerned with the same experience under the denominations of other religions in the sacred world of the East. Yet it seems to me that in what has been called the "general and popular world" of thoughtful and literate people, there is still only a very slight and imperfect understanding of the whole subject. There is, I think, none on which statements are looser and fundamental misconceptions more frequent. The terms Mysticism and Mystical are still used to characterize the dealings of "occult science" and as synonyms for the scheme of things, which are usually connoted by the title of "new thought." They are labels in commonly used indifferently by friends and enemies of both. Those who affirm that there are no occult sciences, though there are many grades of self-induced hallucination, are apt to term them mystical as a by-word of reproach. Those in whose view the literary ventures which carry the mark of new thought are goods that are labelled falsely, regard it as the last word of condemnation to describe them as mystical. On the other hand, both literatures belong, in the opinion of many defenders, to the realm of mysticism, which they understand to mean higher thought. The point of union between the two parties resides in the fact that they are indifferently misusing words.

It happens that mysticism is the world-old science of the soul's return to God and that those who apply it to (1) any form of conventional metaphysics, (2) any branch of mental philosophy, (3) any reveries high or low, are no less mistaken than those who use it as a term of scorn. I care nothing in this connection for the etymological significance of the word, as denoting what is secret and withdrawn. It has come in the course of the years to have one meaning only in the accurate use thereof, and we must abide by this and no other—for the sake of ordered thought—unless and until the keepers of mystical science shall agree between themselves on another and more definite term as an expression of the whole subject.

I have been speaking of the outer circles, from whom it seems idle at present, to expect accuracy; but there is a more extraordinary want of understanding on the part of some whom we should expect to be capable at least of thinking rightly within the elementary measures of mysticism. Here it is no longer a question concerning the mere word, or the use of denominations in the sense of the mystical path when they belong more properly to the end, after all the traveling's are over. I refer especially at the moment to misapprehensions respecting the place of the science in the life of modem man and woman, and this involves a consideration of the now recurring question whether that science can be acquired by practice in the daily life of the world. There can be no expectation of presenting in a brief space any views that will differ materially from those which I have expressed already in much longer studies; but it may be possible to offer something simply, for understanding on the part of those who cannot examine the subject in ordered and lengthy books The question is, therefore, whether those excellent people are right who seem to think that the principles of mystical science may be so put forward that they can be taken into the heart, not indeed of the men in the street—though no one wishes to exclude them—but of men and women everywhere who have turned already to God, or are disposed in that direction. Alternatively, is it—shall I say?—a science which is reserved to experts only? We know that it is not possible to become acquainted readily and easily with the higher mathematics with chemistry or biology. There are certain natural qualifications in virtue of which the poet is born, as well as made subsequently; there is also the scientific mind, which presupposes gift and faculty, as well as opportunity and application. In the science of the mystics, in their peculiar art of life, are there certain essential qualifications to be postulated in every case, and is there a long apprenticeship? Before attempting to answer, let us see what is being said and how far it exhibits any adequate acquaintance with the problems belonging to the debate.

It has been suggested recently that religion is at work revising institutions and theology, that reconstruction is in the air every–where and that mysticism needs reconstruction as much as anything else. In the face of this statement, a certain caution is necessary lest we begin to talk foolishly. It appears, however, that the remark applies rather to notions, theories and systems, to "the spell of mediaeval mysticism" and to the reconstruction of these. Yet the tendency is to regard mysticism as a mode of thought, an attitude—if you like—towards the universal, so that we can have done with archaic forms and devise others which are modem. It is, however, as I have said, a science, the end of which is attained in the following of certain methods. One does not change sciences—as, for example, mathematics—but we can reconstruct and, it may be, improve our way of acquiring them. Mediaeval mysticism is the same as modem mysticism—if any—but there may be other ways of reaching it, in respect of the externals, than were known and practiced in convents. Fundamentally speaking, however, the ways are one—whether in the East or West, for those who follow Vedanta and those to whom the Imitation is a source in chief of leading. The only change that we can make is by taking out of the way that which is unnecessary thereto. As I tried to show some four or five years since, in The Way of Divine Union, there is no question that the end of mysticism was reached by the ascetic path during many past centuries of Christendom, but it belonged to the accidents of the quest; and other ways are possible, which I tried also to indicate.

The alleged reconstruction of religion is taking place only in a subsidiary sense, within narrow measures, or here and there in the comers. The great Latin Church is revising nothing, while the Greek—I suppose—is stewing in the waters of its own incapacity. But if they were both at the work of remaking and at one in their activity with the sects and the Anglican Church, the case of the mystics would still differ, because pure mysticism has no institutions to revise and no conventional or official theology to expand, reduce, or vary. It is a path of advancement towards a certain end, and the path is one: the variations are found only in the modes of travelling. Having in this manner cleared the issues, there must be something said of the end and the way thereto.

There is a great experiment possible in this life and there is a great crown of the experiment, but in the nature of things it is not to be bought cheaply, for it demands the whole man. It has been said that the life of the mystic is one of awareness of God, and as to this we must remember that we are dealing with a question of life and a life-problem. But what is awareness of God? It is a certain inward realization, a consciousness of the Divine—not only without us, but within. The word awareness is therefore good and true, but it is one of those intimations which—as I have suggested already—are of the path and not of the end. It is of the learner and not of the scientist. The proof can be put in a nutshell by an appeal to the perfect analogy of that experience which is human love. Can we say to the human over that an awareness of the beloved must content him here and now? But that which he seeks is possession, after the manner of all in all—possession which is reciprocal and mutual. In Divine Things, the word is realization, and mystical realization is the state of being possessed and possessing. Otherwise, it is God in us and we in God: O state of the ineffable, beyond all words and thoughts, deeper than tears of the heart and higher than all its raptures. The science of the mystic is that of the peculiar life-cultus, life-practice, or quest of life which leads to this state. In respect both of path and state, the word is love. The kind of loving is summarized in the grand old counsel: "With all thy heart and with all thy soul." The rewards of love are not those which can be earned by divided allegiance. There is also another saying—about the desire of a certain house having eaten one up. There is no eye on two worlds in this and no Sabbath dedication except in the long Sabbath of undivided life. Here, too, is no art of making the best of both worlds and especially of this one, as if with one eye on the dollars and another on God. In this kind of dedication, the world goes by and the pageants of all its temples: there are no half-measures respecting it. The motto of the path is sub specie aeternitatis, and it connotes the awakening and subsequent activity of a particular inward faculty. We know well enough by experience the power of a ruling passion, and it may happen to be one that is lawful. The man who is ruled thereby is living sub specie illa; it colors all his ways and days: it is the very motive of his life. Now, if we postulate in certain persons a ruling passion for God, it is then sub illa specie aeternitatis that they live and move and have their being.

As regards this state and as regards its gifts and fruits, even at the early stages, I testify that the Divine in the universe answers to the Divine in man. There does take place that which maintains and feeds the passion. A life which is turned to the keynote of the eternal mode knows of the things that are eternal. It knows very soon that it is not on a false quest: that God is and that He recompenses those who seek Him out is verified by a valid experience. It grows from more to more, an ever-expanding equipment in the highest sanity of mind. Two things are certain: (1) apart from this high passion there can be no practical mystic; but (2) no one can teach another how to acquire it. Once it has been kindled in the heart, the secret of the path is its maintenance, and many devices have been tried—among others, those of the ascetics. The only excellent way is that of love in its activity towards all in God and God in all. This is the sense of St. Augustine's: Love and do what you will. Hatred is a canker in the heart and eats up this passion. Universal love maintains the passion for God till that time when God enters and takes over the work: it is then the beginning of the end, and that end is the still activity of union in the Eternal Center. It is inevitable that vocation must be postulated, but this signifies an inward possibility of response to an ever-recurring call. It is thus that the divine passion is kindled which—as I have said—no one can communicate to another. There is something in the individual fount by which some are poets and some are called to the priesthood. For the same inscrutable reason, there are some who receive and answer the call to mystic life. It may be a consequence of antecedent lives or of hidden leading from spiritual spheres: I do not know. It follows that the mystic life is reserved to those who can lead it, but unlike all other sciences, the only technique connected with it is the technique of love; the apprenticeship is that of love; the science is love; and the end is love's guerdon. All this being so, I am sure that there are more true mystics than we can dream, and yet they are few enough. They will grow from more to more, for love always conquers. But as to when this science of love can appeal to all classes, I make no pretense of knowing: it is for those who are able to acquire it; and so are the questions answered.

CHRISTIANITY AND SPIRITUALISM

February, 1920

WE are almost weary of hearing that common sense is, comparatively speaking at least, rather a rare quality, but it should be understood perhaps of that sense in one of its superior degrees. I mention the point to introduce a conclusion which I have reached on my own part about the analogous region of commonplace, having found that some of its examples call for continued repetition because few persons have any realization about them. It is, of course, a commonplace to say that the realm of religious doctrine can only go counter to the world of things as they are—the domain of actual fact—at its own peril, or that Christian Theology, as an established science of dogma, has been much too well planned to fall into obvious pitfalls of this kind. In the doctrine of a Trinity in Unity there may be grave difficulties, but it does not contradict mathematics, as it belongs to another order, and—cæteris paribus—so also of the rest. They stand or fall in their relation to intellectual truth and by the hypotheses of the scheme of revelation, not by a supposititious place in the world of external facts. If these patents, yet often unnoticed, considerations are granted, we see at once that the question of relation between Christianity and Spiritualism is grave for both sides, because the warrants of both are in the unseen, by way of revelation therefrom. In so far as Spiritualism is a philosophy—which it claims to be—it stands or falls by its relation to intellectual truth; in so far as it is a revelation of life from the unseen, it is of necessity a challenge to other systems which are held to have emanated from the same source. In one sense it is the most important of all challenges because, in place of news from the invisible world and gospel tidings coming through divinely elected channels, it is offered on all sides, is placed in the hands of all, and directly or indirectly the supposed source of revelation can be tapped by anyone who follows the proper lines of communication.

Now, this is a ground on which the Churches as official spokesmen of Christianity have every title to be concerned in respect of Spiritualism. There are people in the past who have set out quite sincerely to explain its identity with primitive faith and practice during the first Christian centuries. Save only as an index of intention, their findings are without value. There are people who believe themselves in communication under the aegis of Spiritualism with friends and kinsfolk now on the other side, as also with guides and instructors, yet they are living members of one Church or another, even regular and devout communicants. But what—if any—is the light which "spirit intercourse" casts upon the field of Christian doctrine and its peculiar quality of faith in a future state of being? The answer is that there could be no two schemes more completely independent of each other. In the orthodox sense, there is neither heaven nor hell; there is no entrance into a supernatural mode of being; there is no. vision of God; there are no tidings of Christ, unless—and then rarely—as a teacher of olden times who, with many that are like Him, is now in some high sphere. The official scheme of redemption has passed utterly away. In place of it, the world beyond is a reflection or reproduction in psychic terms of that world in which we live. If such testimony be true, the whole body of Christian theology belongs to the region of intellectual conventions, and when we pass into disembodied life it falls away, as fell the cloak and scallop-shell of old from the pilgrim who reached his borne.

I do not know how far this position of affairs has been realized clearly by Miss Stoddart in writing her Case against Spiritualism. It seems lost amidst the miscellaneous considerations of her chapter devoted to the comparison, yet it constitutes the only vital case, so far as Churches are concerned, and it has the benefit attaching to a clear issue. By all its hypotheses and on all the basis of its evidence, the world opened up by intercourse with disembodied spirits knows nothing of so-called Christian evidences, and is implicitly an undesigned witness against them. On the other hand, the case of the Churches against Spiritualism is that of the custodians of a rigidly defined faith against a sphere of experience in which that faith has become of no effect. The papers collected into Miss Stoddart's volume appeared originally in the British Weekly, but they represent quite adequately the general thesis of the Churches outside that of Rome. It can be said with sincerity that she has put it in a clear and ordered manner. It is one at the same time which is usually fair and moderate, careful on the side of justice, and making few points in respect of the evidences or their criticism for which authorities are wanting. It seems to me of considerable value regarded as an ex parte statement, and it is eminently desirable at the present time to know what is being thought and said on the official side of religion in respect of this momentous subject.

There is a sense in which, as a mystic, I stand apart from both schools, and can look upon them therefore independently, more especially as regards their reaction upon each other at the present time. I am entirely certain that the fact of their co-existence is the most important fact of this age, and if I did not bear my witness when a need arises, I should be guilty of disservice to my own standpoint as well as to the two interests which are here contrasted. Miss Stoddart has had occasion to quote various passages from my Studies in Mysticism, which appeared so far back as 1906, and it must be said in the first place that there is nothing to alter or withdraw either in respect of those passages or of the papers to which they belong, within their own measures. But, in the second place, the subject has extended greatly during the thirteen years which stand between this date and the year 1906. To cite only specific examples, we have on one side the three epoch-making volumes of the American Society for Psychical Research concerning the case of Doris Fischer, and on another the records of such investigations as those of Sir Oliver Lodge and Dr. W. T. Crawford. Miss Stoddart suggests that Spiritualism is like a tidal wave which ebbs and flow?, and this is true as a point of fact, but I believe that we stand on the threshold of more ordered experiment, and in any case those who account—like her—for the existing concern in the subject as owing to a "need for distraction" during the great war can have only a most inadequate realization of the things that are at stake. So also, it should be impossible any longer to speak of Spiritualism as rushing in "with its false and fatal comfort" presumably interrupting the words of Divine consolation which are uttered by the Churches. The question at issue is precisely whether the comfort is false and whether its results are fatal. On what grounds soever I have challenged and must still challenge the validity of most messages, they are not of this order, nor do I find that the wardens of official religion communicate anything except as an echo from the past. About the dangers which loom in certain quarters of research, there is indeed no question, but the voices of warning must sound a clearer note if they are to call for hearing.

I agree with Miss Stoddart that "table-turning" must be set aside as evidence of any intelligence outside that of the medium or circle, until we know better concerning our own inward nature. I agree that most, if not all, automatic writing must be set aside in like manner, and for the same reason. Miss Stoddart's remarks on this subject command provisional assent. But for what the speculation may signify to those who can receive it, I feel that we stand here on the threshold of things unrealized, that the day may come when a consecrated and ordained "automatist" assisted by a dedicated circle—in the plenary sense of these expressions—will obtain records from "dissociated personality" or from "the other side," and that they will carry an authentic, note. If there are deeps unsounded beneath our average humanity, there are also heights above. The prophets spoke of old in virtue of a power within them, and there is nothing to tell us that it was only for once and for all. We need them no less at this day than did that crooked generation of old which was called Israel, and it is the kind of need which is an open door of opportunity for the only kind of help. Meanwhile, as I have intimated, there is danger from the other side, and it is of all that which tends to befall the unsanctified. I am quite sure that Catherine of Siena was what we call a medium, but her protection was that Catherine of Siena was a saint. Even so, we are not at an end of the problems for—outside the Latin Church—no one can say that her Guide was That which he called himself, the Christ of Nazareth, though his intention to help the Church of the period may not have taken place without high authority beyond the normal bar.

As regards the fact of communications on the part of disembodied intelligence, the evidences have extended since 1906, when I felt that it might be admitted provisionally: whether in the nature of things an absolute demonstration may be obtainable is another question, but I do not see that we have reached it. As regards the modes and status of being on the other side of this life, the subject seems getting gradually away from the Summerland spheres of Andrew Jackson Davis, and is the more in nubibus accordingly. Meanwhile, it is not the messages of Spiritualism which signify, save indeed in respect of a single conclusion that they tend to justify, and to which I shall advert at the end. It is the phenomena which really matter: I mean, of course, those which take place under circumstances that are beyond challenge and above all certain amazing records in Germany just prior to the war, and more recently in Paris. They show that there is yet untrodden ground in psychology and physiology, that here also we stand on the threshold of discovery—in things that are psychic, things of mind and things of the body also. Beyond and above these is "the holy spirit of man," where lies another ground, untrodden by the great majority of men. Some of its vistas opened to Greek philosophers, to Christian and Vedic saints. I have to say in conclusion as to this part that outside the closely woven circle of Roman doctrine, a significant change has passed over Christian eschatology. The idea of redemptive processes beyond the gate of death is replacing within the Churches those old theological dogmas of heaven and hell: I believe it to be a reflection from Spiritualism and from the peculiar congeries of hypothesis and intimation connoted thereby.

I should like to add a word in conclusion about Mrs. Travers. Smith and her Voices from the Void issued a few months since with an introduction by Sir William Barrett, who describes her as "a gifted psychic and automatist." She is also his personal friend of many years' standing. Amidst the great output of psychic books, records of spiritualistic research and essays in automatic writing, it seems to me that its importance has been overlooked. It is to my mind of considerable value as a transparently sincere and unpretending statement of first-hand experience by a lady of considerable mental ability, who has weighed with care and discrimination the results obtained during six or seven years of regular communications received by herself. She has considered the various explanations and has concluded that the choice lies between a theory that in some inexplicable way she has read the minds of persons who have not been in touch with her, and for no assignable reason, or that there has been actual communication with those who have "passed through the experience which we call death." While keeping an open mind and confessing that she is by no means convinced, Mrs. Travers Smith inclines to the second view, as on the whole more natural and less marvelous than the first. I think that Voices from the Void is a book to be read and considered by inquirers for its simple account of the facts, its temperate conclusions thereon and its anxious recognition of the dangers which attend to research. Many qualified experimenters will agree when it is said that "the subliminal self-accounts for much and many things, but not for everything."

OCCULT FREEMASONRY AND THE JEWISH PERIL

September, 1920

FOR seventeen days in succession, ending July 30, The Morning Post published a remarkable series of articles on The Cause of World Unrest, the work of two anonymous writers, with occasional intervention on the part of leading articles, generalizing on the subjects treated, and of occasional correspondents, chief among whom is Mrs. Nesta H. Webster, author of a book issued in 1919 under the title of The French Revolution. As expressed in a short announcement of July 12, the articles claim to disclose "the existence of a revolutionary movement in which Jews and secret societies play a leading part."

On July 24, another announcement stated that "thousands of new readers have been taking The Morning Post during the publication of the series." Accepting this implicitly on the honorable assurance of the oldest morning paper, I regard it as incumbent on myself to review the whole question, in softer as it affects the things for which I stand and the dedications of my literary life. The nature of the secret societies incriminated emerges in another passage which appeared on July 21 and affirmed (1) that for a long period of time a conspiracy has been gradually developing for the overthrowing of the existing Christian form of civilization; (2) that the prime agents of this conspiracy are Jews and revolutionary Freemasons; and (3), that its object "is to pave the way for the-world supremacy of a chosen people." I propose on my part to show that the writers are utterly misinformed, where it is possible for an individual critic to check them, and that it would be curious therefore—as well as difficult to suppose—if they are mainly or substantially correct over their findings in those political realms which lie beyond my field of research.

It is to be observed that the existence of a plot for "the destruction of all Christian Empires, Altars and Thrones" is an old Roman Catholic thesis, put forward long prior to the War. One of the forms which it took was a review of the Dreyfus case, and it not only made common cause with the activities of the Latin Church against Freemasonry, but seems to have been part of that cause. A periodical, called La Revue des Sociétés Secrètes, was filled with the case against Freemasonry and the case against Israel. The management of both issues was of similar value, being the enumeration and repetition of various less or more familiar facts on which a false construction was placed, or of statements that were probably untrue. Both forms being equally effective in impressing those who were unversed, the first was pursued when possible. My thesis is that the revelations in The Morning Post on "the cause of world unrest," the "most formidable sect in the world" and "the terror in France," but especially on "the red curtain in Freemasonry," the "arrière Loges" and the "ritual of revenge" bear all the marks and signs of derivation from the same mint, appeal to the same sources, and are speaking the same language as the French anti-Masonry of the last thirty years and over. They are the work of writers belonging to the Latin Church or alternatively content to depend—so far as Freemasonry is concerned—solely on material which, during the period specified, has been dished up in various forms for the one purpose with which Rome is concerned on this side of its activity—namely, the forlorn hope of destroying the "iniquitous sect" of Masonry, and presumably to maintain at white heat the old hostility of France to Jewry and all connoted thereby. I speak with a certain authority, for it happens that I know the leading literature of anti-Masonry, on what it has depended from the beginning, and the contentions which it will sustain to the end. It happens also that I am a Freemason, holding the chief Rites and Degrees, under one or other obedience, that I know the literature of Freemasonry, its history ab origine symboli and the great cloud of its Rituals. If I flourish, for once in my life, a trumpet of this kind, it is in order that the anti-Masonic sect, wheresoever dispersed over the world, in whichever of its disguises, and in this or that of its regular or casual journals, may learn exactly where they are. Finally, I am a Christian and Catholic Mystic, and my Catholicism embraces all that belongs to the eternal in the symbolism of Roman Doctrine and Ritual. It comes about in this manner that, for me, Emblematic Freemasonry is a Mystery of the relations between God,

Man and the Universe, set forth in the figurative and sacramental forms of sacred ceremonial. It will be understood on this basis that those various associations which, in France and other Latin countries, while still wearing an outward guise of Freemasonry, regard the belief in God and immortality, the intercourse between God and the soul represented by the Bible and other Sacred Books as matters of personal opinion—to be held or not according to mental predilection—have made void their Masonic titles. They are cut off from communion with the vital and spiritual source: they may be political or not, revolutionary or not, monarchical and otherwise "reactionary," or the reverse of these; they are in no case part of my concern. The question is whether the writers in The Morning Post have followed a line of accusation which incriminates all Freemasonry even when it offers a distinction; and the answer is that they have. Out of this there arises the further question of whether they and the Roman Catholic crusaders, on whom they depend, are competent witnesses on the Masonic side of their subject; and the answer is that they are not.

It is obvious and goes without saying that the articles are not written by Masons holding under any obedience, and my thesis is that they betray the most extraordinary ignorance on elementary matters respecting the Craft and its developments. It is recognized from the beginning that English Freemasonry is not to be included by their sweeping thesis concerning universal revolution, but it is affirmed that "there is Freemasonry and Freemasonry." More correctly, there is Freemasonry and there are things which masquerade in its likeness but do not belong thereto. Anyone acquainted with the subject would know that true Freemasonry is neither English nor English-speaking only, neither British, Colonial nor American, to the exclusion of other countries. It is certain that prior to the War, Germanic Freemasonry had no poisoned wells of political concern. There are also other countries—and I should place Sweden among them—where pure and ancient Freemasonry," with some flowers of its later development, are equally uncontaminated as to root and branch and blossom. But having made the distinction in question, like a proverbial sop to Cerberus, the articles proceed to ingarner some time-immemorial charges of French origin against Templar Freemasonry and the Scottish Rite as one of its custodians, which is a charge against English as well as continental bodies. The writers seem unaware that there are great Templar jurisdictions in England, Scotland and Ireland, and also Supreme Councils of the Thirty-third Degree. I have said therefore that their line of accusation incriminates all Freemasonry, even when it claims to do otherwise. It is not that there is "malice aforethought," of which I find no signs; but the writers have entered a field which calls for special knowledge, and they have not even a smattering. They affirm, for example, that there are at least thirty-three degrees of Masonry, whereas there are fourteen hundred in the historical list of Ragon, and over two hundred less or more in activity at the present day.

It is impossible within the limits of this study to enumerate all the misconceptions, but the following examples may stand for the whole, (1) To illustrate an alleged vengeance formula in the Craft Rituals, it is said that the Candidate for the Grade of Master hears for the first time of a murdered founder, whose fate has to be avenged. This is erroneous. The legend is concerned with an assassination which is represented as duly expiated in the order of law and justice. There is no arrière pensée and there is no consequence in the life of Craft Masonry. It will be seen that this invention inculpates English Masonry as associated with a vendetta which is foisted on Masonry abroad. (2) It is said correctly that there is the quest of a Lost Word in Masonry, which Word is arbitrarily affirmed to be Jehovah, and explained—with unthinkable logic—to signify natural religion. There is no such meaning tolerated by the orthodox Grades. There are various Sacred Names, carrying their proper philological import; in branches of Masonry belonging to the symbolical time of the Old Covenant, they are derived for the most part from the Old Testament; but in those which belong to the New and Eternal Covenant, the Name is Christ. (3) The last misconception which I shall notice among points of ritual and symbolism is the folly that terms the Craft Degrees Jewish, thus implicitly connecting them—under all their obedience's, English and continental—with an alleged Jewish peril. It is obvious that allegories dealing with Solomon's Temple must contain Jewish material in the nature of things. The imbecility is to draw any inference therefrom as to the work of Jews in Masonry. Even "the Word of God" is Jewish in the Old Testament, yet I fail to see that the circulation of the Scriptures is playing into the hands of Israel, in order that it may possess the world. The Craft Rituals as we have them are the work of Christian hands, Protestant enough in all conscience and therefore suspect by Rome; but Jewry had no share therein.

(4) Passing now from ceremonial questions to matters of external fact, it is affirmed that Philippe Egalité, Duc d'Orléans, was not only Grand Master of the Grand Orient—a creation, by the way, of 1773—

but of the Templars also. Now, it so happens that The Morning Post does not know what it means when it speaks of Templar Grades. There was something like six Rites incorporating this element, all independent in origin, working and history. Philippe Égalité stood at the head of none. The only purely Templar Rite in France during his reign as Master was the Strict Observance, the titular patron of which was in Germany, not in France, where a Lyonnese merchant, named J. B. Willermoz, was Provincial Grand Master of Auvergne. A certain Council of Emperors possessed the Templar Kadosh Grade, but it was not a Templar Rite. Philippe Egalité took, such an active interest in Masonry and had so great a faith in its possibilities that when he was elected Grand Master in 1771 his presence could be hardly secured for installation; and he exhibited the uttermost negligence in that capacity, while in 1793 he repudiated Freemasonry in the Journal de Paris! He affirmed that it had once presented to his mind "an image of equality," but that he had found the reality and so left the phantom. He was further of the opinion that there should be no mystery and no secret assembly in a republic. The Grand Orient declared the headship vacant, and a few months later, the guillotine closed the question so far as the quondam Grand Master was concerned. These are the facts, with which we may compare the long since exploded fictions reproduced by The Morning Post on the subject of Philippe Egalité engineering his vast machine of Masonry to consummate revolution.

(5) It is affirmed that Frederick the Great of Prussia was Grand Master of a world-wide system of Freemasonry. He was nothing of the kind. Masonic historians would take a natural pride in giving such a celebrated, if not illustrious, personality an important position in the Order; but the most that can be shown is that he was President of the Grand Lodge of the Three Globes at Berlin, his correspondence with which remains to exhibit how far away the connection was. The old, old story of the old false charter which represents him creating a Supreme Council of the Scottish Rite as a system of Thirty-three Degrees is put forward as a historical fact, but it has been abandoned long since by Masonic scholarship worthy of the name. (6) Reflecting here as elsewhere the parti pris of Abbé Barruel, the Lodge of Les Amis Réunis and the Rite of the Philalèthes are represented as arrières Loges in which the Revolution was plotted. They were an open Lodge and an open Rite existing in the face of day. The account is otherwise muddled, representing Savalette de Langes as belonging to the former and not the latter, whereas he be-

longed to both, and was so much the moving spirit of the second that it is supposed to have suspended its labors when he died. As a matter of fact, the Rite was founded within the bosom of the Lodge, and the Convention of Paris, held in 1784, indicates at full length the real nature of its concerns. Fortunately, the chief documents on which Barruel relies for his foolish account are in my possession: they are concerned with the occult sciences, not with Revolution.

(7) There is another and to me more important matter. The great French mystic, Louis Claude de Saint-Martin, is represented as a political "fanatic" and a member of the alleged revolutionary Lodges. This is partly on the authority of Barruel and partly on that of a converted Jew, named Lémann, who became a Roman Catholic priest. The latter affirms that SaintMartin "developed" the "sect" of Pasqually after the latter's death. I cast back the statements into the mouths of their makers. The French mystic had no sect, no Rite, though he had a great number of unincorporated disciples. He did not belong to the Rite of the Philalèthes or Les Amis Réunis. He became a Mason in his youth, but left the Order to follow "the inward way." I appeal to my Life of Louis Claude de Saint-Martin, published in 1900. (8) As regards Martines de Pasqually—whose very name is blundered, still following Barruel—The Morning Post affirms that he "worked in France on very much the same lines as Weishaupt," founder of the Illuminati, "worked in Germany." In reply to this amazing rubbish, I appeal to the same work of twenty years since, and need only add here that in such case Weishaupt worked in "occult communications" by virtue of which it was supposed that the Christ of Palestine instructed the Brethren of Pasqually's Masonic Rite of Elect Priests—Rit des Élus Cohens—according to that which was called in their terminology la voie sensible. It is a new view of the German revolution-monger, and The Morning Post will find that "second thoughts are best." As against some other misstatements of Lémann and Abbé Barruel, Pasqually was not a Jew. He was born in the parish of Notre Dame (Saint-Hugues), town and diocese of Grenoble. The baptism of one of his children on June 20, 1768, is on record in the municipal archives of Bordeaux. (9) In or about the year 1780 that brilliant adventurer who called himself Count Cagliostro, founded a Rite of Egyptian Masonry, which filled for a brief period the Masonic world of France with wonder. This also is garnered by The Morning Post into its indiscriminate net of revolution-plots. There could be nothing more antecedently ridiculous, and again it happens that the Rituals are in my posses-

sion, while I am acquainted otherwise at first hand with the written laws and constitutions. Egyptian Masonry was an occult Rite, belonging to Hermetic Masonry and more especially designed to sustain the claims of Cagliostro as possessing the Great Secret of the Universal Medicine. I observe that the author of the article under notice identifies the "Grand Copht" with Joseph Balsamo, so he has not read the evidence against this view produced by Mr. W. R. Trowbridge, who is not a Mason and has no job in Romanism or revolution questions.

After this enumeration, there remain over three matters which deserve studies set apart to each. I have indicated a root-opinion on the part of The Morning Post that the Templar Movement in Masonry is contained within the measures of a single system, being in fact the Scottish Rite—a somewhat inchoate collection of thirty High Grades superposed on those of the Craft. It is a development from that Council of Emperors, which superposed twenty-two Grades, and as regards both, they are not Templar Rites in the proper sense of the words. The Rite of the Strict Observance was solely and militantly Templar, ab origine symboli. It superposed three Grades, of which the first—or Master of St. Andrew's—formed a connecting link between the Craft and two exceedingly important modes of Templar chivalry. It used to be said that it was Jacobite at the inception, but was certainly not. Here, for the first time—albeit by implication only—it is accused of political purpose, under the Duke of Brunswick. As a fact the writer in The Morning Post does not know that he is impeaching the Strict Observance: he seems to think in his state of confusion that the Duke of Brunswick was "Grand Master of the German Freemasons" because he was Grand Master of certain Ecossais Lodges. As regards the Scottish Rite—Antiquus Scoticus Rilus Acceptus, as it is called in the forged Constitutions—it did not come into existence till 1801, and then at Charleston, U.S.A. In this connection the articles remind us that Stephen Morin carried a warrant from Grand Consistory of Masons, countersigned by the Grand Orient, to America, and there began to confer High Grade powers on a number of Jews, among them Hippolyto Joseph Da Costa, who was not a Jew at all, and at a subsequent date would have died in the hands of the Holy Inquisition at Lisbon, if he had not been rescued by English Masons, facts perhaps naturally omitted by writers in The Morning Post. So much for Morin. We hear also in 1801 of the first Supreme Council in Charleston when Jews were again prominent, among them being Frederick Dalcho. Our contemporary is unfortunate, for Dalcho, who was of

Prussian origin and English birth, was for twenty-two years a priest of the American Episcopal Church, and a monument to his memory is still standing in the vestry of St. Michael's at Charleston. These are the kind of qualifications which pronounce on "Red Masonry" and presume to talk of revolution in connection with the Scottish Rite. The same fatal blundering pursues the articles when they proceed to Albert Pike and his work in the Southern Jurisdiction of that obedience. The writer is of course unaware that Pike reconstructed the Rituals and that they stand therefore at his value as a symbolist and critical scholar the value is unfortunately very slight. But those who suggest that he imported revolutionary notions into his Masonic Order are talkers of rank nonsense, and the quotation from his Morals and Dogma which is made in Article IV, on the profanation of Masonry by plotters of anarchy—whatever its value as history—is sufficient as to his own position. Among the evidences offered to the contrary are Ritual counsels to destroy Ignorance, Tyranny and Fanaticism. Very well: be it agreed that this is part of the design of Masonry. Does The Morning Post stand for Ignorance, stand for Tyranny, and stand for Fanaticism? No; but Roman Anti-Masonry—which it reflects throughout the Masonic part of these articles—invariably regards every plan for their removal as a siege laid against the walls of its particular Spiritual City. As one who knows all the Rituals of the Scottish Rite and has made a long critical study of many codices of each, I am in a position to check wild statements respecting their content. For example, I am familiar with some twenty separate and independent versions of the Rose Croix, and I affirm that Barruel lied when he said that the French Ritual current at his period represents, Christ as "a common Jew crucified for his crimes." I challenge The Morning Post and its anonymous contributors to produce any codex which does. In France then, as in England now, Christ—for the Rose Croix—is the Son of God and Lord of Glory. I lay down the same challenge respecting alleged "subversive forms of Freemasonry" working "a Ritual of hatred for the Cross." Templar or non-Templar, there are no such Grades. The Cross is an object of veneration in Christian Masonry, and in some of the "philosophized" Degrees it is treated as a universal symbol. Now the Templar Rituals were Christian in all their forms during the eighteenth century, but a few were philosophized afterwards. The Rite of the Strict Observance has been always Christian. Here again I know all its Rituals, including those which are held in great secrecy. They were communicated to me after the same long delay and under the same great reserves as was done presumably in the past. They are neither of Stuart legitimacy nor of continental anarchy: they belong to things of the spirit and God known of the heart; and the Templar Order in Britain—where it is governed by Great Priory—in the Colonies and America, belongs to the same category. This notwithstanding, the claim to descend from the old Knights Templar is a myth and pure invention. Couteulx de Canteleu is a false witness on this subject, just as Copin Albancelli is an hystérique insatiable about the Jews.

I pass now to the German Order of Illuminati. It may have been observed that the root-authority on which The Morning Post depends for its case against Masonry is Abbé Barruel, in an almost forgotten work, entitled Memoirs of Jacobinism. He is said to trace the origin of the French Revolution through a bewildering maze of secret societies; but as a fact, his societies are Masonic, plus German Illuminism, the position regarding the latter being one of extreme simplicity. The Bavarian Order of Illuminati was founded by Adam Weishaupt in 1776, and it was suppressed by the Elector of Bavaria in 1789, some of its active members and the author of its more advanced Rituals having withdrawn previously. Those who say that "it was continued in more secret forms" have never produced one item of real evidence. The Morning Post affirms that the Illuminati came out of their seclusion and attempted a revolution at Berlin in 1918. There is again not a shadow of proof that they did anything of the kind, though a few revolutionaries of that date took over some catchwords adopted by the original gang. Weishaupt assumed in his Order the name of Spartacus, and The Morning Post reproduces a question raised by Mrs. Webster—namely, whether it was "mere coincidence" that the Spartacists of modem Germany "adopted the pseudonym of their fellow countryman and predecessor of the eighteenth century." The simple and obvious answer is that it was not coincidence but imitation. Mrs. Webster is not of any importance on this part of the subject, but she has been cited often and has intervened at length in the debate. It may be well to point out that she seems to be a member of the Roman Communion, as shown by her invariable allusion to the "Catholic Church," meaning the Latin or Roman Rite. Her historical accuracy appears on August 3, when she quotes an address of Lamartine to "his fellow-Masons." Now, in that speech Lamartine mentioned expressly that he was "not a Freemason," and did not understand "the particular language" of the Order. Mrs. Webster may or may not have read the address which she cites: her evidence is not to be trusted in either case. For the rest, I can tell Mrs. Webster and all others who are concerned that the Order of Illuminati was revived in Germany to my certain knowledge about 1893; that I have all its Rituals, all its Statutes, Constitutions and so forth; that it had nothing to do with politics and nothing with revolution. It follows from all the evidence that Barruel was not "justified by time" in his fantastic thesis of survival. The "formidable sect" mentioned by Mr. Winston Churchill in the House of Commons on November 5, 1919, is certainly not a succession from Adam Weishaupt. As a scheme of universal revolution, German Illuminism looks formidable in the light of those archives which were published by the Bavarian Elector. So also does the Masonic Rite of Mizraim, with its Laws, Statutes and vast mass of arrangements, not to speak of the Rituals representing its ninety Grades, suggest to an unfamiliar mind that it was a thing of great moment and very wide diffusion, but the cumbrous scheme never kept half-a-dozen chapters together, of all its Senates and all its Areopagite Councils. It was and remains a scheme on paper, and this is the description applying to the archives of German Illuminism, which were magnified in the mind of Barruel till they looked like a colossal conspiracy diffused everywhere. I agree with Lord Acton that the "appalling thing" is the design in matters of this kind, but in the present case it is also the thing ridiculous, for Weishaupt's House of Revolution was a house of cards, and the sands on which it was built were the parchments on which he wrote. His scheme was in concealment behind the ignorance of its members, and there was no influential center to move the puppets on the external stage. There was the amiable enthusiast Baron von Knigge, who wrote up the advanced Rituals and retired altogether when Weishaupt wanted to correct them.

It is gross exaggeration to suggest that the Illuminati were "in secret control of a multitude of Lodges throughout Germany," for there was no such multitude in existence; it is gross exaggeration to say that Freemasons were "initiated in shoals" by von Knigge at the Convention of Wilhelmsbad in 1782. But if both statements were literal, no magnitude of external membership would have made Illuminism a living reality when there was no vitality behind it. This is the general answer to the thesis of Barriel and to those who, at this day, have turned to his forgotten book. It answers also the question of the articles, whether the German Illuminati were the only or chief sect which had a hand in the French Revolution. It was too invertebrate from the beginning to have had a practical hand in anything, and it had passed out of existence. The mark which it left upon Masonry was in Southern Germany, where the downfall of the one Order caused the suppression of the other. All that is said about Mirabeau, his visit to Berlin and his plot to "illuminize" French Freemasonry, may be disposed of in one sentence: there is no evidence to show that Mirabeau ever became a Mason. The province of Barriel was to color everything, and he laid on the blacks and the scarlets with lavish brushes. But he was largely confined to the documents, and it is just one of those cases in which documents produce a false impression, for the reasons given.

The next point is possibly the grand divertissement of all. Those who are entitled to speak about secret societies in France at the end of the nineteenth century are aware that Leo Taxil flaunted in the face of Paris his public confession that everything concerned with Diana Vaughan, the Universal Masonic Directorium, its supreme pontificate, Lucifer in the High Grades and Le Diable au XIX Siècle, were impositions of his own invention. Everyone knows that Dr. Bataille, otherwise Dr. Hacks, whose name appears as author of this work, had confessed previously, deriding the credulity of "catholics." I have always felt sure that there would be a recrudescence of these mendacities when people had forgotten the circumstances which led to their public exposure; but I did not expect it to occur in the columns of The Morning Post.

I have now done. On the basis of these findings, I deny that evidence has been produced for the hand of Freemasonry even in the French Revolution. The contrast made by Louis Blanc between Craft Degrees for those who were to be kept in the dark and "occult Lodges" for the elect is opposed by the history of French High Grades. The latter were as much open to those who sought them as anything in the Craft itself. In the sense of Louis Blanc, there were no occult Lodges. I am sure, however, that French Freemasonry was a finger-post pointing in the direction of revolution. The Masonic watchwords of Liberty, Equality and Fraternity were like a passing bell ringing out the old order. And the French Revolution was like the German Reformation, a pretty bad thing, but it had to come. The factory of the one was not in "shadowy sanctuaries" but in the French Court, while in the other the factory was at Rome.

The question of Co-Masonry I leave to those who are concerned are illicit from the stand-point of the Grand lodge of England, under whose obedience I abide as a mason. The reasons are that it initiates women and is empowered by an irregular jurisdiction. But I believe that The Morning Post has discovered another mare's nest, while it is specifically wrong as usual on its points of fact. The French Lodge Libres Penseurs did not transform into Le Droit Humain; the Order is not oriental; and its devotion to the supposed Comte de St. Germain is an incident of theosophical revelations.

As regards Latin Freemasonry in this twentieth century, I hold no brief whatever. Wheresoever dispersed over continental Europe, it may be playing the game of politics, as it is said to do in South America; but there is, of course, no concerted effort as there is no central direction; and I have not heard a single name of importance cited in connection with the alleged doings. It would serve, I should think, no purpose for any serious government to concern itself with the scattered groups unless and until they are caught in overt acts.

I have now reviewed the whole position, and as regards "perils" and "protocols" I make no claim to know; but having spent a great part of my literary life in the criticism and exposure of fraudulent documents, one has acquired a certain instinctive—or shall I say expert?—sense on the subject. The protocols are stolen documents, presumably of French origin and therefore suspect, because in Roman Catholic circles of that country the animus against Israel has ranked second only to that against Masonry. Admittedly also there is no evidence in support of them, though they are taken on faith at their face value by both writers in The Morning Post. For myself, I can say only that if the alleged fact of a Jewish Peril rests on no firmer ground than these documents, we may reach an aureum sæculum redivivum before an universal social cataclysm. For me, they are not suspect; they take their place in the class to which I have referred. I shall believe in the protocols and their Elders of Israel when I believe in the Charter of Cologne, the Charter of Larmenius, and the Ecossais Constitution of Frederick the Great.

THE SUN OF ALCHEMY

March, 1921

PARACELSUS was born on November 26, 1493, and his strange, stormy career closed at the early age of forty-eight years, or in 1541. Among his brilliant contemporaries was Cornelius Agrippa, whom I mention because the instructor of both was Johannes Trithemius, of Spanheim and Wurzburg, an occult philosopher, who is cited as of great importance at his epoch, as an alchemist, magician and authority on secret writing, though he seems for the most part unread, even by those who praise him. There is a sense in which both pupils outgrew their master, for Agrippa lived to discover the vanity of most arts—at least as then practiced—which passed as occult science, while Paracelsus traveled remote untrodden roads in medicine, alchemy and philosophy, leaving Trithemius far behind him—if we can judge by the remains of the latter. There is a story that the German Hermes and beloved Trismegistus—as his ardent disciples called Paracelsus—had another and much more obscure master, in the person of a certain Solomon Trismosin, of whom very little seems to be known, apart from his autobiographical account of adventures and wanderings in search of the Philosopher's Stone. The authority for this fable is a German alchemical treatise by or ascribed to Trismosin under the title of The Golden Fleece, first printed in 1598. It is comparable to that other myth reported by J. B. Van Helmont, according to which the Philosopher's Stone was given to Paracelsus—or its secret communicated—by an unknown adept at Constantinople in 1521. Trismosin himself, by tradition as well as by claim, is accredited with the possession of the Catholic Tincture and Medicine. It is said also (1) that his true name was Pfeiffer and (2) that, according to a French traveler, he was seen alive at the end of the seventeenth century.

So far as alchemy is concerned, Paracelsus served his apprenticeship at Schwatz, in the laboratory of Sigismund Fugger. On the other hand, Trismosin eschewed the individual practitioners and went direct to the mines. There he encountered Flocker, who was alchemist as well as miner, and in Trismosin's opinion he had attained the secret of the art. The evidence was that—apparently in his presence—Flocker took prepared lead and unalloyed silver, put them in flux together and then extracted the silver, half of which proved to be gold when "cast in an ingot." The miner, however, refused to disclose his secret, and therefore, in 1473, Trismosin went further, seeking an artist in alchemy; but he encountered sophisticators only, till he entered the service of a Venetian noble, where he saw all kinds of operations and was entrusted with a translation of some Greek MS., on which he was set to experiment. By closely following its instructions, he affirms that he "tinged three metals into fine gold." Later on, he quitted Venice, proceeding to a place which served his purpose better, but it is not named in his story. By means of Kabalistic and magical books which he caused to be translated from Egyptian into Greek and thence into Latin, he says that he "captured the treasure," learning the subject of the art—otherwise the First Matter—with the mode of extracting the Tincture, one part of which transmuted fifteen hundred parts of silver into gold.

Such in brief summary was the adventurous quest of Trismosin in search of the Art and its Masters; but according to his testimony, the Mastery was found in books. It happens, however, that at the end of the seventeenth century there was no scholar in Europe who could render the "Egyptian language" into Greek or any other tongue. The claim of Trismosin falls to pieces in this manner, and the fiction of his attainment is like the instruction which he gave to Paracelsus or the testimony of that unspecified Frenchman who saw him two hundred years later, possibly "somewhere in France," more probably at a castle in Spain. We may suppose that in reality he was gathered into the Paradise of Hermetists at the more ordinary allotted time, and that as nothing was heard of him in his life, so also there was silence concerning him for something approaching a century, i.e., till The Golden Fleece appeared, as we have seen, at that magical period of Germany when Simon Studion was testifying at Luneberg and bibliography is not likely to determine. In 1602, a portion of the German work was translated into French and was reprinted or reissued in 1612. Partial versions of the French text in an English vesture are available at the British Museum in the Sloane collection of manuscripts. There is also a priceless volume called Splendor Solis in the Harleian collection, with very beautiful painted pictures. Notwithstanding the distinctive title it should be understood that this text forms part of the original German and is therefore extant in three languages, several printed editions and three manuscripts—not to speak of what Oxford possesses, Under the good auspices of Messrs.

PHLOSPH.

Via Vniuersalis particularibus Inclusis creata

MALE AND FEMALE.

Kegan Paul there has just been added to these an English printed text, for which the original-colored designs of the Harleian Splendor Sol is have been reproduced with much care in black and white. It must be said that the decorations and adornments exceed anything else in the pictorial symbols of alchemy, the nearest approach, and yet at a far distance, being some of the illustrations which appeared in The Hermetic Museum under my own editorship, a good many years ago. Our thanks are due to the publishers for the enterprise of such an undertaking and above all for their courtesy in furnishing three of the designs for reproduction with this article. A word of recognition may be extended also to the Editor J.K., even if some of his methods—including his English—are not a little curious and if he has read his proofs so badly that there are serious misprints passed over within the compass of comparatively few pages. He has given us the account of Trismosin's "Alchemical Wanderings," which is not in the Sloane or Harleian MSS., and has brought together various points of scattered information on matters arising from the text at large. Most important of all, to the best of his ability, he has atoned for the enforced absence of coloring by describing the original plates. It must be remembered that alchemical symbolism is largely a color symbolism, in the present case especially, which recalls those other colored designs, less decorative but not less extraordinary, in the Secret Symbols of the Rosicrucian's, published at Altona towards the end of the eighteenth century. It would appear that the symbolical message of Splendor Solis—whatever it may be held to be—is about equally divided between the very individual designs and the colors referred to these. The supplementary descriptions of J.K. are of consequence in this connection; they have been done accurately, and there is no attempt at explanation, which would have confused the issues. In certain prefatory remarks, a suggestion is hazarded (1) that the mystic meanings seem identical with those of the Tarot Trumps Major and (2) that they observe the same order. They do nothing of the sort, and J. K. has been misled by the fact that there happen to be 22 plates, as Eliphas Levi was misled in the same connection by the 22 chapters into which the Apocalypse is divided in late MSS. and by the 22 sections of Saint Martin's Tableau Naturel. The plates of Splendor Solis seem purely and typically alchemical, in the physical sense. The three examples which illustrate the present notice have not been selected on account of their comparative importance; but the first represents the male and female principles in alchemy, called otherwise heaven and earth, the fixed and fluidic qualities, the state of fixation in the male resulting from immersion in the female moisture.

The second represents the separation of gross and subtle, while the third exhibits allegorically the soul in alchemy, the rainbow colors of the work at various successive stages, leading up to that beautiful red state, "such as no scarlet can compare with," which constitutes an ineffable treasure, as Trismosin affirms in his "adventures," following the consensus of adepts.

It seems curious in conclusion that J.K. presents his text as if it appeared in print for the first time. On the contrary, Splendor Solis formed Part III of the original Aureum Vellus of 1598, and of course of the French translation La Toyson d'Or of 1602 and 1612. Kopp, whose authority is considerable, regards the whole collection as spurious and Trismosin as a fictitious personality, in which case the adventures given in the prefatory part of Aureum Vellus were a publisher's device to introduce the tracts that follow. It should be added that the hand-colored designs of the German and French editions are exceedingly rough and crude. The artist of the Harleian MS. performed upon them a veritable work of transmutation, adding also the elaborate borders.

COLOURS OF THE GREAT WORK.

ILLUMINATIONS OF ÉLIPHAS LÉVI

July, 1921

A S Francis Bacon affirmed on his own part that he had taken all learning for his province, so, I think, it may be said with much truth of Eliphas Lévi that he had assumed to himself as an expositor the whole held of occult science and philosophy. The term learning must be understood in a particular sense so far as Bacon is concerned, and in like manner the assumption which I am placing to the credit of the brilliant French littérateur and so-called Magus must not be held to signify that he was a profound and much less an exhaustive exponent of the wide domain connoted by my reference. That which he brought to the subject was not unchallengeable knowledge as the outcome of extraordinary research, but a marked and often illuminating genius of interpretation. In the sense applicable to the word according to its familiar French use, he created a certain kind of occult synthesis. It is provisional and tentative enough from my own standpoint, and I should question further whether there is a real synthesis possible because of the precarious position occupied by the alleged sciences and by the speculative philosophical considerations which have emerged therefrom. But for the present purpose, at least I may call this a personal matter. Eliphas Lévi has given us, in any case, a comprehensive method of surveying the whole field, and one which is original to himself. If we take his precursors, the historians of Magic in the early nineteenth century, like Jules Garinet and Eusèbe Salverte, they are tolerably safe guides on bare questions of fact, so far as facts were before them, but they reflected no light thereon. There was indeed no light to reflect, for in the first place they were annalists and not men of genius in the sense that Lévi may be called a man of genius, by his gifts of divination and insight, while in the second place, for them all—and for Salverte more than all—the occult sciences had only two radical component elements, being those of delusion and imposture in about equal proportions. A little prior to their day the great romance-period represented by Court de Gebelin, Jacques Oazotte, the Hermetic and Kabalistic Grades of Masonry, the Rite of the Philalethes, not to speak of professional Magi like Martines de Pasqually and Cagliostro, had closed in the French Revolution. On the other hand, Eliphas Lévi had enough of the Magus-mentality to discern that behind the follies, enthusiasm and false-seeming of the occult sciences and their exponents there are veridic vestiges which are like portents pointing to a hidden science of the soul.

Baron Dupotet had done something to elucidate the pretensions of Magic in the light of animal magnetism, and the phenomena which are covered by the loose term Spiritualism had come over from America to France when Lévi began to write on the occult sciences and occult happenings of the past, and to offer his authoritative thesis as to that which lay behind them. Within the measures of the present notice, I am not concerned with his thesis but am indicating only how he calls to be regarded and judged, as also and more especially how it comes about that for all French occultism he has taken a place definitely as the exponent-in-chief of its concern. Other names of importance have risen up since he passed from this life in 1875, and other contributions to the subject-general and its particular departments have been made and are held in varying, often in high repute. But Lévi heads the list, is the point of departure for all, and the chief source of authority. He acknowledges a debt on his own part to the mathematician Hoene Wronski—who had also some singular gifts, but was handicapped heavily by his eccentricities—and Wronski counts still, but not in the manner of his pupil, who did not, I think, owe to him so much as he himself supposed, or alternatively had set out to do more than justice to his precursor—in the spirit of chivalry.

I have made Lévi familiar to English readers by a considerable scheme of translation, but only the History of Magic now remains in print. He published during his life-time six volumes in all on the occult sciences, between the years 1860 and 1865, and several others have been issued since his death. There would appear, however, to be quite a collection of MSS. held in various hands, and in the present extraordinary renewal of occult and psychic activities in Paris, they are not unlikely to see the light in rapid succession. We know that Le Voile d'Isis has begun to publish in its pages the voluminous correspondence on Kabalistic subjects with Baron Spedalieri, extending, I believe, to several centuries of letters. Moreover, the proprietors of this magazine—that is, the Bibliothèque Chacomac—have marked the year 1921 by reprinting Le Grand Arcane, while another publisher has issued, within the last few months, an ornate and elaborate work entitled Les Mystères de la Kabbale illustrated by colored and other designs, which are productions of the author. They bear much the same relation to pictorial art that Lévi's occasional metrical exercises bear to poetry. The fact signifies little, and it is possible indeed that the painfully crude figures are in better accord with the strange spirit of Kabalistic and Apocalyptic writings than anything that might be offered by creative art in things of beauty and anthropomorphic joys forever.

It calls to be said that the posthumous writings published previously to this one are not altogether in the same category as some of the earlier texts, especially the Dogme et Rituel, the Histoire de la Magie, or certain sections of La Clef des Grands Mystères and La Science des Esprits. There are naturally pages of considerable moment in Le Livre des Splendeurs, as there are others in Le Grand Arcane; but the little books on Tarot Trump Cards and Le Livre des Sages are not of any real moment. Les Clefs Majeures was addressed to initiates, but if it was received by them in the grandiloquent spirit of its dedication, then it is certain that they belonged as such to no school that matters. Le Livre des Sages, chiefly in dialogue form, is prolonged expatiation and repetition of things that had been said better by the same writer long previously to its appearance. All are interesting in a certain way, for Lévi is eminently readable at best or worst, is suggestive almost always, even when he is least convincing, and is inspired not less invariably with an unflinching zeal of certitude, however often he may happen to be at issue with himself.

Now, the new posthumous publication, which is here especially under notice, though it is actually nothing more than a running commentary on Ezekiel and the Apocalypse of St. John, seems to present Eliphas Lévi in his most persuasive form as interpreter, and would be altogether a work of remarkable insight were it possible to accept his methods and general canon of criticism—which of course it is not. I did not turn to the publisher's preface, at least from this point of view, till I had formed the opinion here noted; but the preface provides an explanation quite unawares, for it puts on record that the work belongs to the year 1861, having been written at that period for Baron Spedalieri. It says also that Lévi was then "in the plenitude of his intelligence and talent," thus recognizing by implication that some of the later productions are of another order. It seems probable that it was produced immediately after La Clef des Grands Mystères and considerably prior to La Science des Esprits. It remained in manuscript, no doubt because Biblical exegesis of an unorthodox and occult kind would have commanded no public in France circa 1861. Perhaps in the last resource, it will command readers now on anything but its own merits—that is to say, on the authority of its author and by the magic of the name of Maître Eliphas, as his admirers and successors call him; since it is a fashion—as I have noted elsewhere—to hold from and appeal to a Master in the occult circles of Paris. For myself, it must be said that I have derived from its pages the same kind of intellectual satisfaction, if not in the same degree, that I have found in the great book of the Zohar. I mean that I have been delighted with its tours de force in the way of interpretation, with the wonderland of its suggestions and the occasional wealth of its images.

The serious intention is to connect Ezekiel and St. John. "It is by the prophecy of Ezekiel that the high theology of Israel joins hands with Christianity. This has furnished St. John in his Apocalypse at once with groundwork and model." But scheme and basis in the view of Eliphas Lévi connote what he calls the Kabalah. The prophet of the Old Testament "develops a Kabalistical theory of the Divine Ideal, conceived in the image and after the likeness of the Mysteries of Nature," and it is under Kabalistic emblems that the prophet and apostle of the New Testament "conceals the most profound secrets of Christian theology." His description of the New Jerusalem is analogous to the Temple of Ezekiel: "It is the pantacle of absolute and universal truth; it is the key of sciences and religion; it is the hieroglyphical synthesis of all the conquests of human genius." Furthermore, as we hear in a later place, it is in analogy with the allegorical city of Thebes and with "the mysterious plan of the Garden of Eden." In other terms, it is no literal city, as the Temple of Ezekiel was not an edifice built with hands: it is a great "hieroglyphic symbol." As such, it is the mystic city of initiation, and its twelve gates are the twelve stations of the sun and the twelve signs of the zodiac, but understood spiritually as the twelve fruits of the Holy Spirit, while the names of the twelve tribes of Israel, inscribed upon the gates, signify presumably twelve schools or classes of the elect, called out of all nations into the light of God, shining in the Lamp of the Lamb—otherwise, that Sun of Intelligence Which is also the Sun of Beauty and of Righteousness.

This is in the characteristic manner of the French Magus, at his best in the chair of seership, and similar suggestive intimations fill the volume. The Word made flesh of the Apocalypse is the Word of Truth, the Man of Light and Creator of the moral world. The seven seals of the Book of the Everlasting Gospel are the seven Christian virtues, corresponding to the Seven Gifts of the Spirit; and the seven heads of the beast are the seven deadly sins. The seven trumpets proclaim the triumph of truth, otherwise the victories of that Lamb Who is the Word. The seven cups or vials contain seven medicines for the diseases of the old world, and after these have been poured out there appear the Sun and Moon of the new heaven and the new earth, otherwise Jesus Christ and His Church, the Angel of the Sun and the Woman clothed with the Sun, having the Moon beneath her feet. The interpretation proceeds after this manner, from chapter to chapter, until Babylon the great has fallen in a last social cataclysm, when the descent of the New Jerusalem from heaven to earth signifies that at such long last the will of God is done on earth, even as it is done in heaven. Thereafter, it is the great Messianic Reign. Such is the outline offered of the great epical mystery in summary form, and I present it as a poet's explanation, without pretending to indicate that it can be accepted in any literal sense. So also, as regards the Seven Churches of Asia, which others before Lévi have regarded as seven ages of the Universal Church. The Church of Ephesus corresponds here to Apostolic times; the Church of Smyrna represents the age of persecutions; the Church of Pergamos is that of Christianity established under the empire of Constantine; the Church of Thyatira is the day of great doctors and great saints, but that also of the bas empire in decadence; the Church of Sardis belongs to the epoch of Attila; Philadelphia corresponds to the Renaissance, an age of mediocrity in virtue and pregnant with a crisis to come; in fine, the Church of Laodicea is that of the seventh epoch, and—one would say—the close of the dispensation, a Church which is neither hot nor cold, poor, miserable blind and deaf, having no power of regeneration within itself, or—as Lévi puts it—a Church without charity, and the enemy of all progressive movement. It was the Church of his day, as he viewed it, and of morrows to follow, looking towards the end of all, but thereafter to a great "new birth of time." Eliphas Lévi claims to have provided an "occult harmony of the two Testaments," because the Apocalypse is planned by his hypothesis upon Ezekiel; but that which he really gives us is a book of his own illuminations on the Scripture texts, and my thesis concerning them is that they move in a strange atmosphere of theosophical enchantment: that is their value, and this is the only possible criticism concerning them. They are not "Mysteries of the Kabalah," their title notwithstanding, not even of that Kabalah which Lévi has made up otherwise to his own image and likeness. There is otherwise nothing like them in exegetical literature, or in the literature called occult.

Like some other writings of Eliphas Lévi, Le Grand Arcane had become very scarce, and the new edition is welcome. It was divided originally into three parts, entitled respectively The Hieratic Mystery, The Royal. Mystery and The Sacerdotal Mystery; but the first of these is now omitted on the ground that it corresponds to Le Livre des Splendeurs, which the publishers hope to re-issue later on. Le Grand Arcane was written in 1868 and is important for comparison with the earlier works. I regard it in fact as a commentary on Le Dogme et Rituel.

THE GREAT GNOSTIC MISCELLANY

May, 1922

THE original edition of this important work, a translation of Pistis Sophia, appeared in 1896 and went quickly out of print. There is no question that the demand for some new issue has continued and grown dining the intervening period of nearly twenty-five years, but Mr. G. R. S. Mead tells us that for a long time he abstained from compliance for reasons which must command our respect, whether we are in full agreement or not. The explanation is that his translation was made, not from the Coptic text, but from a Latin version by M. G. Schwartze which appeared at Berlin in 1851, checked by the French rendering of E. Amelineau, published in 1895. Mr. Mead was and remains too sound a scholar to feel satisfied with the translation of a translation, and he has waited a quarter of a century, "hoping that some English Coptic scholar would take the matter in hand." He has done even more than wait, for he influenced a friend who answers to this description, and a version of Pistis Sophia had been planned as a result, when the war intervened, and this extinguished the project. There is no other in sight, and he decided at last to repeat what he calls the "venture." That which he has produced, however, is a new work rather than a second edition. In the year 1905, the German translation of Carl Schmidt came out at Leipzig and is, in Mr. Mead's opinion, "deserving of the highest praise." It has rendered him valuable help, and he has revised his text thereby. We have therefore a rendering based on three authoritative versions, and when the time at last comes, as come it may, to compare what now lies before me with one that is done into English direct from the Coptic document, we shall be prepared to find that to all intents and purposes the work has been performed already by Mr. Mead. It is perhaps beside the root-matter of the question, but he reminds us that the Pistis Sophia is, in the judgment of practically all scholarship, itself translated matter, the unknown original being Greek. There are two things more to be noted respecting this new edition: the introduction has been rewritten, and the bibliography has been brought up to date, as well as revised throughout. It may be regarded as a full survey of the literature, both in books and periodicals, which has grown up round the Gnostic document, from 1770 to 1920. It is of the utmost value and interest, enabling the unpracticed reader to become casually acquainted, at least with all that has been thought and said upon the subject since criticism began thereon.

In the residuum of this brief notice, my design is to provide an outline of materials which are necessary to the study of the text on the part of those who will be making their first acquaintance with it in the present English form. There is a considerable public awaiting it, and this avant courier will tell them what they are looking for and what they should know at the beginning. In the first place, Pistis Sophia is represented for us by a single Coptic manuscript, known as the Askew Codex, which was bought by the British Museum in 1785 from the beneficiaries of Dr. A. Askew, who on his part is supposed to have obtained it from a London bookseller. It is written in double columns on parchment and contains 356 pages in quarto, eight pages being wanting just before the end. It has no antecedent bibliographical history. I have intimated that it represents a lost Greek original composed in Egypt during the second half of the third century A.D., according to the latest conclusions of scholarship, a respectable minority inclining, however, towards the first half, which is also Mr. Mead's disposition, for want of "compelling reasons" in favor of the later period. Many other dates have been propounded, from the second to the ninth or tenth century. The "background" of the document is still a debated question and varies with the view of its antiquity. The second-century theory is also Valentinian, referring it to Valentinus himself, or to a disciple of that school. An Ophite origin would favor the first half of the third century, but source and date do not stand or fall together. The Severians of Upper Thebaid, mentioned by Epiphanius as surviving in his day, are tolerated as a source by Schmidt, but Mr. Mead can discover nothing in support of this view. The Barbelo-Gnostics and Sethites have been also mentioned. The question remains open, but it may be noted that in our translator's opinion The Book of the Great Logos in the Bruce Codex at Oxford belongs to the same tradition as Pistis Sophia, though the fact throws no light either on date or origin.

So far, respecting the criticism of the document on what may be called its external side, and the next question is its place in the literature to which it belongs. Mr. Mead tells us that we have three direct sources of information on the Gnosis "according to its Friends." They are (1) the Askew Codex, being Pistis Sophia; (2) the Bruce Codex, containing the Book of the Great Logos according to the Mystery, already mentioned, and an untitled Apocalypse; (3) the Berlin Codex, first heard of in 1896 and containing the Gospel of Mary, an Apocalypse of John and the Wisdom of Jesus Christ. Prior to these, we knew Gnosticism only "according to its foes," that is to say, the Church Fathers. The Bruce Codex was translated into French by Amelineau in 1891, and into German by Carl Schmidt in 1893: its two documents are referred respectively to the first half of the third and to the second half of the second century. Of the Berlin Codex the second document, or Apocalypse of John, is a "pre-Irenæic" work. We are told that Carl Schmidt proves "beyond a shadow of doubt" that its Greek original lay before St. Irenæus, who wrote circa A.D. 190. The two other documents of this Codex are not as yet available to investigation by non-Coptic students, who are awaiting Schmidt's long-promised translation. Meanwhile, my readers who wish to pursue the subject may be referred to the second edition of Mr. Mead's Fragments of a Faith Forgotten, 1906, where there are studies of the Bruce and Berlin Codices. The untitled Apocalypse has been translated into English from the Coptic text and will—I hope—soon be published. Mr. Lamplugh has produced a version at its value—I think, from the French of Amelineau.

And now as to the content and arrangement of Pistis Sophia. Mr. Mead—intentionally or not—indicates how a beginner should read the document, which is not as it appears in the text. The earlier teachings of Jesus contained therein, otherwise the Lesser Mysteries, are found in Division IV. They are supposed to have been delivered on the Mount of Galilee, after the Resurrection, and in certain regions of the invisible world, above and below. The Higher Mysteries are in Divisions I-III, and by the hypothesis of Pistis Sophia were revealed on the Mount of Olives in the twelfth year after the Resurrection. Their formulation was made possible by the fact that in this year Jesus was invested with "the robe of glory," ascended into heaven and returned after thirty hours to give His final messages. In the course of these it is promised that the disciples shall be taken into "the spheres and heavens," to learn their nature, quality and inhabitants, but this does not come to pass in the text as we have it, or in the fragments belonging thereto. It will be understood that the work as a whole exists to incorporate the teachings and the questionings of the disciples arising therefrom, the chief of these interlocutors being St. Mary Magdalene, who experiences the jealousy of apostles, or of some at least among them, partly on account of the hearing which she thus secures, but perhaps in part also on account of her extraordinary aptitude. She is justified, however, by the Master. The others are Mary, the Mother, Peter, James and John, Philip and Andrew.

In the Fourth Division, after the Master's invocations and the convulsions in heaven which follow, Jesus and the disciples are transported to "the ways of the midst," which are set over great chastisements, meaning rulers of the ways. These are Paraptex,Ariouth the Ethiopian, triple-faced Hekate, Parhedron Typhon and Yachthanabas, under all of whom are multitudes of demons, dispensing the measures of torture on the classes of sinful souls. When the Company has returned to earth, there is an instruction on Mystic Rites, Baptisms of Water and Fire, Baptisms of the Holy Spirit of Light and Spiritual Chrism, by which the disciples shall be led into the Light of lights and shall afterwards lead others. Of such are the Lesser Mysteries, and the Greater cover a much wider field, in part cosmic, in part eschatological, but dealing also at length with conditions appertaining to initiation and non-initiation, purifying Rites and Mysteries within the Mystery.

The story of Pistis Sophia is introduced at the request of Mary Magdalene and occupies part only of the first two Divisions. Mr. Mead says that she seems to represent "the type of the faithful, repentant individual soul." Her sorrows, aspirations, ambition and final triumph are told therein. Mr. Mead compares it also with the "tragic myth" of the world-soul, according to Valentinus. For myself, I am reminded continually of the expulsion and return of Shekinah, her separation from the great Adam of the universe and her restoration into the life of union, according to Zoharic lore. It may be indeed that something from the Gnostic fountain has been reflected into the great storehouse of Kabalism, which is a little like Alexandria in the early Christian centuries, the meeting-place of many systems of thought, of several wisdom-religions. However, this may be, the story of Pistis Sophia is only an episode, as I have indicated, and the proper title of the whole work, according to the evidence of the first three Divisions, is "Portions of the Books of the Savior" rather than Pistis Sophia. It was intended for "initiated disciples" and not as "a public gospel." Mr. Mead says with great truth that it contains things "of rare, if exotic, beauty, things of profound ethical significance, things of delicate spiritual texture." As a Christian Mystic, I must confess that I can see nothing but confusion and dismay in its spheres and sons, its four-and-twenty Invisibles, its Ineffable and the spaces thereof, or in its hierarchy of demons and the fantastic terrors of its eschatology. It goes without saying that I do not connect these things with the Christ of the Fourth Gospel, and much less of the Synoptics. But I speak as one who prefers Ruysbroeck to the Gnosis, and I do not claim to understand the Gnosis. At the same time, there are great casual lights in Pistis Sophia, and so I have agreed with Mr. Mead in his view. Historically, it is a document of the first importance, and to make it thus available, and shining in all the light of its translator's knowledge, is a noble piece of work.

COMTE DE SAINT-GERMAIN
AS AN HISTORICAL PERSONALITY

April, 1923

AMONG occult personalities of the eighteenth century there is no question that Martines de Pasqually, with his Masonic Rite devoted to a Higher Magia, is of more real consequence than any, while Count Cagliostro is the most obvious and perhaps the cheapest as a professional man of mystery, and Saint-Germain, who came upon the scene before him and quitted it earlier, is the most romantic, unaccountable and attractive. The field on which the pageants of all deployed was the France of Louis Quinze and his successor—in things occult as in others, France being the world's center, so to speak, at that time. I have been led rather unexpectedly to look at the problem of Comte de Saint-Germain, firstly, because of certain alleged Rosicrucian connections, but, secondly, and at the present moment more especially, because it has been pointed out that a portrait which appeared over his name in my Secret Tradition in Freemasonry, published in 1911, is not that of the reputed occult adept but of Claude Louis de Saint-Germain, a French general and field marshal, whose chequered career is extant in every biographical dictionary. The indication is correct beyond cavil, and the explanation is that when the volumes in question were passing through the press, a professional Masonic collector was employed by the publishers to furnish portraits, which was done in the case under notice either with insufficient instructions or without due care. It calls to be added that I am likely to be worthy of blame on my own part, as it is probable or possible that I saw the illustrations in proof, and in this case did not realize that an inscription below the portrait itself made evident the blunder. My work has been long out of print, and there the matter must remain, pending the new and revised edition which I have in my mind. It may be noted meanwhile that in the opinion of Lane and Browne there would appear to be no extant portrait of the occult Saint-Germain, real or alleged, as none is cited in their well-known Portrait Index. At the same time, the late Mrs. Cooper Oakley prints one—which I am giving in the present article—as the frontispiece to her monograph on the Count, which appeared at Milan in 1912. She gives no account of its source in connection with the reproduction itself, but mentions in the course of her narrative a portrait engraved on copper in the d'Urfe collection, and it may derive therefrom. The question is otherwise not of importance, and it is not unfit that even an alleged likeness of the adept should remain encompassed by mystery, like his personality and his occult claims.

Leaving out Rosicrucian matters, to which I owe the first impulse of my brief exploration, and leaving also Masonic activities aside because they happen to be of no consequence, there are three aspects under which Saint-Germain is presented to our view: (1) In the light of his recorded claims and the exaggerations to which they led in contemporary and later memoirs; (2) in that of ascertainable historical facts, which are more considerable than might have been expected; and (3) in regard to the present cultus of which he is a subject in certain quasi-Masonic and theosophical centers. We shall see that there is no cultus which is so utterly its own and no other as that of Saint-Germain. Upon the first of these aspects, I do not conceive that it is necessary to dwell, for they are matters of general knowledge. We are left, however, to distinguish as best we can between the lying inventions of the Chroniques de l'Œil de Bæuf or the Souvenirs sur Marie-Antoinette of the Comtesse d'Adhemar and the claims which are or may have been advanced by Saint-Germain himself. It is quite certain that he represented himself as a son of Prince Rakoczy of Transylvania, from which it might follow that he was born about 1690, and was therefore some eighty-eight years old when he stayed with Prince Karl of Hesse circa 1780, and this is the age which he gave to the Prince in question, though in appearance he was always a man in the middle prime of life.

On the validity of this claim, my proposal is that every person must be left to rule as he pleases, for there is no evidence in its favor that can be called worthy of the name. They must decide also for themselves whether a person of the considerable age alleged could have carried his years in the way that Saint-Germain did, granting his acquaintance with elixirs and with medicinal and chemical secrets. I am satisfied on my own part in either case, as it relieves Saint-Germain of the ridiculous stories that are attributed to him—for example, that he was alive and in Palestine in the days of Jesus of Nazareth. There should be no need to add that personally I put no faith in stories apart from evidence, where historical matters are concerned, whosoever may bring them forward, and least of all, when the unsupported witness happens to be a professional adept. Whatever the age and origin of Saint-Germain, there is no question that when he was a wanderer for a very considerable period over the face of Europe, he had the entree to most Courts in the countries which he visited, and this could not have been the case apart from personal and other high credentials.

As regards his familiarity with occult arts, we have the authority of Madame de Genlis that her father was a great admirer of his skill in chemistry. There is extant also a letter of the Graf Karl Coblenz which affirms that he witnessed Saint-Germain's transmutation of iron "into a metal as beautiful as gold," his preparation and dyeing of skins, silk and wool, all carried to an extraordinary degree of perfection, as also his composition of colors for painting, If the Memoirs of Madame de Hausset can be trusted in such a connection, it would seem also that he had—as indeed he claimed—an equally singular knowledge of precious stones and the art by which they might be improved, the removal of flaws included.

So far on the claims, and now as to the historical facts mentioned in my schedule. I have made for another purpose a kind of Saint-Germain itinerary, showing the wanderings of my subject from the time of his actual appearance on the public stage to that of his death in 1784. It is too long for reproduction here and is not in correspondence with the more simple purpose which is now in view. He has been variously regarded as a mere adventurer, an occult quack, and a political agent.

I propose to glance, however, at unquestioned matters of fact, contained in certain diplomatic correspondence preserved in the British Museum under the title of Mitchell Papers. (1) On March 14, 1760, Major-General Joseph Yorke, English Envoy at The Hague, wrote to the Earl of Holdernesse, reminding him that he was acquainted with the history of an extraordinary man, known as the Comte de Saint-Germain, who had resided some time in England, where, however, he had done nothing. Since that period, and during a space of two or three years, he had been living in France, on the most familiar footing with the French King, Mme. de Pompadour, M. de Belleisle and others. He had been granted an apartment in the Castle of Chambord and had made a certain figure in the country. More recently he had been at Amsterdam, "where he was much-caressed and talked of," and on the marriage of Princess Caroline he had arrived at The Hague, where he called on General Yorke, who returned his visit. Subsequently, he desired to speak with the English Envoy, and the appointment was kept on the date of Yorke's letter. Saint-Germain produced two communications from Marshal Belleisle, by way of credentials, and proceeded to explain that the French King, the Dauphin, Madame de Pompadour, and practically all the Court except the Due de Choiseul, desired peace with England. They wished to know the real feeling of England and to adjust matters with some honor.

Madame de Pompadour and Marshal Belleisle had sent this "political adventurer" with the King's knowledge.

(2) On March 21, the Earl of Holdernesse informed General Yorke that George II entirely approved the manner in which he had conducted the conversation with Comte de Saint-Germain. The King did not regard it as improbable that the latter was authorized to talk as he had done by persons of weight in the Councils of France, and even possibly with the King's knowledge. Yorke was directed, however, to inform Saint-Germain that he could not discuss further such "interesting subjects" unless he produced some authentic proof that he was "being really employed with the knowledge and consent of His Most Christian Majesty." On that understanding, only King George II would be ready to "open Himself" on the conditions of a peace.

(3) On April 4 General Yorke reported that Saint-Germain was still at The Hague, but that the Due de Choiseulhad instructed the French Ambassador to forbid his interference with anything relating to the political affairs of France, and to threaten him with the consequences if he did.

(4) On May 6, the Earl of Holdernesse wrote to Mr. Andrew Mitchell, the English Envoy in Prussia, referring to all that had passed between General Yorke and Comte de Saint-Germain at The Hague; to the formal disavowal of Saint-Germain by the Due de Choiseul; and to Saint-Germain's decision that he would pass over to England, "in order to avoid the further resentment of the French minister." The Earl mentioned further the fact of his arrival; his immediate apprehension on the ground that he was not authorized, "even by that part of the French Ministry in whose name he pretended to talk"; his examination, which produced little, his conduct and language being "artful"; and the decision that he should not be allowed to remain in England, in accordance with which he had apparently been released and had set out "with an intention to take shelter in some part of his Prussian Majesty's Dominions," which intention Mr. Andrew Mitchell was desired, on the King of England's part, to communicate to the King of Prussia.

The Mitchell papers by no means stand alone. There is also extant in the French Record Office of Foreign Affairs certain correspondence on the same subject at the same period between the Due de Choiseul and Comte d'Affrey, French ambassador at The Hague. It appears from this (1) that Saint-Germain claimed to be entrusted with an important mission on the financial position of France, the peace question passing entirely out of view; (2) that he intended to save the Kingdom by securing credit for France from the principal Dutch bankers; (3) that he was threatened by de Choiseul with an underground dungeon if he chose to meddle in politics; (4) that Louis XV required his ambassador to discredit Saint-Germain in the most humiliating manner and arrange for his arrest; (5) that Saint-Germain fled to England, only to be arrested in London on the order of Pitt; (6) that after examination he was regarded as a kind of lunatic who had no evil intention; (7) that he was released under orders to quit England, and that he went apparently to Prussia.

So began and so ended the only political mission of which we have authentic particulars in connection with the name of Saint-Germain. There is full documentary evidence for the fact that Louis XV assigned him the Castle of Chambord as a place of abode in 1758. There is extant also a letter from Saint Germain to the Marquise de Pompadour, dated March 11, 1760, which exhibits his relations with the Court of Versailles, but does not indicate that he was accredited politically after any manner, however informal. This notwithstanding, at the value of such a tentative view, it seems to me quite possible that he had a private verbal commission to see if he could arrange anything in the matter of peace with England behind the back of the Due de Choiseul, and that when his attempted intervention became known to that minister he was thrown over by the French King, after the best manner of Louis XV. Whether Saint-Germain showed any considerable ability and tact on his own part is another question. Experience in these later days tells us that the role of the professional occultist is seldom set aside by those who have once adopted it, and it would appear that he had failed signally at interviews with Pitt's clerk. However, this may be, Saint-Germain comes before us as an unsuccessful political emissary who was used at best as a cat's-paw, and it must be added that when he addressed the King's mistress it was not ut adeptis appareat me illis parem et fratrem, or

Lofty and passionless as date-palm's bride,

Set on the topmost summit of his soul.

He tells her that he has spoken to Bentinck of "the charming Marquise de Pompadour" from "the fullness of a heart" whose sentiments have been long known to herself, reminds her of the "loyalty" that he has sworn to her and alludes to Louis XV as "the best and worthiest of Kings." It is not at such cost that adeptship repays the favor even of a palace at Chambord.

It follows from evidence published at Copenhagen in 1898 by Louis

Bobe that Saint-Germain died at Erckenforde, according to the following entry in the Church Register of that town: "Deceased on February 27th, buried on March 2nd, 1784, the so-called Comte de Saint-Germain and Weldon—further information not known—privately deposited in this Church." On April 3, the Mayor and Council of the town certified that "his effects have been legally sealed," that nothing had been ascertained as to the existence of a will, and that his creditors were called upon to come forward on October 14. The result of this notice is unknown, and it remains only to add that Welldown, otherwise Weldon, was one of the Count's numerous assumed names.

There are foolish persons who challenge these records because, according to the Protestant anti-Mason Eckert, Saint-Germain was invited to attend the Masonic Congress at Paris in 1785, and that of Wilhelmsbad in February of the same year, according to another account. It has not occurred to them that such invitations could be issued without knowledge that a mysterious and unaccountable individual, ever on the wing under various styles and titles and sometimes vanishing altogether with great suddenness, had at length departed this life in a private manner. The sum of the whole business is that we can trace him historically on the stage of public affairs for something like twenty-six years, and that this period was closed by his death. Here is the plain story, which invention has colored to its liking.

So far as evidence is concerned, I am of opinion otherwise that Saint-Germain was not an adventurer in the common sense of the term, that he was not living by his wits, and that no dishonorable conduct has been charged against him. On the other hand, there is also no evidence that he was a man of spiritual experience, and much less a mystic, as he is miscalled continually by Mrs. Oakley. He was a professional occultist of his period, and though some of his disguises may have been dictated by prudence, others may be referred to a love of mystery for its own sake. If the connotation of this is a passion for pose, he would seem to have had obvious dispositions of the kind. For these reasons and on these grounds, I do not accept the judgment of his friend Karl of Hesse, who called him" perhaps one of the greatest philosophers who ever lived": it is open to question whether Prince Karl had a valid canon of distinction on such a subject. But I accept it when the same witness calls Saint-Germain "the friend of humanity," a friend to animals, and one with a heart "concerned only for the happiness of others." The authentic records do not belie this view, and, moreover, it postulates nothing that is in the least unlikely or the least uncommon.

And now as to the third aspect in which the adept is presented to our notice. I approach it from the evidential standpoint, detached from all other issues. It is known that Saint Germain is an object of particular devotion in circles of modern theosophy, and I am told that in Co-Masonic Lodges connected with this movement his portrait is saluted as that of a Master who has taken the Woman Movement in Freemasonry under his special charge. Out of a casual and unsupported statement of Madame Blavatsky, who says that he was in possession of a Rosicrucian cipher-manuscript, Mrs. Cooper Oakley leaps to the conclusion that he occupied a high position in that Order, and talks vaguely of his connection with branches in Austria and Hungary. She maintains that these things are proven, but in what manner she omits to indicate. The legend has grown from more to more in successive fantastic memorials, including a foolish account of the Brotherhood, published as No. 2 of the Golden Rule Manuals. If we ask what it is that has led to such a cultus, encompassed by such inventions, the answer is that it is not in records of the historical past but in those which are called Akashic. Obviously, therefore, it must be accepted or set aside as such, and for our assistance in making a choice it happens fortunately that we know the kind of deponent who skries in that psychic sea, who is acquainted at this day with the alleged Graf Rakoczy in a physical body, who affirms that the said Graf is the Comte de Saint-Germain, who antecedently was Francis Lord Verulam, and yet earlier was Christian Rosy Cross. But outside the Akashic records, there are those of German Rosicrucianism at the end of the eighteenth century, and they have not one word to tell us concerning the Comte de Saint-Germain. In this dilemma, I am content to leave the issue.

LEGENDS OF THE HORSE

May, 1923

A BOOK about Horses in Faerie and the Horse in magic and myth can scarcely help being a good book because of its subject; but Miss Howey's comprehensive collection will be appreciated not only as the first attempt of its kind on record, for it is also well arranged and puts all its facts and narratives with simple force and clearness. It is not, of course, exhaustive, but a representative part of the old dreams and traditions have been brought together and they can be said to stand for the whole. The collector is, moreover, an artist and has provided most of the pleasant illustrations which make up a beautiful volume, very creditable to all concerned.

The Horse in Faerie stands first in the gamer, and I have been reminded of many things far back in my old readings, including Baron Osbert's encounter with a ghostly knight riding a black horse, which the Baron took from his opponent, but it vanished next morning at cock's-crow. This is from the Minstrelsy of the Scottish Border. Heywood's Hierarchy of the Blessed Angels, that strange old book which has been so long awaiting an editor and may yet, as I hope, find one, is the source of a Bohemian story concerning a faerie host and their champion who slew an earthly rider, as well as his steed. But what of that other version, in which the rider comes out of a swoon, to behold—in the mist and the moonlight—the host and its banners passing between the hills, while the horse follows behind? It is on record that this adventurer was haunted of Faerie through all his after days. The Horse of Monk's Heath, the Horse of Eildon Hills, and Papillon the Faerie Horse of Ogier the Dane, are old familiar favorites with some of us, but there are many others in Miss Howey's first and perhaps most delightful chapter.

Other divisions of the volume tell us of Angel Horses, like those seen in the vision by prophets of Israel and in the Apocalypse by St. John, in the spirit on the Lord's Day at Patmos; but AI Borak is also included, "the fine-limbed, high-standing Horse" on which Mahomet ascended to heaven. They tell us of ghostly Horses, as those which draw phantom hearses or spectral coaches at night; of Demon Horses, like that which was summoned from Sheol by Michael Scott when he went on an embassy to France, or the Horse of the Wild Huntsman; of Horses that go headless, carrying headless riders; and of Horses ridden by witches. So far on the side of legend, but there are those of myth and allegory,

Sun-Horse and Moon-Horse, Horses of Wind and Sea, and those which draw the dark chariot of night or carry the death-goddess. It will be seen that there is a goodly collection, not to speak of some effigies in wood, the Bridal, the Hobby, the Hooden Horse, and that which figured in the Siege of Troy. In fine, there are chapters on the lore of Horse-shoes, on the Horse in charm and incantation and in creation-myths.

The Horse in folk-lore and generally in traditional stories is naturally a much wider field than is likely to be covered within the measures of any single volume, and it is not the least office of a book of this kind, as of nearly all such researches, to awaken memories of other instances which it does not happen to include but which have come within one's own notice in the following of kindred paths. Some at least of my readers will know the beautiful story of the Knight Launfal, whom a queen of the woodland world, in haunts remote, enchanted with her talismans of beauty, so that he was wiled away into Faerie and the music of its life, beyond all years of sorrow. There are many versions, and that which may count as the earliest belongs to that great lady of legends who is like the Irish Swan of Endless Tales—I mean, Marie de France. But the point of my own story is that the Horse of the good knight loved his master, according to later texts, and when he received no command to enter the charmed precincts of Avalon in the West Country, it is said that he tarried without, ever and continually calling with loud neighs. But because there is a spell of silence woven about the place and a sleep as of outward senses is set thereon, the Horse was not heard within. The legend says that he is there unto this day; and seeing that all such tales, at one epoch or another, must come to a good end, we may look for a time to follow when the Horse of the Knight Launfal shall find his master. I should think that then also there will be an end to the sleep of Arthur, who will come forth out of Avalon.

There is another Horse as dear, and made in the same likeness: it is that of King Roderick, denominated "the last of the Goths in Southey's romantic poem of that name, the noblest of all his efforts. The Horse was called Orelio, "a milk-white steed," whom Roderick styled "my beautiful." After the last battle, when the Moorish power was broken, in the great day of the King, it is said in the poem and in the old Chronica de Rey Don Rodrigo that the latter vanished—as if he also, like Launfal, might have been taken into Avalon. But as to the faithful Battle-Horse:

Upon the banks

Of Sella was Orelio found, his legs

And flanks incarnadined, his poitrel smear'd

With froth and foam and gore, his silver mane

Sprinkled with blood, which hung on every hair.

Aspersed like dew-drops: trembling there he stood

From the toil of battle, and at times sent forth

His tremulous voice far-echoing loud and shrill,

A frequent, anxious cry, with which he seem'd

To call the master whom he loved so well.

This is Southey at his best and carrying the "seal of simplicity," which is that of Nature and Art, as a wise Hermetist says. The banks of that Spanish stream, Sella, are surely at no great distance, in the radiant mind of myth, from the walls of Faerie, so that Orelio may yet meet with the Horse of the Knight Launfal. "Life is not a dream, but it ought to become one, and will perhaps," says Novalis, the German seer and poet. In the spirit of that dreaming we can see even now the Breton chevalier coming out of Avalon and also the return of the Goth.

Miss Howey gives two instances of St. James, the patron saint of Spain, intervening to help the Christian armies against Moors and Mexican Indians. In the first case, he was mounted on a snow-white Battle-Horse, and on a gray in the second. There is a third example in Southey's introduction to his Chronicle of the Cid, according to which King Ramiro had fought all day long with the Moors and kept the field at night with a broken army. "The King called them together, and told them that Santiago had appeared to him in a dream, and had promised to be with them in the battle. . . on a white steed, bearing a white banner with a red cross." He appeared accordingly, and the Moors were defeated utterly. Southey regards both dream and vision as part of a pious fraud, a point of view which was inevitable amidst the regnant protestantism of 1808.

But this reminds me of the great hero whose life is told in this Chronicle, Rodrigo Diaz de Bivar, and of his Horse, Bavieca. "Who can tell the goodness of. . . Bavieca, and of the Cid who rode him?" He rode him in battle through many years of life, and the charger carried him in death, erect and armed, as if a living warrior, from Valencia to San Pedro de Cardena, while the Cid's army scattered the Moorish hosts and their six-and-thirty kings. "And from the day in which the dead body of the Cid was taken off his back, never man was suffered to bestride that horse," which is said in the legend to have lived altogether "full forty years."

Here are a few recollections which have been brought back to a single reader, turning over and dwelling on the pages of Miss Howey's book. There are others which might expand this notice, but these must stand for the whole. As it has been greatly suggestive to me, so may it prove to many who know the field, while to those who enter it for the first time, I have said enough to show that they have a capable guide. She is one also who believes that there is something behind folk-lore which belongs to the soul of man. This is true indeed, and it communicates to those who can receive. I think that some of us in these "foremost files of time" can share in its gift of the ages with inward eyes more open than was usual in Victorian days. Among many lamps which bum in the sanctuary of the soul before the Inward Presence, I am sure that the lamp of folk-lore is not the last or least.

THE HOLY KABBALAH

September, 1924

AS the esoteric reception, the Secret Tradition of Israel, emerges by stages in the direction of a greater knowledge, the problem of its textual side confronts the general reader and grows from more to more, full of disturbing elements. A recent issue of The Quest has a contribution of four pages addressed to students of the literature by one of our foremost encyclopedic scholars, Dr. Robert Eisler; and with the best intentions in the world, it cannot be felt that they are likely to bring peace of mind to those who are concerned, though it is true that they offer good news in the first instance. It is said that "a series of translated and annotated texts of the principal remains of Jewish Mystic Literature" has begun publication at Leipzig under his editorship, with the title of Corpus Cabbalisticum, and that the first volume contains a translation of The Bahir into German and a commentary thereupon. It is expected also that a German rendering of Sepher Yetzirah will follow later on and will be made, I infer, by Dr. Eisler himself, who says that he has been studying it for years in conjunction with "the parallel and Contemporary remains of Greek number-mysticism." Its most recent translation into English accepts the traditional authorship of R. Akiba ben Joseph, but Dr. Eisler believes firmly that it was "the work of the famous Jewish arch-heretic Elisha ben Abuia." This is by no means a new hypothesis, but it is not, I believe, familiar to general students in

England.

They will be unprepared still more and much more seriously concerned when they learn what Dr. Eisler teils them on the subject of Sepher Ha Zohar, its translation into French by the late Jean de Pauly and its issue in seven beautiful volumes, between 1906 and 1911. The revelation is as follows: (1) that it is "absolutely unreliable," "full of mistakes," "crammed with intentional alterations," "unacknowledged omissions, and (2) that Jean de Pauly was in all probability a "renegade named Paulus Meyer, "whose infamous attitude in the Prague alleged blood-ritual murder case is not forgotten in Eastern and Central Europe." It is submitted that for English students of Kabbalah, who do not know Aramaic and few of them Hebrew, and therefore for readers at large of The Occult Review, this is disturbing news, apart from the question of identity and that "murder case," about which they will remember little. As readers possibly of Latin, they will have surrendered cheerfully any reliance they may have once had on certain Zohar excerpts presented by Baron von Rosenroth; they know by report and are satisfied that some casual specimens of Adolphe Franck are much worse than Rosenroth's; and that the Kabbalah Unveiled of Mathers collapses with Kabbala Denudata, as it depends from the Latin of Rosenroth.

But they will have thought that Pauly's rendering of the Zohar was at least a terminus a quo, instead of a text which has now at last earned a sweeping condemnation from those who speak with authority. I mention these matters to show how difficult it is for "students" of the subject to know at all where they are. Every translation of the Sepher Yetzirah differs widely from those which preceded it, and the end is not yet. There is marked disagreement, moreover, as to what portions constitute the original tract and what has been interpolated. Finally, there is no critical edition. But if this is the position as regards the minute Book of Formation, what is the case of the Zohar, in Aramaic and not in Hebrew, and sealed therefore to those who are conversant only with the latter? It is also a vast work, in which many texts are embedded, and—with all its omissions—Pauly's Version extends to six imperial octavo volumes and then does not touch the Supplements.

I was pondering upon these matters when M. Paul Vulhaud's La Kabbale Juive came to me, full of learning and interest, the most elaborate study of its subject which has ever appeared in the French language. It has drawn me from these problems into enchanted fields of speculation and research, where I have been reminded of things innumerable and have learned continually as I traveled. It has brought me also, I fear, not a little satisfaction, which might be called malicious, thinking of les ecoles esoteriques of Paris; of their devotion to Eliphas Levi, their grand Kabbaliste; of his Mysteres de la Kabbale, issued by the same publisher; of the excellent Dr. Papus; and of M. Chateau. There is one at the gates carrying titles of knowledge and he has utterly set aside their "masters." Les ecoles sent Karppe to Coventry long ago, and M. Vulliaud will be diverted with me at the conspiracy of silence which awaits him in those directions.

It is impossible in a short notice to say anything adequate or descriptive of so large a work: I can note only here and there, but with difficulty even then, for one tends to be drawn into side issues through predilections arising from old personal traveling's in the same paths. An early chapter on generalities of Jewish Mysticism is full of such temptations, while another is the question of so-called Kabbalistic precursors and the position—among others—of Ibn Gebirol. I should like to compare at some length what is said of him from this point of view by M. Vulliaud with the study of Isaac Myer, long ago now in America. However, the chapter on Sepher Yetzirah must set all these aside, and it proves thoroughly informing, though—for once in M. Vulliaud's pages— there is little that can be called new. Those who are acquainted with Mr. Knut Stenring's translation, introduced recently by myself, will find it most interesting. The conclusion is that Sepher Yetzirah is not a "preface" to Sepher Ha Zohar, but that the two works belong to one and the same tradition, the first being more explicit than the second and a summary of certain Kabbalistic themes, "notably that of Divine Revelation considered under the form of symbolical writing," and of emanation and cosmic evolution, contemplated from both the mystical and natural standpoint and developed in the Order of harmonious analogy. The possible authorship of Elisha ben Abuia is passed over with a mocking reference, in dismissing a hypothesis of Epstein which regards the tract as designed for the instruction of youth.

The antiquity of the Zohar is considered in a long chapter, which embodies an acute analysis of salient points in hostile criticism and seems to dispose of them effectually. They are taken in succession and examined in their different aspects, variously put forward as their Champions followed one another, from the date of the vowel-points—which are mentioned in the Zohar—to the antiquity of the first theosophical intimations on En—Soph. and the Sephiroth. Thereafter follows the story of Isaac de Acco and the quest which he attempted concerning the great text, as I gave it long since in one of my early studies, and with much the same results. M. Vulliaud concludes, like some others, including Prof. Schiller-Szinessy, the Talmudic scholar, that the work is not an imposture of R. Moses de Leon in the thirteenth Century; that it is a collection of many texts belonging to various dates; that the arguments against it are of anything but irresistible force; that it represents an ancient tradition, a school, and is the "authentic expression" of old Jewish wisdom, notwithstanding "interpolations, suppressions and changes" in the actual form, which is an outcome of successive developments. In this connection it is to be inferred from Dr. Eisler's address to students that another defender of the Zohar may be expected in the person of Dr. Scholem, already cited. He has prepared a glossary of the text and seems now engaged on the philological analysis of authentic writings under the name of Moses de Leon. Meanwhile, M. Vulliaud, who also knows something of these texts and has cited them to the confusion of hostile critics, seems also aware of omissions in De Pauly's Version and mentions one of them at least. This notwithstanding, his "critical essay" is dedicated with lively affection and gratitude to Emile Lafuma, to whose editorial labors we owe the publication of the French Zohar, after the death of its translator. Moreover, one of his longest extracts (Vol. I, pp. 272-274) from the text follows the Pauly Version, though elsewhere he translates on his own part.

I have dealt with two matters about which my readers are most likely to desire the views of a new expositor in the field. For the rest, M. Vulliaud gives us studies on Sephirotic doctrine; the relation of the Kabbalah to Pantheism; on Shekinah the Indwelling Glory and Metatron the Angel of the Presence; on Messianic theosophy, more especially in the Zoharic school, the sects which have arisen therefrom, the Sabbatai Zevi movement and the excesses of the later Hassidim. A chapter on the influence exercised by the Kabbalah on Christian Kabbalists is exceedingly full and informing, though I miss a few names which in old days were of some consequence to myself, and in a few cases the folios which they brought into being are still on my shelves. One of the most curious considerations, developed at a certain length, is on the Kabbalah and Freemasonry. For Benamozegh and many others, "Masonic theology" is identical with the Secret Tradition in Israel. Authors of note and all the posy of zanies are quoted in this connection, with a sufficient realization of a distinction between the two classes, and of the more important fact that the said theology amounts to peu de chose. M. Vulliaud has a good time and offers as much to his readers among all the follies and nonsense, but he is probably not a Mason and he misses the root-matter of the whole correspondence, such as it is and such as I have sought to develop it on several occasions on my own part. He misses, moreover, a broader occasion for distraction, being unacquainted with High Grade Rites and Orders which claim derivation from Kabbalism.

One of the charms of the work, though it may not appeal to all, is a curiously discursive style: it does not mean that the author is diverging from his main issues, but he is at ease about them, is never in haste to proceed and always finds an opportunity to look at the various aspects. It may be said that the theme throughout is one of Zoharic Kabbalism, while the impression which is left on the reader is that unquestionably which it is intended to convey, namely, that the best evidence for the age of the Secret Tradition for which the word Kabbalism Stands in the language of Jewry is the milieu, the environment, the atmosphere amidst which Christianity itself happened to be born and in which it grew up at the beginning. The cosmic matter and nebulae, so to speak, crystallized in the main Kabbalistic text, is the age-long story of the theosophical mind of Israel, in Palestine, in Babylon, and at that great meeting-place of life and thought, Alexandria.

It does not appear that M. Vulliaud is himself a son of Israel, though he is in a sense a son of its doctrine. Moreover, he has described his work exactly in the parenthesis beneath its title: it is a critical essay, full of apprehension as such, but I do not find evidence that he is aware of a life and reality deep in the heart of the doctrine. His contemplation of Shekinah, as Our Lady of Israel comes before us in the Zohar, offers proof of this: it is well enough done and is not apart from sympathy, but as it begins so also it remains, an enlightened critical appreciation. Of Zoharic sex-doctrine he says little, and that there is something very deep in its intimations—as if a strange key were being offered to those, a few, who might use it—he does not dream. The work, taken as a whole, is a study of that which has environed the central thing rather than of the thing itself. This is why it is so informing externally, but why also, as it seems to me, there is something missed, and it belongs to the secret life of the subject.

MEISTERECKHART

October, 1925

THE publication of this book marks an epoch in the literature of Christian Mysticism, so far as England and the English-speaking world are concerned. The great Strassburg mystic of the late thirteenth and early fourteenth Century had Suso, Tauler and Ruysbroeck as his contemporaries of a younger generation; but while their memorials remained in evidence for those who sought, Eckhart was not only withdrawn literally and historically into a cloud of unknowing regarding his personal fate, but his writings were taken into the hiddenness, and so far as they were available at all to the generations which succeeded his death it was in virtue of secret circulation. The Flemish of Ruysbroeck and the German of Tauler were turned by Surius into Latin, of which it may be said almost that he who runs can read; Suso, if I remember rightly, wrote in that tongue; but no one translated Eckhart from his Alemannic Originals because of condemned propositions and the excommunication which befell their author. Prior to the present undertaking, he has been known in England by Mr. Claude Field's rendering of a very few sermons, by some three excerpts from the Version here given which are found in a pamphlet series entitled The Porch, and by Miss N. Leeson's translation of certain instructions which appeared, anno 1917, in a minute volume called After Supper in the Refectory.

The object in this case seems to have been entirely devotional; the selection is utterly colorless; while the absence of bibliographical particulars makes it impossible to identify sources. For example, we do not know whether the Version is made from Pfeiffer's text or from the modern German of Büttner. I have taken some pains to collate and have failed. It remains only in these preliminary words to offer on behalf of many my appreciation of a great task fulfilled successfully on the part of Miss Evans, as the first real translator of the famous Dominican, and to Mr. J. M. Watkins, as publisher, for the production of a noble volume, the manner of which reflects the worth of the matter. And now concerning these Sermons, Collations, Tractates, Philosophical and Theological Questions which are here drawn together, presenting the message at large of the Strassburg Master. When Eckhart proceeds to debate he is the greatest analytical mind of his own age, and the peer of all in any. One is overwhelmed continually by his brilliant unexpectedness and his searching gift. But in this respect, it is, I think, comparatively seldom that he begets any conviction. His real titles will be found in a multitude of lights which are brought forth apart from argument into dogmatic expression, and as such are to be taken or left. They will be left by those who are not of his spiritual consanguinity: they will be appropriated and will fructify in the deep heart of those who belong to God, in the sense and the spirit that he himself belonged. It must be remembered, however, that he adopted—which means something more and fuller than affected—an almost militant external conformity with current doctrine, to maintain his place and peace with the regnant orthodoxy of his day, which had the power and will to crush all distinctions which raised their voice against it and all variations which, soon or late, might make for living distinctions. But the theses of reality can be affixed to many doors, and I hold that Eckhart acted in sincerity with the end of his work in view, as I hold also that the hierarchic ruffianism at the Roman center was sincere after its own manner, that which it taught and that also which it did being the logical outcome of its proper Claims and the implicits of doctrine that had grown up through the centuries. When Eckhart says that it is "ours to be God by grace as God is God by nature," we know that this cannot be true in what Thomas Vaughan names the eternal foundation, but it was a sop for the ecclesiastical Cerberus of that nightmare time to express deep mystical intimations in these stultifying terms.

In the eternal foundation, if the soul is God at the root—meaning spirit of soul—it is because life all the wide world over is life of the unbeginning, unending cosmos; while grace—so denominated—is the realization of that which we are and of that which is hidden from us normally because our ground is clouded among the play-scenes of the sense-life. In the realization of her pure being she comes to know, and then—as Eckhart says—she lives no more by grace but is grace itself. He says also that "we attain to actual Deity"—which can mean only that we know in realization that which we are in essence—and that the soul becomes Deity "to every creature as well as to herself." Hereof is the Provincial of the Dominican Order in Saxony, Vicar-General of Bohemia and Prior of Frankfurt, when he utters the naked truth as he understood it; and the counterstatements are like foils to shield it, diverting attention at need. It came about that he who received his title of Meister from Pope Boniface VIII was far more nobly dignified by those who revered his memorials. "This is Meister Eckhart, from whom God nothing hid" appears on old parchments and papers; "this too is Meister Eckhart, who always taught the truth"; and for others who treasured his writings, full of incense fragrance, he was counted as one who was "in league with Deity."

By those who knew him, he was well loved because of it; but those who knew were those who had eyes within them, having stood themselves between two pillars which are called the nowhere and the naught in Dionysian terminology. As one who "preached to the multitude in the German tongue," he has been termed "father of the German language" and "father of German philosophic prose." Miss Evans reminds us also of Dean Inge's dictum, that Eckhart is, "next to Plotinus, the greatest philosopher-mystic." But he who had "conceived the then novel idea" of instructing Beguines, Beghards and Friends of God—the "semi-religious communities and brotherhoods of that date"—in their own language, and on topics which have been described as "bristling with difficulties for the orthodox faith," found that his reward was with him when he may have been approaching his seventieth year. The Inquisition of Venice began a process against him circa 1326, and if it be true that he died in 1327—and was not spirited away by the Holy Office—he was excommunicated post mortem by a Bull of Pope John XXII, to which was appended a list of seventeen heretical doctrines and eleven others characterized as "objectionable." Now that the great bulk of his writings has become available in English, it seems to me that his collations and treatises might have provided substantial warrant for a baker's dozen of Bulls done at Avignon; but the point of living interest is the kind of pope who pronounced against him who wrote "text-books of God-intoxicated piety." For this same John XXII is he who left gold in millions and jewels to the value of millions, not indeed manufactured by alchemy, as a fraudulent story tells, but by the sale of indulgences. By such practices was dogma then exemplified.

THE GREAT SYMBOLS OF THE TAROT

February, 1926

O N the hypothesis that there is or may be a deeper meaning in the chief Tarot Symbols than attaches thereto on the surface, it becomes necessary to establish certain preliminary points as an initial clearance of issues, and I will premise in the first place that by chief Symbols I mean those only which I have been in the habit of denominating Trumps Major in other writings on the subject. First among the preliminary points there is the simple fact that we know nothing certainly concerning the origin of Tarot cards. As usual, however, in matters belonging to occult arts and so-called Science, the place of knowledge has been occupied by uncritical reveries and invention which is not less fraudulent because the fraud may be frequently unconscious. When the artist Gringonneur, in or about the year 1393, is affirmed to have produced a set of picture-cards for the amusement of King Charles VI of France, it has been affirmed that some of their designs were identical with Tarot Trumps Major. The evidence is the fact of certain beautiful and antique card-specimens—in all about twenty-six—which are scattered through different Continental museums and were attributed in the past to Gringonneur. They are now held to be of Italian origin, more or less in the early years of the fifteenth Century, and there are no extant examples prior to that period. But to establish this point on expert authority at its value is not to fix the origin of Tarot cards in respect of date or place. It is idle, I mean, to affirm that Venetian, Bolognese and Florentine vestiges of sets allocated to 1400-1418 are the first that were ever designed. In view, however, of the generations of nonsense which we have heard testifying on the subject, it must be said that it is equally idle and more mischievous to affirm that they are not. When, towards the close of the eighteenth Century, Court de Gebelin first drew attention, as a man of learning and an antiquary, to the fact of Tarot cards, he produced sketches of the Trumps Major in the eighth volume of Le Monde Primitif. In the form that he had met with they were not priceless works of art like those in the Bibliotheque Nationale, but rough, primitive and barbarous, or precisely of that kind which might be expected to circulate in country places, among lower classes of players and gamblers, or among gypsies for purposes of fortunetelling. Supposing that they had been designed and invented originally about the period mentioned, nearly four centuries had elapsed, which were more than ample time for them to get into general circulation throughout the countries in which they were traced by Court de Gebelin—namely, Southern France, Spain, Italy and Germany. If the Trumps Major were originally distinct from the minor emblems, there was also full opportunity for them to be joined together. But alternatively, the designs, perhaps even in several styles, may have been old already in the year 1400—I am speaking of the Trumps Major—in which case they were married much later to the fifteenth Century prototypes of our modern playing-cards. It will be seen that the field is open, but that no one is entitled in reason to maintain either view unless evidence should be found to warrant it in the designs themselves, apart from the real or presumptive age of the oldest extant copies.

Having done something in this summary manner to define the historical position, the next point is to estimate the validity of those speculations to which I have referred already. It is not possible on this occasion, nor do I find that it would serve a purpose, to do more than recapitulate my own previous decisions, reached as the result of researches made prior to 1910. The first and most favored hypothesis concerning Tarot cards is that they are of Egyptian origin, and it was put forward by him who to all intents and purposes may be called their discoverer, namely, Court de Gebelin. It has been set aside long since by authorities, apart from predispositions and ulterior purposes in view. De Gebelin was an Egyptologist of his day, when Egyptology was in its cradle, if indeed it can be said to have been born, and that which he did was to excogitate impressions and formulate them in terms of certitude. They have not been borne out, and their doom from the standpoint of sane scholarship may be said to have been sealed when they fell into the hands of French occult dreamers and were espoused zealously by them. The most salient and amazing elaborations were those of Eliphas Levi in 1856 and onward. The designs were for him not only Egyptian in the sense of the earliest dynasties, but referable to the mythical Hermes and to the prediluvian wisdom of Enoch. They formed otherwise the traditional Book of Adam which was brought to him in Paradise by an angel, was removed from him at the Fall, but was restored subsequently in response to his earnest supplications. Eliphas Levi did more, however, than theorize on the subject. He gave pictorial illustrations of the cards restored to their proper primeval forms, in which they appeared as pseudo-Egyptian designs, the work of an amateur hand. The same practice prevailed after Levi had ceased to publish. It was developed further by Christian, while long after him, under the auspices of Oswald Wirth and others, the Trumps Major appears in all the panoply of imitative Delta art. These things are to all intents and purposes of a dishonest device, but very characteristic unfortunately after their own manner, for the marriage of speculative occultism and intellectual sincerity has hardly ever been made in France and seldom enough elsewhere.

These are the preliminary points which are placed here for consideration—as I have said, to clear the issues. In the complete absence of all evidence on the subject, we must be content to carry an open mind as to where the Tarot originated, remembering that the earliest designs with which we are acquainted do not connote antiquity, unless possibly in one case, and unless the early fifteenth Century may be regarded as old enough in the absence of a parti-pris. The Statement obtains also respecting cards of any kind, including the Baldini emblems, which are neither Tarots nor counters for divination, or games of chance.

I satisfied myself some years ago, and do not stand alone, that the Trumps Major existed originally independently of the other arcana and that they were combined for gambling purposes at a date which it is possible to fix roughly. I am concerned only on the present occasion with what may be called the Great Symbols. They are twenty-two in number, and there is no doubt that some of them correspond to estates and types. The Emperor and Empress, the Pope and Juggler belong obviously to this order, but if we put them back speculatively even to mediaeval times, we cannot account in this manner for the so-called Pope Joan or High Priestess. She must be allocated to another sequence of conditions, another scheme of human Community at large. It is to be noted that though Venetian, Florentine and French packs differ somewhat clearly, between narrow limits of course, Pope Joan has never been termed the Abbess many, nor can I recall that she has been so depicted that such a Denomination could apply and thus include the design among ecclesiastical estates in Christendom. She comes, therefore, as I have intimated, from another region and another order of things. This is the one Tarot Trump Major which suggests a derivation from antiquity, not however in the sense of Court de Gebelin, who referred it to Isis, but to an obscure perpetuation of pagan faith and rite in Italy which the inquiries of Leland seem to have established as a matter of fact. In this case, and at the value of his researches, on which I have commented elsewhere, Pope Joan represents not improbably a vestige of the old Astarte cultus. I do not pretend to be satisfied with the explanation, but it may be accepted tentatively perhaps and does not necessarily carry the question of antiquity behind mediaeval times. In the midst of all the obscurity, one only point emerges in all certainty: whatever the card may have stood for originally, it was not the mythical female pope, an ascription which arose as a leap in the dark of ignorance on the part of people—whether in France or Italy—who knew the Pope Joan legend but had never heard of Astarte and much less of Isis. I should regard it as a rather old leap.

I have spoken of Classification under types, estates or classes, but it obtains only in respect of a few designs, seeing that the majority of the Trumps Major are occasionally allegorical and, in several cases, can be understood only as belonging to a world of Symbols, while a few are doctrinal in character—in the sense of crude Christian doctrine. The Resurrection card and the Devil belong to this last class. Death, on the other hand, is a very simple allegorical picture-emblem, like the Lovers, Justice and Strength. The symbolical cards, which must be so termed because certainly they do not correspond to the admitted notions of allegory, are the Hanged Man, Chariot, the so-called card of Temperance, the Tower, the Star, the Sun and Moon, and that which passes under several names, one of which is the World. The Wheel of Fortune is seemingly of a composite character, partaking of both allegory and symbolism, while the Fool is very difficult to class. On the surface, he may be referable to that estate which inhabits the low-life deeps—the mendicant and vagabond type. He suggests the Italian lazzaroni, except that he carries a wallet, as if he were on his way through the world. He recalls, therefore, the indescribable rabble which followed the armies in crusading and later times. He is the antithesis of the Juggler, who flourishes at the expense of others by following a knavish trade, or who profits alternatively by the lower kind of skill.

When Court de Gebelin described the Trumps Major in Connection with the rest of the Tarot pack, he gave an account of their use in games of hazard, but he had heard also of their divinatory value and was at some pains to ascertain the process by which they were adapted to this purpose, in which way he is our first authority for the traditional meanings of the cards as counters in the telling of fortune. He represents in this manner another landmark in the obscure history of the subject. It is to be assumed that his knowledge was confined to the practice in France, and there are no means of knowing whether Spain, Italy and Germany followed other methods at that time. I believe that Alliette or Eteilla varied the divinatory meanings on the threshold of the nineteenth Century in accordance with his own predilections, as he altered the Trumps Major themselves in respect of their arrangement and changed the original names in certain cases. In the year 1856, as we have seen, Eliphas Levi began to issue his occult revelations, based largely on the Trumps Major, developing their philosophical meanings in a most elaborate manner. They are at times exceedingly suggestive and always curious, but it must be understood that in occult matters, he depended solely on personal intuitions and invention. There was a time, over twenty years since, when I was led to think otherwise, in view of evidence which has proved worthless on further and fuller investigation. Levi said on his own part that he owed his "initiation" only to God and his personal researches, but some of his French admirers have not hesitated, this notwithstanding, to affirm his direct connection with Masonic Rites and Orders. The question does not signify, for initiations of this kind would not have communicated occult knowledge. It follows that his Tarot System—if such it can be called—is at best a work of ingenuity but often a medley of notions, and it owes, so far as can be ascertained, nothing whatever to the past which extends behind Court de Gebelin. The point is not without importance, because he speaks with an accent of great authority and certitude. When P. Christian went still further in L'Homme Rougedes Tuileries and in his Histoire de la Magie, the same criticism applies, as there is no need to say that it does in the labored excogitations of Papus, Stanislas de Guaita and others of the French school.

Now, there are twenty-two Trumps Major arranged more or less in a sequence but subject to certain variations as the packs differ, respecting time and place of origin. There are also twenty-two letters of the Hebrew alphabet, and it occurred to Eliphas Levi that it was desirable to effect a marriage between the letters and cards. It seems impossible to make a combination of this kind, however arbitrary, and not find some accidents in its favor, and there is better authority in Kabalism than Eliphas Levi ever produced in writing to connect the Hebrew letter Beth with the so-called Pope Joan or Sovereign Priestess of the Tarot. But he was concerned very little with any root in analogy, or he might have redistributed the Trumps Major, seeing that their sequence is—as I have said—subject to Variation in different sets and that there seems no particular reason to suppose that any arrangement of the past had a conscious purpose in view. In this manner, he might have found some curious points by taking the old Yetziratic Classification of the Hebrew letters and placing those cards against them, which corresponded to their conventional allocations. It was sufficient, however, for his purpose that there are twenty-two letters and twenty-two palmary Symbols, and if he remembered, he cared nothing apparently for the fact that the numerical significance of Hebrew letters belies his artificial combination after the letter Yod. We can say if we choose that the eleventh Trump is that which is called Strength, though it depends on the arrangement adopted in the particular pack; but the letter Caph is not eleven in the alphabet, for it corresponds to the number 20. Death is the thirteenth card and seems placed well in the Tarot sequence because thirteen is the number of mortality; but the letter Nun is 40 and has no such fatal connection. The folly of the whole comparison is best illustrated by the card which is called the Fool and is not numbered in the series, the cipher Nought being usually placed against it. In Levi's arrangement it corresponds to the letter Skin, the number of which is 300. But wherever it is placed in the series, the correspondence between Trumps Major and the Hebrew alphabet is ipso facto destroyed.

It is to be noticed further that Levi allocated meanings to each letter individually of the Hebrew alphabet, but they are his own irresponsible invention, except in two or three very obvious cases—e.g., that Beth, the second letter, corresponds to the duad, Ghimel to the triad, and Daleth to the tetrad. It may be interesting to note that his number 15, which answers to the Tarot Symbol of the Devil, is explained to be so-called occult Science, an eloquent tribute to his own fantastic Claims in respect of the subject which he followed. As an explanation unawares it is otherwise of some value, for there is of course no ordered occult Science, though there are certain forms of practice which bring into operation those psychic powers of which we know darkly in the way of their manifestation only, and it is a matter of experience that they are more likely to open the abyss rather than the Path to Heaven.

Levi's instituted connection between Tarot cards and the Hebrew alphabet has proved convincing to later occultism in France and elsewhere. He is also the originator of another scheme which creates a correspondence of an equally artificial kind between the four suits, namely, Clubs, Cups, Swords and Pantacles, which make up the Lesser Arcana of the Tarot, and the Ten Sephiroth of Kabalistic theosophy. Because of the number four, it was inevitable that in a mind like his they should be referred to the four letters of the Sacred Tetragram—Jod, He, Vau, He— which are commonly pronounced Jehovah. It is the uttermost fantasy as usual, as exhibited by his attempted identification of Jod with Clubs, while Cups and Pantacles or Deniers are both coerced into correspondence with the letter He. As regards the constituent cards of the four suits, even his ingenuity failed to discover a ground of comparison between the Sephiroth and the Court-cards, so he offers the following couplet as a commentary on the King, Queen, Knight and Knave or Squire:

The married pair, the youth, the child, the race:

Thy path by these to unity retrace.

But this comes to nothing, for the Knight is not necessarily a youth, nor does the ancient or modern Jack correspond to the idea of a child. Had Levi understood Sephirotic Kabalism better, again he could have done better by affirming—as it would have been easy for him—that the French damoiseau had replaced a primitive damoiselle, the Squire Court-card being really feminine. He could then have allocated correctly as follows: the King to Chokmah, the Queen to Binah, the Knight to the six lower Sephiroth from Chesed to Yesod inclusive, governed by the semi-Sephira Daath, and the Damoiselle to Malkuth. He would have found also in this manner a complete correspondence between these Trumps Minor and the four letters of the Tetragram.

Finally, he would have established the Operation of the Sacred Name in the four Kabalistic worlds and would have exhibited the distinctions and analogies between Shekinah in transcendence and the Shekinah manifested in life and time. But Levi was the magus of a world of fancy and not of a world of knowledge. He found his opportunity, however, with the so-called pips, points or numbered cards, for he had the clear and talismanic fact that there are ten numbered cards in each suit, while the Sephiroth are also ten. But because there is no other correspondence in the nature of things, he did badly enough in the development and produced the following nonsense rhymes, which are borrowed from the literal translation that I have made elsewhere.

Four signs present the Name of every name.

Four brilliant beams adorn His crown of flame.

Four rivers ever from His wisdom flow.

Four proofs of His intelligence we know.

Four benefactions from His mercy come.

Four times four sins avenged His justice sum.

Four rays unclouded make His beauty known.

Four times His conquest shall in song be shown.

Four times He triumphs on the timeless plane.

Foundations four His great white throne maintain.

One fourfold kingdom owns His endless sway,

As from His crown there streams a fourfold ray.

In this manner, the four Aces correspond to Kether because it is the first Sephira in the mystery of coming forth from Ain Soph Aour, the Limitless Light; the four twos to Chokmah, four threes to Binah and so forward till the denary is completed. But what is to be understood by the four proofs of Divine Understanding, the four Divine Benefactions and the sixteen sins which are avenged by Geburah or Justice we know as little as of the reason for believing that the Divine Victories shall be celebrated only four times in song, or how in the philosophy of things it is possible to triumph four times on a plane where no time exists. If Eliphas Levi could have furnished the omitted explanations, it is certain that Zoharic Kabalism knows nothing about them.

At the back of all these reveries is the well-known fact that the Ten Sephiroth are inter-connected in the Kabalistic Tree of Life by means of twenty-two paths, to which the Hebrew letters are attributed, Kether communicating with Chokmah by the Path of Aleph, with Binah by that of Beth, and so downward. A diagram showing these allocations was published by Athanasius Kircher in Œdipus Œgyptiacus. The allocation of the Tarot Trumps Major to the Paths of the Tree of Life is obviously the next step, and attempts have been made in this direction by blundering symbolists, but they have forgotten that in the Mystical Tree the Sephiroth are also Paths, making thirty-two Paths of Wisdom, from which it follows that in the logic of things there ought to be thirty-two Trumps.

The study of the Tarot has been pursued since the days of Levi in France, England and America, the developments being sometimes along lines established by him and sometimes the result of an independent departure. Speaking generally, he has been followed more or less. I have shown that his allocations are for the most part without any roots in the real things of analogy, while as to later students of the subject, all that they have to offer is ingenuities of their own excogitation. We have to recognize, in a word, that there is no canon of authority in the interpretation of Tarot symbolism. The field is open therefore: it is indeed so open that any one of my readers is free to produce an entirely new explanation, making no appeal to past speculations: but the adventure will be at his and her own risk and peril as to whether they can make it work and thus produce a harmony of interpretation throughout. The sentence to be pronounced on previous attempts is either that they do not work, because of their false analogies, or that the scheme of evolved significance is of no real consequence. There is an explanation of the Trumps Major which obtains throughout the whole series and belongs to the highest order of spiritual truth: it is not occult but mystical; it is not of public communication and belongs to its own Sanctuary. I can say only concerning it that some of the Symbols have suffered a pregnant change. Here is the only answer to the question whether there is a deeper meaning in the Trumps Major than is found on their surface.

And this leads up to my final point. If anyone feels drawn in these days to the consideration of Tarot symbolism, they will do well to select the Trumps Major produced under my supervision by Miss Pamela Coleman Smith. I am at liberty to mention these as I have no interest in their sale. If they seek to place upon each individually the highest meaning that may dawn upon them in a mood of reflection, then to combine the messages, modifying their formulation until the whole series moves together in harmony, the result may be something of living value to themselves and therefore true for them. It should be understood in conclusion that I have been dealing with pictured images; but the way of the mystics ultimately leaves behind it the figured representations of the mind, for it is behind the kaleidoscope of external things that the still light shines in and from within the mind, in that state of pure being which is the life of the soul in God.

RAYMUND LULLY

September, 1926

WHEN at the beginning of my literary life, it happened that there was some attraction towards one who was termed by his admirers the Doctor Illuminatus, an explanation is to be sought in his legend and in the supposed fact that he was an alchemist who claimed in his records to have accomplished the Great Work. It will be understood that such a concern took me in the first place to encyclopedias and biographical dictionaries and secondly to such of his writings, as appeared most prominently in these sources of knowledge. Some acquaintance was made in this manner with the Raymund Lully who devised and taught an Ars Magna Sciendi, an Ars Universalis, which attained a certain vogue, so that it is possible to speak of a school of Lullists and even of two or three Colleges perpetuating his method, for a not inconsiderable period, under the less ambitious title of Ars Lulliana. I have quoted elsewhere a definition of G. H. Lewes, according to whom the Art was "a new method of dialectics." Howsoever denominated—Ars Magna, Ars Compendiaria, Ars Demonstrativa and even the Universal Science—it is like millstones about the neck or a dead weight piled on the head of a modern Student; but there was a possible refuge in that alternative Lully who was Doctor Hermeticus and wrote those cryptic texts which were of the highest repute in Alchemy for the space of several centuries. There was enough to be learned concerning him and his pretensions, including the fact, ascertained as a result of long investigations, that he was another and very different claimant in the mask of an identical name. These are personal reminiscences of more than thirty years since, but they serve a purpose, indicating that at this period it was possible to learn readily enough about a Latin-writing Lully, but of Lully the Catalan poet, and author in that language of a didactic romance which Stands alone in literature, one gleaned very little indeed, even if one heard of Blanquerna at a far distance and sometimes as if here also might be a Latin text. All this has now passed away; the Universal Doctor has given place to the poet, and the romance has taken its proper and very high place among prose fictions of its epoch.

There is before me a translation in full of Blanquerna by Mr. E. Allison Peers in a noble volume, which has brought joy to the heart of one who loves Lully but who does not know Catalan and to whom it has been therefore a sealed book, though available for others in two editions published at Majorca, respectively in 1904 and 1914. Mr. Peers speaks also of a text printed at Valencia in the sixteenth Century, but of this I have not heard previously. I have said that the story Stands alone and in the limpid simplicity of the English Version it is difficult, from my own point of view, to find a dull page, though the translator speaks of its longueurs, its leisurely pace and the prolixity of certain parts. All this is true enough and indeed manifest, but every part and chapter belongs so inevitably to the purpose which informs the whole that those who are sympathetic could scarcely spare anything. This is how it strikes a reader, but it is admissible that he who put the text into English must have had occasional times of weariness, the fact notwithstanding that Mr. Peers confesses in his preface only to work "full of enjoyment from beginning to end."

Of the story itself, there is a need to speak at some length, because it is more than a mere setting for things introduced therein or interlinked therewith. Blanquerna was born of parents in the uttermost state of dedication to Divine things, and because the chronicle of his life is for every place and time, we do not hear of the country and much less of the precise place, except that it was a certain city. He was brought up as one chosen out of thousands to do the work of God, and hence it came to pass that when he was of marriageable age and was desired by his parents to take a wife, he resolved rather on the life of a hermit, to their great distress. It was so arranged accordingly, and while he sought a place for his purpose, they stripped themselves of their possessions and built a hospital in which they ministered to the poor. In this manner, they are held to have mortified the seven deadly sins, and this gives rise to seven intervening episodes in the illustration of these and their conquest. Meanwhile, a youthful and fair lady, who might have been wife to Blanquerna, seeing that he was called otherwise, entered the life of religion, and was ultimately elected abbess, which gives rise to twelve further episodes, concerned with the ruling of the five corporal senses and the exemplification of seven virtues. It is a long time; therefore, we hear again of the proposed hermit, who is seeking in a forest for a place of contemplation and worship. It proves to be a realm of allegory, wherein he reaches a palace which is the habitation of the ten commandments and is consoled and blessed by them. He meets subsequently with Faith, Truth, Understanding and Diligence, while later episodes are so much successive instruction on worth or velour, on consolation, fortitude, temptation and penitence. When he comes at last to an abbey, that which happens therein belongs to matters of perseverance, counsel, the ordering of studies, vainglory and lessons arising from accusation. But the end of all is that Blanquerna is elected Abbot, much against his will, and so rules his convent that it becomes like a living book in exposition—clause by clause—of the Ave Maria. The result of this is a bishopric, which is also against his grain, and the manner in which he Orders his diocese is like a study at large in poverty, meekness, mercy, purity, peace and so forth, with Blanquerna as one who practices while he teaches, and teaches most in practice. In fine, however, against all his own judgments, he is elected Pope, whereupon he assigns to himself and his Cardinals the clauses of the Gloria in Excelsis Deo, one for each, as an office, "to the end that through their good works glory might be given to God in the Heavens." The history of these clauses, the life and work therein occupies eighty pages. But Blanquerna renounced the Papacy, that he might at last become a hermit, as he desired from the beginning and had been forestalled throughout. In this solitude he wrote a Book of the Lover and the Beloved and an Art of Contemplation, which follows in due course, and then a final chapter ends the spiritual romance.

Having gone through the great text once again for the purpose of my summary, I feel more assured than ever that it is throughout a living memorial, that its disquisitions belong to the narrative, and that the narrative enlightens these. It is a great book of its period and a great illustration of doctrine as it obtained therein. Over and over, it is worth the whole Ars Magna and its appalling mechanism. I think also that Mr. Peers' translation will live long among a few, to whom such things have a message. But I am writing here for a special class of readers, and they must not look in Lully for any light of the spirit which may be thought to lie behind the thirteenth century doctrine of the Latin Church. They will find, e.g., that unbelievers who "die in the sin of ignorance" are delivered to "everlasting fire." It must be added on my own part that, so far, I have known the books on the Lover and Beloved and Contemplation only under Latin veils and that in the better light of their English Version I should qualify two or three things which have been said previously. They are works of a mystical class but not of a real mystic, the end of whom is neither in contemplation nor in vision but in the unity behind Union. The Art of Contemplation is a didactic treatise, confessedly on the search for "new argument" and "lengthier matter." In the prologue to the Lover and Beloved, there is a valuable light on the way in which it was composed. Its author "considered the manner wherein to contemplate God and His virtues"; thereafter, he "wrote down the manner wherein he had contemplated," and then added further "arguments" daily. The result is a delight to read and have, but it is "about it and about" and not of the oneness beyond the one in one. Yet the method is characteristic of the man, for in his external life Lully was comparable himself to a great debater going from place to place and "a challenge to all the field." But he was also a Knight of God, and Blanquerna is a high romance of Spiritual Chivalry.

THE SERPENT MYTH

October, 1926

It is said in the prefatory words of a book which lies before me that the serpent, with its sinuous movements, may be regarded as emblematic of thought forms or objects unfolding in a continuous procession. The idea is suggestive after its own manner, but the Symbol reminds me on my own part of serpent lore itself. That great procession and pageant coming down through the ages, ever and continually casting oft old skins or vestures and over assuming new, but remaining that which it was in the life and essence, from the first even to the last. The myth in its generic sense is perhaps not unduly described on the same page as the most widespread and comprehensive, if not indeed the most marvelous "conceived by the human race." I know that it has intervened continually in my own explorations and researches, when I have been least aware of its presence. When, therefore, a work on the subject is placed before me, it will not be surprising if I am reminded of many things, whether or not they may happen to be found subsequently enshrined within its covers. It is like an evocation of pictures, persons and notions in a seeing-glass.

I remember the rabbins of old for one, at least of whom Satan was hold to have tempted God "under the form of one of those resplendent winged serpents which are denominated Seraphim. "But to speak of rabbins is to recall the greatest of rabbinical books and this is the immortal Midrash, which is termed "ZOHAR": it teils us that the serpent was female and was and is she whose "feet go down to death," according to Proverbs. v. 5, in other words, the "strange woman" or harlot, while he who rode the serpent was Samael, the angel of death. Now, this is exotic lore and must be left as such, though it is developed in the text at some length and with many variations. The pictures crowd otherwise through the glass of memory. There is Taliesin describing his "quick, gliding train of radiant Seraphim" who are serpents and move in due order to the liberation of Elphin; but we conclude that this has been foisted on the old Welsh bard who knew nothing of Jewish angelology. It is to be questioned also whether any will feel satisfied at this day about the fabled baptism of the Mysteries and the golden serpent said to have been lodged thereafter in the bosom of the neophyte. These things and others like them were done according to the story in the name of Mithras, to the scandal and wrath of Tertullian, who may well have heard at second-hand. It is to be understood that we are in a realm of fables and inventions as well as of world-old lore. There is the Greek serpent god which is said to have been a guardian of the Acropolis, but I have not found the authority; there is the dragon which Demeter is supposed to have put on watch at Eleusis, but modern scholarship seems to know nothing concerning it; we hear nothing also to-day of the ancient Amonian Metis, whose countenance was encompassed by serpents.

It is good, therefore, to pass from the field of reminiscences and from old collections like those of Bryant and Faber, not excepting our excellent friend Godfrey Higgins, who sought in anacalypsis, "to draw aside the veil of the Saitic Isis," and have recourse to a modern ingarnering, even if from time to time it may cite the old literati, who after all worked zealously enough in their time. Some three or four years ago Miss M. Oldfield Howey gave us a charming book on the "Horse in Magic and Myth," which should have appealed widely to those who love that friend and servant of man and the legends which have gathered about him. Its adornments, moreover, made it a book of beauty, and I remember writing about it at some length. She has now brought us another more elaborate and more important offering in a study of serpent symbolism, which reminds me inevitably of Ferguson s vast treatise on Tree and Serpent Worship, now a rare thing in the market and highly priced. Her account, however, is not intended for specialists but for readers at large who are drawn to such a study, and it has not been compiled or written in Support of a particular thesis, though it glances at many in passing, leaving them to stand at their value for those who would go further. It comes about in this manner that there is not as a rule any considerable excursion in critical comment. As a storehouse of lore and myth, it has drawn me through all its wealth of pages and high adornment of pictures, when I might have dealt summarily enough with a new hypothesis and a great argument thereupon. At the same time, it is sufficiently and clearly ordered under forty heads of its subject. If they are very nearly exhaustive but not quite, and if personally I could at need have added a section on the serpent Symbol in alchemical literature, the point of fact helps one to realize in no unpleasant way that after all the traveling's something remains to be said upon a world-wide mythos, as it does indeed and always upon other themes innumerable.

Meanwhile, as the sub-title Claims, we have a study of serpent symbolism in all countries and ages, from that of the Egyptian pantheon to the great Midgard "worm" of Scandinavian mythology and the victory of Thor. Cambodia, India, Palestine, China and Japan, the Americas—North and South—are searched throughout their records. Greece and the healing serpent of Æsculapius, Hermes and his Caduceus, Apollo and the Python, bring their contributions from the classical world, to be contrasted by those who will with the aboriginal ophiolatry of Africa, Australia and Polynesia. A vast field is therefore covered, and—as the publishers teil us—it is in "a readable and accessible form." The illustrations—which are nearly one hundred—are excellent throughout, and there is a colored frontispiece of Stonehenge as seen from the south-east.

In conclusion, and on my own part, there is one aspect of serpent symbolism which finds explanation but rarely in the records, so far as I am able to learn, though its connotations are on every side. The fascination of the serpent, to which Miss Howey devotes a chapter, in so far as it belongs to the myth of the Earthly Paradise, is an allegory of the Maga or illusion by which the soul of man, according to secret theosophical doctrine, was drawn into the circle of generation and left thus for this earthly life the far and favored land lying under a fair skyr or the spiritual and prenatal state.

THE TEMPLAR ORDERS IN FREEMASONRY

February, 1927

HAVING regard to the fact that Emblematic Freemasonry, as it is known and practiced at this day, arose from an Operative Guild and within the bosom of a development from certain London Lodges which prior to the year 1717 had their titles in the past of the Guild and recognized its Old Charges, it would seem outside the reasonable likelihood of things that less than forty years after the foundation of Grand Lodge Knightly Orders should begin to be heard of developing under the ægis of the Craft, their titles in some cases being borrowed from the old institutions of Christian Chivalry. It is this, however, which occurred, and the inventions were so successful that they multiplied on every side, from 1754 to the threshold of the French Revolution, new denominations being devised when the old titles were exhausted. There arose in this manner a great tree of Ritual, and it happens, moreover, that we are in a position to affirm the kind of root from which it sprang. Twenty years after the date of the London Grand Lodge, and when that of Scotland may not have been twelve months old, the memorable Scottish Freemason, Andrew Michael Ramsay, delivered a historical address in a French Lodge, in the course of which he explained that the Masonic Brotherhood arose in Palestine during the period of the Crusades, under the protection of Christian Knights, with the object of restoring Christian Churches which had been destroyed by Saracens in the Holy Land. For some reason which does not emerge, the foster-mother of Masonry, according to the mind of the hypothesis, was the Chivalry of St. John. Ramsay appears to have left the Masonic arena, and he died in the early part of 1743, but his discourse produced a profound impression on French Freemasonry. He offered no evidence, but France undertook to produce it after its own manner and conformably to the spirit of the time by the creation of Rites and Degrees of Masonic Knighthood, no trace of which is to be found prior to the thesis of Ramsay. Their prototypes, of course, were extant, the Knights of Malta, Knights of the Holy Sepulcher, Knights of St. Lazarus, in the gift of the Papal See, and the Order of Christ in Portugal, in the gift of the Portuguese Crown. There is no need to say that these Religious and Military Orders have nothing in common with the Operative Masonry of the past, and when their titles were borrowed for the institution of Masonic Chivalries, it is curious how little the latter owed to the ceremonial of their precursors, in their manners of making and installing Knights, except in so far as the general prototype of all is found in the Roman Pontifical. There are, of course, reflections and analogies: (1) in the old knightly corporations the candidate was required to produce proofs of noble birth, and the Strict Observance demanded these at the beginning, but owing to obvious difficulties is said to have ended by furnishing patents at need; (2) in the Military Order of Hospitallers of the Holy Sepulcher of Jerusalem, he undertook, as in others, to protect the Church of God, with which may be compared modern Masonic injunctions in the Temple and Holy Sepulcher to maintain and defend the Holy Christian Faith; (3) again at his Knighting he was "made, created and constituted now and forever," which is identical, word for word, with the formula of another Masonic Chivalry, and will not be unknown to many.

But the appeal of the new foundations was set in another direction, and was either to show that they derived from Masonry or were Masonry itself at the highest, in the proper understanding thereof. When the story of a secret perpetuation of the old Knights Templar—outside the Order of Christ—arose in France or Germany, but as I tend to conclude in France, it was and remains the most notable case in point of this appeal and Claim. It rose up within Masonry, and it came about that the Templar element overshadowed the dreams and pretensions of other Masonic Chivalries, or, more correctly, outshone them all. I am dealing here with matters of fact and not proposing to account for the facts themselves within the limits of a single study. The Chevalier Ramsay never spoke of the Templars: his affirmation was that the hypothetical building confraternity of Palestine united ultimately with the Knights of St. John of Jerusalem; that it became established in various countries of Europe as the Crusaders drifted back; and that its chief center in the thirteenth Century was Kilwinning in Scotland. But the French or otherwise German Masonic mind went to work upon this thesis, and in presenting the Craft with the credentials of Knightly Connections, it substituted the Order of the Temple for the chivalry chosen by Ramsay. The Battle of Lepanto and the Siege of Vienna had invested the annals of the St. John Knighthood with a great light of valor; but this was as little and next to nothing in comparison with the talismanic attraction which for some reason attached to the Templar name and was obviously thrice magnified when the proposition arose that the great chivalry had continued to exist in secret from the days of Philippe le Bel even to the second half of the eighteenth Century. There were other considerations, however, which loomed largely, and especially in regard to the sudden proscription which befell the Order in 1307. Of the trial which followed, there were records available to all, in successive editions of the French work of Dupuy, first published in 1685; in the German Historical Tractatus of Petrus Puteamus published at Frankfort in 1665; in Gurther's Latin Historia Templariorum of 1691; and in yet other publications prior to 1750. There is not a little evidence of one impression which was produced by these memorials, the notion, namely, of an unexplored realm of mystery extending behind the charges. It was the day of Voltaire, and it happened that a shallow infidelity was characterized by the kind of license which fosters intellectual extravagance, by a leaning in directions which are generally termed superstitious—though Superstition itself was pilloried—and in particular by attraction towards occult arts and supposed hidden knowledge. Advanced persons were ceasing to believe in the priest but were disposed to believe in the sorcerer, and the Templars had been accused of magic, of worshipping a strange idol, the last Suggestion—for some obscure reason—being not altogether indifferent to many who had slipped the anchor of their faith in God. Beyond these frivolities and the foolish minds that cherished them, there were other persons who were neither in the school of a rather cheap infidelity nor in that of common Superstition, but who looked seriously for light to the East and for its imagined traditional wisdom handed down from past ages. They may have been dreamers also, but they were less or more zealous students after their own manner, within their proper measures, and the Templar Chivalry drew them because they deemed it not unlikely that its condemnation by the paramount orthodoxy connoted a suspicion that the old Knighthood had learned in Palestine more than the West could teach. Out of such elements were begotten some at least of the Templar Rites and they grew from more to more, till this particular aspect culminated in the Templar dramas of Werner, in which an Order concealed through the ages and perpetuated through saintly Custodians reveals to a chosen few among Knights Templar some part of its secret doctrine—the identity of Christ and Horus, of Mary the Mother of God, and Isis the Queen of Heaven. The root of these dreams on doctrine and myth transfigured through the ages—with a heart of reality behind it—will be found, as it seems to me, in occult derivations from Templar Ritual which belong to circa 1782 and are still in vigilant custody on the continent of Europe. I mention this lest it should be thought that the intimations of a German poet, though he was an active member of the Strict Observance, were mere inventions of an imaginative mind.

There is no historical evidence for the existence of any Templar per-petuation story prior to the Oration of Ramsay, just as there is no ques-tion that all documents produced by the French non-Masonic Order of the Temple, founded in the early years of the nineteenth Century, are inventions of that period and are fraudulent like the rest of its Claims, its list of Grand Masters included. There is further—as we have observed—no evidence of any Rite or Degree of Masonic Chivalry prior to 1737, to which date is referred the discourse of Ramsay. That this was the orig-inal impetus which led to their production may be regarded as beyond dispute, and it was the case, especially with Masonic Templar revivals. Their thesis was his thesis varied. For example, according to the Rite of the Strict Observance, the proscribed Order was carried by its Marshal, Pierre d'Aumont, who escaped with a few other Knights to the Isles of Scotland, disguised as Operative Masons. They remained there and un-der the same veil; the Templars continued to exist in secret from gener-ation to generation under the shadow of the mythical Mount Herodom of Kilwinning. To whatever date the old dreams ascribe it, when Em-blematic Freemasonry emerged, it was—ex hypothesi—a product of the Union between Knights Templar and ancient Scottish Masonry. Such is the story told.

The Strict Observance was founded by Baron von Hund in Germany between about 1751 and 1754 or 1755, and is usually regarded as the first Masonic Chivalry which put forward the story of Templar perpetu-ation. I have accepted this view on my own part, but subject to his Claim at its value—if any—that he had been made a Knight of the Temple in France, some twelve years previously. The question arises, therefore, as to the fact or possibility of antecedent Degrees of the kind in that coun-try, and we are confronted at once by many stories afloat concerning the Chapter of Clermont, the foundation of which at Paris is referred to several dates. It was in existence, according to Yarker, terised the First Temple. The discovery explains also the wealth acquired by the Tem-plars, but it led in the end to their destruction. Traitors who knew of the secret, though they had not themselves attained it, revealed the fact to Clement V and Philip the Fair of France, and the real purpose of the persecution which followed was to wrest the transmuting process from the hands of its Custodians. Jacques de Molay and his co-heirs died to preserve it, but three of the initiated Knights made their escape and after long wandering from country to country, they found refuge in the caves of Mount Heredom. They were succored by Knights of St. Andrew of the

Thistle, with whom they made an alliance and on whom they conferred their knowledge. To conceal it from others and yet transmit it through the ages they created the Masonic Order in 1340; but the alchemical secret, which is the physical term of the Mystery, has been ever reserved to those who can emerge from the veils of allegory—that is to say, for the chiefs of St. Andrew of the Thistle, who are Princes of the Rosy Cross, and the Grand Council of the Chapter.

The alchemical side of this story is in a similar position to that of the perpetuation myth, of which it is an early version. There is nothing that can be taken seriously. But this is not to say that in either case, there is no vestige of possibilities behind. Modern Science tends more and more to show us that the transmutation of metals is not an idle dream and—speaking on my own part—there are well-known testimonies in the past on the literal point of fact which I and others have found it difficult to set utterly aside. So also, there are few things more certain in history than is the survival of Knights Templar after their proscription and Suspension as an Order. With this fact in front of us, it is not as a hypothesis improbable that there or here the chivalry may have been continued in secret by the making of new Knights. It is purely a question of evidence, and this is unhappily wanting. The traditional histories of Knightly Masonic Degrees—like those of the Chapter of Clermont, the Strict Observance and the Swedish Rite—bear all the marks of manufacture, the most that can be said concerning them—and then in the most tentative manner—is that by bare possibility there may have been somewhere in the world a rumor of secret survival, in which case the root matter of their stories would not have been pure invention. The antecedent material would then have been worked over and adapted to Masonic purposes, inspired by the Oration of Ramsay.

It is to be presumed that when this speculation is left to stand at its value, there is no critical mind which will dream of an authentic element in Hugh de Payen's supposed discovery of the Powder of Projection at or about the site of the Jewish Temple. This romantic episode Stands last in a series of similar fictions which are to be found in the history of Alchemy. When we are led to infer therefore by the records before me that the Chapter of Clermont reached its end circa 1763, we shall infer that it was in a position no longer to carry on the pretense of possessing and being able to communicate at will the Great Secret of Alchemy. It is evident from the Ritual that this was not disclosed to those who, being called in their turn, were admitted to the highest rank and became Knights of

God. It was certainly promised, however, at a due season as a reward of merit. From a false pretense of this kind, the only way of escape would be found by falling back upon renounced and abjured allegory. Now, we have seen that the Chapter in its last Degree represented the New Jerusalem, and therefore its alchemy might well be transferred from a common work in metals to the spiritual side of Hermeticism. Those who have read Robert Fludd and Jacob Böhme will be acquainted with this aspect; but it may not have satisfied the figurative Knights of God, who had come so far in their journey from the Lodge of Entered Apprentice to a Temple of supposed adeptship. The Chapter therefore died.

THE TEMPLAR ORDERS IN FREEMASONRY
An Historical Consideration of their Origin and Development

March, 1927

I HAVE met with another French Ritual in a great manuscript collection and again—so far as ascertained—it seems to be the sole copy in England, though it is not unknown by name, in view of the bibliographies of Kloss and Wolfsteig. It is called Le Chevalier du Temple, and is of high importance to our subject. The collection to which I refer is in twelve volumes, written on old rag paper, the watermark of which shows royal arms and the lilies of France: it is pre-French Revolution and post 1768—say, on a venture, about 1772. The Ritual to which I refer extends from p. 73 to 202 of the fifth volume, in a size corresponding to what is termed crown octavo among us. The hand is clear and educated. The particular Templar Chivalry is represented as an Order connected with and acknowledging nothing else in Freemasonry except the Craft Degrees. In respect of antiquity, it Claims descent by succession from certain Canons or Knights of the Holy Sepulcher, who first bore the Red Cross on their hearts, and were founded by James the First, brother of the first Bishop of Jerusalem. These Canons became the Knights Hospitallers of a much later date. On these followed the Templars, from whom the Masonic Knights of the Temple more especially claimed derivation, though in some obscure manner they held descent from all, possibly in virtue of spiritual consanguinity postulated between the various Christian chivalries of Palestine. The traditional history of the Grade is given at unusual length and is firstly that of the Templars, from their foundation to their sudden fall, the accusations against them included; it is a moderately accurate summary, all things considered. There is presented in the second place a peculiar Version of the perpetuation story which is designed on the one hand to indicate the fact of survival in several directions, and on the other to make it clear that Templar Masonry had in view no scheme of vengeance against Popes and Kings. After the proscription of the chivalry, it is affirmed that those who remained over were scattered through various countries, desolate and rejected everywhere. A few, in their desperation, joined together for reprisals, but their conspiracy is characterized as detestable, and its memory is held in horror. It fell to pieces speedily for want of recruits. Among the other unfortunate Knights who had escaped destruction, a certain number entered also into a secret alliance and chose as time went on their suitable successors among persons of noble and gentle birth, with a view to perpetuate the Order and in the hope at some favorable epoch that they would be restored to their former glory and reenter into their possessions. We hear nothing of Kilwinning or Herodom, and indeed no one country is designated as a place of asylum; but it is affirmed that this group of survivors created Freemasonry and its three Craft Degrees to conceal from their enemies the fact that the Chivalry was still in being and to test aspirants who entered the ranks, so that none but those who were found to be of true worth and fidelity should be advanced from the Third Degree into that which lay beyond. To such as were successful, the existence of the secret chivalry became known only at the end of seven years, three of which were passed as Apprentice, two as Companion or Fellow Craft, and two as Master Mason. It was on the same conditions and with the same objects that the Order in the eighteenth Century was prepared to receive Masons who had been proved into that which was denominated the Illustrious Grade and Order of Knights of the Temple of Jerusalem.

The Candidate undertakes in his Obligation to do all in his power for the glorious restoration of the Order; to succor his Brethren in their need; to visit the poor, the sick and the imprisoned; to love his King and his religion; to maintain the State; to be ever ready in his heart for all sacrifice in the cause of the faith of Christ, for the good of His Church and its faithful. The Pledge is taken on the knees, facing a tomb of black marble which represents that of Molay, the last Grand Master and martyr-in-chief of the Order. Thereafter, the inward meaning of the three Craft Degrees is explained to the Candidate. That of Apprentice recalls the earliest of Christian chivalries, being the Canons or Knights of the Holy Sepulcher, who for long had no distinctive clothing and hence the divested state of the Masonic Postulant. But this state signified also that his arm is ever ready to do battle with the enemies of the Holy Christian Religion and his heart for the sacrifice of his entire being to Jesus Christ. The alleged correspondences and meanings are developed at some length, but it will be sufficient to mention that the Masonic Candidate enters the Lodge poor and penniless, because that was the condition at their beginning of the Templars and the other Orders of Christian Knighthood. The Candidate is prepared for the Second Craft Degree in a somewhat different manner from that of the First, and this has reference to certain distinctions between the clothing of a Knight of the Holy Sepulcher and that of a Knight of St. John. The seven steps are emblematic of the seven sacraments of the Holy Church, by the help of which the Christian Chivalries maintained their faith against the infidel, and also of the seven deadly sins which they trampled under their feet. The Blazing Star inscribed with the letter Yod, being the initial letter of the Name of God in Hebrew, signified the Divine Light which enlightened the Chivalries and was ever before their eyes, as it must be also present for ever before the mind's eye of the Masonic Templars, a sacred Symbol placed in the center of the building. In French Freemasonry, the Pillar B belonged to the Second Degree and was marked with this letter, which had reference to Baldwin, King of Jerusalem, who provided a House for the Templars in the Holy City.

The Traditional History of the Master Grade is that of the martyrdom of Jacques de Molay, the last Grand Master of the Temple. The three assassins answered to Philip the Fair, Pope Clement V and the Prior of Montfaucon, a Templar of Toulouse, who is represented as undergoing a sentence of imprisonment for life at Paris on account of his crimes, by the authority of the Grand Master. He is said to have betrayed the Order by making false accusations and thus secured his release. The initials of certain Master Words are J.B.M., and they are those also of Jacobus Burgundus Molay.

The Chevalier du Temple has, unfortunately, no history, so far as I have been able to trace. I have met with it as a bare title in one other early collection, which has become known to me by means of a Dutch list of MSS., and there is no need to say that it occurs in the nomenclature of Ragon. It is numbered 69 in the archives of the Metropolitan Chapter of France, and 8 in the Rite of the Philalethes: they may or may not refer to the same Ritual as that which I have summarized here. There is no means of knowing. In any case the 30th Grade of Mizraim and the 34th of Memphis, which became No. 13 in the Antient and Primitive Rite, is to be distinguished utterly: it is called Knight of the Temple, but has no concern with the Templars and is quite worthless. It should be added that in one of the discourses belonging to Le Chevalier du Temple, there is a hostile allusion to the existing multiplicity of Masonic and pseudo-Masonic Grades, and this may suggest that it is late in the order of time. A great many were, however, in evidence by and before the year 1759. We should remember Gould's opinion that there was an early and extensive propagation of Ecossais Grades, and the source of these was obviously in the Ramsay hypothesis. It is certain also that Elu Grades were not far in the rear. The date of the particular Collection Maconnique on which I depend is, of course, not that of its contents. On the whole there seems nothing to militate against a tentative or provisional hypothesis that Chevalier du Temple was no later and may have been a little earlier than the Clermont Knight of God, thus giving further color to the idea that Templar Masonry and its perpetuation story arose where it might have been expected that they would arise, in France and not in Germany. I have said that the Grade under notice has no reference to Scotland or to any specific place of Templar refuge after the proscription. But the chivalrous origin of Masonry is not less a Ramsay myth, and it characterizes almost every variant of Templar perpetuation which has arisen under a Masonic aegis, from that of the Knights of God and the Chevalier du Temple to that of Werner and his Sons of the Valley, belonging to the year 1803. There stand apart only the English Religious and Military Order and the late French Order of the Temple which depends from the Charter of Larmenius, but this was not Masonic, though its pretense of Templar perpetuation and succession is most obviously borrowed from Masonry. In conclusion, I shall think always that Baron von Hund drew from France, whether directly at Paris or via Hamburgin his own country.

We have seen that the Strict Observance appeared in Germany between 1751 and 1755, a development according to its founder of something which he had received in France so far back as 1743. No reliance can be placed on this Statement, nor is the year 1751 in a much better position. Hund is supposed to have founded a Chapter of his Templar Rite about that time on his own estate at Unwurdi, where the scheme of the Order was worked out. We hear also of a later scheme, belonging to 1755 and dealing with financial matters. But the first evidential document is a Plan of the Strict Observance, laying claim on January 13, 1766, as its date of formulation, and there is a record of the Observance Master Grade, with a Catechism attached thereto, belonging to the same year. But as 1751 seems too early for anything in the definite sense, so 1766 is much too late. A memoir of Herr von Kleefeld by J. C. Schubert bears witness to the former's activities on behalf of the Strict Observance between 1763 and 1768. The Rite, moreover, was sufficiently important in 1763 for an impostor named Johnson to advance his Claims upon it and to summon a Congress at Altenberg in May, 1764, as an authorized ambassador of the Secret Headship or Sovereign Chapter in Scotland. His mission was to organize the Order in Germany, and for a time Von Hund accepted and submitted, from which it follows that his own Rite was still in very early stages. I make no doubt that it made a beginning privately circa 1755, and that a few persons were knighted, but Von Hund had enough on his hands owing to the seven years' war, so that from 1756 to 1763 there could have been little opportunity for Templar Grades under his custody, either on his own estates or elsewhere. Meanwhile, the Clermont Rite was spreading in Germany and in 1763 there were fifteen Chapters in all. There is hence an element which seems nearer certitude rather than mere speculation in proposing that the Templar claim on Masonry was imported from France into Germany, that Von Hund's business was to derive and vary, not to create the thesis. Of the great success which awaited the Strict Observance, once it was fairly launched, of its bid for supremacy over all Continental Masonry and of the doom which befell it because no investigation could substantiate any of its Claims, there is no opportunity to speak here. It may be said that a final judgment was pronounced against it in 1782 when the Congress of Wilhelmsbad set aside the Templar claim and approved the Rectified Rite, otherwise a transformed Strict Observance, created within the bosom of the Loge de Bienfaisance at Lyons and ratified at a Congress held in that city prior to the assembly at Wilhelmsbad. The Grades of the Strict Observance superposed on the Craft were those of Scottish Master, Novice and Knight Templar; those of the revision comprised a Regime Ecossais, described as Ancient and Rectified, and an Ordre Interieur, being Novice and Knight Beneficent of the Holy City. It laid claim on a spiritual consanguinity only in respect of the Templar Chivalry, apart from succession and historical connection, but it retained a certain root, the poetic development of which is in Werner's Sons of the Valley already mentioned, being the existence from time immemorial of a Secret Order of Wise Masters in Palestine devoted to the work of initiation for the building of a spiritual city and as such the power behind the Temple, as it was also behind Masonry.

In conclusion, as to this part of my subject, the combined influence of the Templar element in the Chapter of Clermont and that of the Strict Observance which superseded it had an influence on all Continental Masonry which was not only wide and general, but lasting in the sense that some part of it has persisted there and here to the present day. The eighth Degree of the Swedish Rite, being that of Master of the Temple, communicated its particular Version of the perpetuation myth, being (1) that Molay revealed to his nephew Beaujeu, shortly before his death, the Rituals and Treasures of the Order; (2) that the latter escaped, apparently, with these and with the disinterred ashes of the master, and was accompanied by nine other Knights, all disguised as Masons; (3) that they found refuge among the stonemasons. It is said that in Denmark the history of Masonry, owing to the activity of a Mason named Schubert, became practically that of the Observance, until 1785, when the Rectified Rite was introduced as an outcome of the Congress of Wilhelmsbad. It was not until 1853 that the Swedish Rite replaced all others, by reason of a royal decree. So late as 1817, the Rectified Rite erected a central body in Brussels. In 1765, the Observance entered Russia and was followed by the Swedish Rite on an authorized basis in 1775. Poland and Lithuania became a diocese of the Observance Order in 1770, and it took over the Warsaw Lodges in 1773. The story of its influence in Germany itself is beyond my scope. It is written at large everywhere: at Hamburg from 1765, when Schubert founded an independent Prefectory, to 1781 (when the Rectified Rite was established for a brief period by Prince Karl von Hesse); at Nuremberg in 1765, under the same auspices; in the Grand Lodge of Saxony from circa 1762 to 1782; at Berlin, in the Mother Lodge of the Three Globes, from 5766 to 1779, when the Rosicrucian's intervened; at Königsberg from 1769 to 1799 in the Provincial Grand Lodge; in the Kingdom of Hanover, at the English Provincial Grand Lodge, from 1766 to 1778; and even now, the list is not exhausted. The explanation of this influence through all its period and everywhere is (1) that which lay behind the romantic thesis of Ramsay, as shown by his work on the Philosophical Principles of Natural and Revealed Religion, published in 1748, I refer to the notion that there was a Mystery of Hidden Knowledge perpetuated in the East from the days of Noah and the Flood; (2) that which lay behind, as already mentioned, the talismanic attraction exercised on Masonic minds in the eighteenth Century by the name of Knights Templar, because the Church had accused them. They had learned strange things in the East: for some it corresponded to the view of Ramsay, for others to occult knowledge on the side of Magic, and for the Chapter of Clermont to Alchemy. The collapse of the Strict Observance was not so much because it could not produce its hypothetical unknown superiors, but because it could not exhibit one shred or vestige of the desired secret knowledge.

I have now accounted at length for that which antecedes the present English Military and Religious Order of the Temple and Holy Sepulcher, so far as possible within the limits at my disposal. The Clerical Knights Templar, which originated at Weimar with the Lutheran theologian, J. A. von Starck, and presented its Claims on superior and exclusive knowledge to the consideration of the Strict Observance about 1770, represent an intervention of that period which has been judged—justly or not—without any knowledge of the vast mass of material which belongs thereto and of which I in particular had not even dreamed. The fact at least of its existence is now before me, and I await an opportunity to examine it. I can say only at the moment that it was devised, as my reference shows, to create an impression that an alleged Spiritual Branch of the old Knights Templar possessed their real secrets and had been perpetuated to modern times. It was, therefore, in a position to supply what the Strict Observance itself wanted; but the alleged Mysteries of the Order appear to be those of Paracelsus and of Kabalism on the magical side. I have left over also: (1) Les Chevaliers de la Palestine, otherwise Knights of Jerusalem, because although it is a Templar Grade, it is concerned with the old chivalry at an early period of its history, and not with its transmission to modern times; (2) the Grade of Grand Inspector, otherwise Kadosh, though I am acquainted with a very early and unknown Ritual, because it does not add to our knowledge in respect of the Templar Claim on Masonry. In the earliest form, it shows that the judgment incurred by those who betrayed, spoliated and destroyed the Order had been imposed Divinely; that the hour of vengeance was therefore fulfilled, and that the call of Kadosh Knights was to extirpate within them those evil tendencies which would betray, spoliate and destroy the soul. (3) Sublime Prince of the Royal Secret, because in the sources with which I am acquainted it recites the migrations of Templars and only concerns us in so far as it reproduces and varies the Ramsay thesis in respect of Masonic Connections. It is important from this point of view.

(4) Sovereign Grand Inspector General, because I have failed so far to meet with any early codex, and that of Ragon is a Templar Grade indeed but concerned more especially with wreaking a ridiculous vengeance on the Knights of Malta, to whom some of the Templar possessions were assigned. (5) Knight Commander of the Templar, because, according to the plenary Ritual in manuscript of Albert Pike, it is exceedingly late and is concerned in his Version with the foundation and history of the Teutonic Chivalry, which is beside our purpose. In respect of the English Military and Religious Order I have met with nothing which gives the least color to a supposition of Gould that it arose in France: the Chevalier du Temple is its nearest analogy in that country, but the likeness resides in the fact that both Orders or Degrees have a certain memorial in the center of the Chapter or Preceptory: we know that which it represents in at least one case and in the other, as we have seen, it is the tomb of the last Grand Master. But failing an origin in France, it is still less likely that it originated elsewhere on the continent, as, for example, in Germany. I conclude, therefore, that it is of British birth and growth, though so far as records are concerned it is first mentioned in America, in the Minutes of a Royal Arch Chapter, dated August 28, 1769. I have sought to go further back and so far, have failed. It was certainly working at Bristol in 1772, and two years later is heard of in Ireland. It is a matter of deep regret that I can contribute nothing to so interesting and vital a question, which appeals especially to myself on account of the beauty and spiritual significance of the Ritual in all its varied forms. The number of these may be a source of surprise to many, and I have pointed out elsewhere that however widely and strangely they differ from each other they have two points of agreement: there is no traditional history presenting a perpetuation myth or a claim on the past of chivalry, while except in one very late instance, there is no historical account whatever; and they are concerned with the one original Templar purpose, that of guarding the Holy Sepulcher and pilgrims to the Holy Places. They offer no Version of Masonic origins, no explanation of Craft Symbolism, no Suggestion of a secret Science behind the Temple, no plan of restoring the Order to its former glory, and, above all, to its former possessions. The issue is direct and simple, much too simple and far too direct for a Continental source. Moreover, the kind of issue would have found no appeal in France, for example, or Germany, because there was no longer any need in fact to guard the tomb of Christ, and there were no pilgrims in the sense of crusading times. Finally, they would not have allegorized on subjects of this kind.

I am acquainted personally with nine Codices of the Ritual, outside those which belong to Irish workings, past and present, an opportunity to examine which I am hoping to find. The most important are briefly these: (1) That of the Baldwyn Encampment at Bristol, which is probably the oldest of all: the procedure takes place while a vast army of Saracens is massing outside the Encampment. (2) That of the Early Grand Rite of Scotland, subsequently merged in the Scottish Chapter General: The Pilgrim comes to lay the sins and follies of a life-time at the foot of the Cross, and he passes through various symbolical veils by which the encampment is guarded. (3) That connected with the name of Canongate Kilwinning under the title of Knight Templar Masonry, in which there is a pilgrimage to Jericho and the Jordan. (4) That of St. George Aboyne Templar Encampment at Aberdeen, a Strange elaborate pageant, in which the Candidate has a searching examination on matters of Christian doctrine. (5) That of the Royal, Exalted, Military and Holy Order of Knights of the Temple, in the library of Grand Lodge. It represents a revision of working and belongs to the year 1830. It is of importance as a stage in the development of the English Military Order. (6) That which Matthew Cooke presented to Albert Pike, by whom it was printed in the year 1851. It is practically the same as ours and was ratified at Grand Conclave on April, 11 of that year. (7) That of the Religious and Military Order, of the grace and beauty of which I have no need to speak. The two that remain over are Dominion Rituals of the Order of the Temple, being that in use by the Sovereign Great Prior of Canada prior to 1876, and that which was adopted at this date under the auspices of the Grand Master, Wm. J. B. MacLeod Moore. They are of considerable interest as variants of the English original, but the second differs from all other Codices by the introduction of three historical discourses, dealing with the origin of the Templar Chivalry, its destruction and its alleged Masonic Connections, which are subject to critical examination, the conclusion reached being that the Templar System is Masonic only in the sense that none, but Masons are admitted. The appeal of the entire sequence is one and the same throughout, an allegory of human life considered as pilgrimage and warfare, with a reward at the end in Christ for those who have walked after His commandments under the Standard of Christian Chivalry.

We have very little need to make a choice between them, either on the score of antiquity or that of Ritual appeal. A descent from the Knights Templar is, of course, implied throughout, but it is possible to accept this, not indeed according to the literal and historical sense, but in that of the relation of Symbols. The old Chivalry was founded and existed to defend the Church and its Hallows, and Masonic Knights Templar are dedicated to the same ends though official obedience's alter and Hallows transform. The Holy Sepulcher for them is the Church of Christ, however understood, and if there is anything in the old notion that the Christian Chivalry in the past had sounded strange wells of doctrine, far in the holy East, there are such wells awaiting our own exploration, to the extent that we can enter into the life behind doctrine, and this is the life which is in Christ. Finally, the modern chivalry is of Masons as well as Templars, because in both Orders there is a quest to follow and attain. But this Quest is one, a Quest for the Word, which is Christ, and a Quest for the Abodes of the Blessed, where the Word and the Soul are one.

THE QUEEN OF STILL WATERS

April, 1928

THE setting sun is like incense, a clouded fragrance of many dyes and tinctures; and the breath of the earth in Faerie goes out to it, an aromatic oblation, lifting up hands of flowers. The morning sun, drawing out life and moisture, is like a priest with holy water who sprinkles the dew of morning. O the evenings and mornings in Faerie, the swoon of its enchantments, the gifts of prophecy in awakening, and the power of the rose in Faerie. O the vintage and the winepress of the roses, vineyards of white lilies, and the red and white wine of flowers. And O the meetings and the marriages, the brides in their winning, the espousals made in Faerie, the jeweled contracts and dowries, the places of many marriages and the mystery of bridals therein. I, being a guest unbidden but a lover of beauty, came with a heart exalted to the nuptials of Prince Hyle, in all the splendor of restitution, and of her who is styled most fair and the Queen of Still Waters in the titles of Faerie nobility.

Now, Prince Hyle had been gifted at his birth by Seven Powers of Faerie with as many treasures of wonder, videlicet, the Harp of Life, the Star of Love, the Blessed Vision, the Crown of Youth, the Key of Immortality, the Sacred Lamp which is called the Light of the Earth, and the Secret of the Lone Road leading to the Hidden Temple. But his honorable and royal parents, finding no service for treasures of this degree—yet being willing to do honor to the givers—assigned them a worshipful place in the innermost room of the palace. It came about, however, that when he was still growing in the grace of youth, Prince Hyle was visited by one wearing a gray mantle, who asked to leave as a traveler to look upon the Gifts of Faerie. When these had been shown to him, he said: "They are fair and good; and the Secret of the Lone Road is golden; but not even the Key of Immortality can compare with this which I hold in my hand, because it is the Key of Death."

The terrific talisman shone with a dull red light, and that stranger, taking the Prince by the arm, led him forth from the Palace and in the end out of the whole country—as if it were, to the world's verge or a term of being. He brought him in this way to a Ghostly House in the Hiddenness, where there were six windows which seemed to look upon hither and thither, over the whole world, but a seventh looked onward and past it. Through one of these windows—under the sorcery of an inward luster—Prince Hyle beheld a spell-bound body on its violet bier, having the aspect of a beautiful maiden, reposing like a mystery of death, wherein is also the secret of life. There were candles in the dark of this Faerie, burning sacredly about the bier and its pageant, while the wind encompassing the mansion chanted its Tenebrae.

Then said the Man in the Grey Cloak, turning to the Prince: "There are no right lines in Faerie. I have drawn thee far through the distance, and never shalt thou find a way back till the Mysteries of this House are made known to thee."

He left him abruptly, and the Prince loitered about the moat till morning, when he crossed it by a narrow drawbridge and read—on an oaken door covered with other inscriptions and having a certain sign in the center—the message of a red tablet, inscribed with golden letters. He learned after this manner that a Queen of Still Waters was holden of bonds within, and that it was a work of the powers which cause sleep and death in Faerie. Beside her was an ancient book, containing seven words. Whosoever pronounced those words would break the death-spell which bound her; but the law of compensation in Faerie is of such kind that the locust would eat up his years, as if a century were heaped over his age. O golden-haired pages, who dwell on the threshold of Faerie. O hauntings on its skirts and fringes. O secrets known therein. Where is he who will venture on this doom for the love of a maid in the toils and durance of spells? Let him stand by the door, said the legend, and cry: "Open: it is the hour and the man."

It is known that there are interventions in this Magian world, which so long gives Nature the slip, and that—all sorceries notwithstanding—there remains a way of escape, if you can take opportunity by the forelock. But the hard terms of the adventure in this case had put back all comers from the threshold, wiping the dust off their feet. It was long before Prince Hyle could call up from heights or deeps his courage to sustain the trial. He had been carried away from his place of birthright in Faerie, and there shone no Key of Immortality to open for him a house of refuge. He reflected, however, that it would be truly a mournful fate for this maid who was queen to remain enspelled through the ages, and that if he uttered the words, there might still be time to reach the Hidden Temple, which must be best of all places to die in; though the Secret of the Lone Road was written in a strange tongue which none in his palace could render. It came about that the sun looked down from the Zenith when the Prince gave the Battery of a Neophyte on the door of doom, crying: "Open: it is the hour and the man."

Was it long also before his invocation was answered? Be this as it may, the door opened, though I know not when, nor how, and he was presently in a great throne-room looking at the Queen of Still Waters, with all worship in his heart. Thereafter he turned and saw through his soul in Faerie that open Book of the Mystery which contained the Seven Words. Whose tears, do you dream, had wiped them out of the pages, when marriage bells brought me thither? The memory of many secrets is stored up on the shelves of the heart; but if I had seen those words, I question whether I should recall them. There is a law called deliverance, as when spells break in Faerie; but there is one which is named expediency and it is a guard against the privilege of spells.

Now, it was because of the Star of Love and the Blessed Vision thereof that Prince Hyle pronounced the Seven Words, as if they were uttered on a cross. So, he sang his Swan-Song; and concerning that spell, I can testify that it broke in music. After the sleep of Faerie cometh a waking time, and the Queen of Still Waters rose in the peace of her beauty, as a gospel revealed in the heart. But the locusts had eaten his years, and if there be one in this world of transformation who knows less of what follows than Prince Hyle, it is I who went to his marriage. It seemed that already in his pilgrimage he had followed the Lone Road and was now in the Hidden Temple, in the presence of a Blessed Vision—as a radiant Star of Love. She who was Queen of Still Waters gave back to him that which he lost, even in Waters of Life, for Faerie has also its baptisms in fonts not made with hands. There is a healing by shadow in Faerie, a healing by light, a healing by music heard over heaven and earth, and there is the healing by waters of love. They are all healings by mercy, and it is known that this is better than medicine.

How did Prince Hyle pass—as it were—through death and sacrifice to his bridal? I know scarcely, but I was there at the sacred pomp, and I—even I—was not forgotten in the kissing of hands and lips. Hereof is therefore his story; but it may be observed that it does not finish, because of what follows on bridals of this kind, like all the wooing's in Faerie and the aftermath of those wooing's. It seems to me that the Key of Death opens other doors. And what of his remaining birthrights? He had found the Star and the Vision, with the Crown of his Youth therein; and he had taken a High Grade in the Hidden Temple. He knew their meaning and purpose. But you do not overlook, I conclude, the Harp of Life, the Key of Immortality and that Lamp which is a Light of the Earth, even for the Light of a Star. It is the Star which leads on to these. So, I think that he returned to that palace out of which he came at first, on the quest of new treasures of meaning, and that the Queen of Still Waters— who is known by other titles—showed him a shorter way.

I do not testify that the Man in a Grey Mantle went before them on the road; but I have been in strange places. There is a harp that moves through Faerie, but who is the harper? The lights go out on earth, but lamps burn ever in Faerie. I believe that a strain of string-music was about the Man in Grey and that he carried his star in a lantern. Was it that blithe procession when I saw the Banners of Faerie plunging in a violet mist, on the world's verge in the sunset? I am no longer with them in Faerie; but I know that their story continues in a land that is very far away—yet nearer than heart to heart when lovers meet at the tryst. I have held in my hand the Key which opens the Golden Gate thereof, and this is a Land of Immortals.

TOUCHSTONE

July, 1928

THE destiny of Faerie is a gilt-edged security for those who are faithful and true. After days and weeks and months of quest and venture, I was licensed to look into the Law of Fate in Faerie and to learn how it is consulted by means of a Dial of Flowers. The inward working of spells is made known thereby, but the way out of them is not declared. I learned it in another place and long after: it is one of the secret laws. You follow the course of destiny in Faerie, as you do on this earth of ours: but it is thus only till you have learned to disentangle its skein. It is then in your hands, and—if you are wise—it can be woven at your own will so that the Law follows you thenceforward. For destiny is consequence, and that upon which it is consequent is we ourselves alone. So, it is true that the Book of Fate in Faerie is the Book of the Art of its Ruling.

There was a Prince who had lost his history through the service of a spell, so that no name is given him. It is needful, on occasion, to be lost before you can find your way; but when I met with him in Faerie, I did not know without seeking whether that which had bechanced him was of evil, which passes, or of hidden goodness, unfolding like a flower from within. He had no memory of his birthplace, his forbears and heritage, or aught of his opening life. A mournful gift of divination was mine in Faerie, and the same is a gift of second sight. Now, there is a certain bond of concord between these kinds of workings and the fall of the evening dew, for which reason I made use of my oracles under the first star. I consulted my Book of Fate, the reading of which is like the sleep of beauty and of magic. I must not tell you my method; but I found that the Prince was heir to a throne in the Kingdom over the way, and he had great treasures in birthright. He was the descendant of a faerie race, full of powers and privileges. Over his cradle, the Houses of Heaven—which are twelve shone as new houses in a renewed heaven, looking as if over a virgin earth. Yet was he deprived of his history, but with you well, it was because of great things which might be fulfilled concerning him. As to these, I did not see in my glass. I had awakened in Faerie and was learned in mysteries of silken couches, of tapestried rooms and ladders of golden rope, of secret keys, of ivory gates and the paths that lead therefrom. I knew also of a certain mysterious repose in Faerie, when the powers of enchantment soften and Nature moves in her sleep. In this manner I had one key of enchantment, but of the way out of all enchantments—which goes due east and explains them all as you go—I had learned nothing as yet.

So further concerning this Prince: he was brought from a far and blessed country, to be abandoned in the dark labyrinth of a forest, which is more full of glamor and misdirection than is a picture of painted images. Like a child made by magic, he discovered himself awake therein. You might judge that he was a Prince by the golden fillet on his head, and another traveler from a land that is very far away—having been once in like case—uncovered the misfortune that had come over the high Prince by means of the heart's remembrance and obvious tests. He sent him through the world in search of a second history, testifying that something of his old estate should unfold in every loyal and sacred venture undertaken and carried to its term by him who was bewrayed.

I know not how long this Prince lingered over the vintages and winepress of Faerie or with maids created for joy who fool some travelers therein. But he came to himself on a day and was presently in a quest of stars, which is a good beginning anywhere. A call in the heart of a star; a star which sings in its calling; the star and its call shall lead. He found some stars, moreover—yes, even in the sandhills and the marshes. But they were not worlds, unhappily; and though one by one the scenes of his past came back, they were only as ghosts or dreams—like tales told in the twilight, which are not believed in day. Then he was counseled to discover the Stone called Touchstone, which opens all doors of mystery. My companion and fellow traveler, seeking for treasure of gold, does it happen that you possess the Touchstone? Do you dream what it is, my child of wonder? It tests and tries everything, and nothing of all resists. It is like a dream which is behind dream; it leads to the Land of Reality, on God's side of the Land of Dream; it brings the good dreams true. By its aid you can find the meaning in Tales of Faerie. It comes to you on the blade of a drawn sword, and that sword is like the parting of ways for ever.

The Prince who has lost his history has been to the Valley of Vision, but the King sleeps therein. He has been to the Land of Irem, but the hidden City is still empty and desolate. He has drunk at the Fountain of Borico, where a man may find his youth, though he has left it long since at a corner of streets remote. He has knelt in the Temple of Isis, which has a girdle of mysteries and a Holy Place within it, about which the mysteries worship. He has watched in the Gloves of Dodona, where the trees—which are old as the world—whisper with human voices, and he has ascended the highest peak of the Holy Mountain Kaf. He has spoken with Harut and Marut, the fallen angels who first taught magic to man. He has been to the tombs of the Magian Kings, which are watched by the Star of Bethlehem—till the second dawn of the day of Christ. He has sorrowed with Vathek and Solomon in the Hall of Eblis, wherein they suffer until their sins are whitened. He has tarried with Gian ben Gian, the King of the Peris. But he has not found that cube which is called Touchstone. Now this is great sorrow, and I have pledged myself to seek through the whole earth and the whole starry heaven for that which will open the eyes, so that even a Prince— in his passing through pageants like these—may know that it is in his heart already—that white and shining Talisman. I travel in search of this and the water of all-seeing. I am pledged to seek out the Touchstone for a Prince who has lost his history. Are you he for whom I work, tell me, or shall I look for another?

SHELLS FROM THE SANDS OF FAERIE: SHEEN OF WATER

September, 1928

EARTH is not all, but earth is full of its rumors. I might have said that the ways are infinite, for there is no end to my stories of entrance. I have stepped through the frame of a picture into a world that is more than picture, though it is painted and emblazoned strangely. It is, in truth, the place of images and endless forms of thought. It is like a picture gallery, where scenes and portraits have come out of their setting, full of life and motion. It is like a great book of romances turned outward into pageants, full of ventures and fulfilments. Listen, therefore, and know, for that which follows is a sacrament.

I have performed one journey into Faerie in a hay-time sweetness of simplicity. Somewhere in this world of ours—but is it within or without?—there is a little place of the waters, a pool of waters of life, which a blue sky has stilled, so that it is always clear and smooth, and no wind may vex it. The guardian heaven above it is never clouded; it has a soft and dreamful radiance, day long in the daylight—even as the eyes of my Lovers—and stars watch in the night time. The planet of love is the fairest of those which visit it; but this is in the Hour of my Lady, who came to me as a Gift from Faerie and a Messenger from the Gate beyond. Can you spell me these words of my parable—you who are mine and listen? You need not go in search of this place: it is nearer than lips and eyes; it is like the tongue and the word for nearness. There is no Faerie but Faerie, and it is not there but here. You may have only to think for a moment, and you will stand by the pool, on its margin. Do you see my meaning now? When I knew that I could enter that inward realm which is called Faerie in the Chronicles. I found the pool of my parable and paused thereat in a mood of still contemplation, preparing for the mysteries to follow. You are by my side at this moment, eager for what I must tell you, pausing in the same manner. Now, prayer is a work in Faerie, and I recited, or, rather, chanted that which may be called the Incantation, or, better still,

THE LITANY OF FAERIE

Wind of the evening, light grows dim:

Breathe in the pause of the Vesper Hymn.

Light of stars, the night is nigh:

Kindle thy beacon-fires on high.

Star of love, from thy far height,

Shine till the morning dawn is bright.

Sun of the Morning, far away

Faintly blossoms thy Rose of Day.

Light breaking on earth and sea,

Herald the Day of Eternity.

Evening gold and morning red,

Veil of night, betwixt you spread,

Lead us on by star and moon

Unto fullest light of noon.

So may every earthly gleam

Lift us to our Land of Dream.

Stately, spectral, far apart,

Opened to the eager heart,

By thy graces be we brought

Into endless Halls of Thought,

Stretching through a world of rest.

Silver Bells and Faerie spells,

Hear the Speaker, help the Seeker:

All your marvels manifest.

This invocation ended, I fixed my heart steadfastly on that burnished pool, as if on a glass of vision, and awaited without stirring the manifestation of a certain glorious light, which is like the ravishment in the heart of my worshippers when I bring them my latest poem; and through this light I passed easily from the hither to the further side. The simplicity of the experiment is obvious, and it has been practiced in all ages.

SHELLS FROM THE SANDS OF FAERIE—THE GATE AND THE WAY

November, 1928

FROM hither to thither, from the right to the left side, turn me the ring of Faerie; and hither, come hither, combing your golden hair, maids of the world's end. I was glad when they said to me: Let us go through the length of the vista and set eyes on the end thereof, on a blessed world of images. At the end was the World of Faerie, with all its pageant of emblems, all its types of venture, and all the suddenness of its transformations. It follows that I am well qualified to answer your cloud of questions, because—after another fashion of speech—I myself have turned the corner of the street. Hereby I am seeking to show you the exact length of the journey, and that when you have grown accustomed to the manner of change mirrored, it is at most like moving your lodgings from Number 1 in the High Street to the Broad Avenue beyond the Market Place. But as it is a Court of the Mysteries—and you pass from Grade to Grade—so also its modes of entrance can be expressed in the terms of these. The distance from hither to thither is the breadth of a hoodwink. The length of the journey is between the eye and the hoodwink. You are there in the fall of the hoodwink. There are things without number which I can tell you concerning my inquisitions and explorations. I shall do something surely of this kind in the sequel; but I make a beginning only here and now, setting down heads of instruction—a little roughly and hurriedly—for the use of good dreamers and those who see.

Understand, therefore, so far as you travel herein, that this is a record of experience, for you as well as for me, and that it might be supported at need by the evidence of other travelers, drawn from many sources. Yet shall the visitations of heralds empowered by phantasy have need of no other titles for those who are born with a dream in the heart of them. Open the heart in Faerie, and then it will speak to the heart.

The dream draws on, the dream draws on.

The vision points the way:

When vision and dream alike have gone,

The sacred memories stay.

All roads lead to Faerie. Even in your own city, you do not know what it may mean to walk to the end of a garden. There is a sense in which by-paths are everywhere paths of Faerie, and all the open roads are highways of enchantment. But much depends on the traveler. There is a point between two moments, and then a vista may open wherein all is wonder. There is space for going into the unknown between two pillars of hills. At need anything serves as a signal to enter. The floating of wind-driven dandelion-seed across what seems to be a meadow has been proved often. There is a star in the forehead of a white roe, and it may lead from no man's land to ever and ever. One of the best stories is that of a covered wagon, drawn by a belled horse, which is driven at great leisure over a carpet of moss, and draws up on the other side before a woodland of Faerie. The meaning of this may seem to be no better than raillery; but there are certainly more ways of getting a magic ring than by buying it. There are also other devices for spinning hemp into gold than are known to an odd little man who works in a place of lullaby, lilting song-tide and moonlight, which is found in the suburbs of Faerie.

AN ELECT PRIESTHOOD

January, 1931

THE "dead secrets" of French occult history are coming forth gradually into the light of day, and the lesson of recent researches is one of great encouragement as to what may transpire in the future. There was a time when one thought that the past had buried its dead in respect of the thaumaturgic heresiarch Eugène Vintras, his so-called "work of mercy" and his miraculous Masses. But a Parisian barrister, with a gift for unearthing archives, discovered a great dossier, and little is left of this mystery except the last problem, which is how the wonders were worked. There was another time when the end of all knowledge, and little at that seemed reached on the subject of the eighteenth-century alchemist Pernety and his Illuminés d'Avignon, the custodian's ex hypothesi of a Masonic Rite which was one of Hermetic dedications. But M. Joanny Bricaud went to work there and here, at Avignon more especially; he was favored past expectation, and the results are with us. So also, a silence of years on the talismanic problems of Martines de Pasqually and his Order of Elect Priests was interrupted once only, in 1926, by the publication of a correspondence between Willermoz, chief of a circle at Lyons, and a certain Baron de Turkheim. That it has been broken utterly at last, and this to some purpose, will be shown in the present study.

I have said that the subject is talismanic, and there is more than one reason. Under the auspices of their Grand Sovereign Pasqually, the Elect Priesthood figured as a Masonic Rite; but they did not come forward to exhibit any "System of morality, veiled in allegory and illustrated by symbols." They were Theosophists, and as such were depositories of Divine Secrets; they were Magi and practiced Magic; but as such they held Sorcery, Necromancy, and Black Arts in horror; in fine, they were men of religion, and as such the Magic of their Invocations brought to them exalted beings who were not of this world: it seems even to have been held that Christ Himself gave teachings in their Lodge-Temples. But the subject was talismanic, also in the eyes of many for a very different reason. For long years, an interest in the School of Pasqually signified a concern in Louis Claude de Saint-Martin, the chief French Mystic at the close of the eighteenth century. Apart from him, it might have remained always among the byways of Masonic history, commemorated briefly in a few records but explored in none. The bibliography of the School, almost till this day, has been practically a bibliography of Saint-Martin. On the side of appreciation and criticism, the expository literature began so far back as 1852, with an essay on his doctrine and his life. M. Caro, its author, is utterly unknown now, but if his monograph was denied consideration, the latter had at least been earned if not obtained. The next evaluation was coincident with the first appearance of Saint-Martin's important correspondence with Baron KirchBerger in 1862, the same year being marked by M. Matter's suggestive study of the mystic and the circle to which he belonged. It is the work of most permanent interest which attaches to the name of Matter. Adolphe Franck followed in 1866. He has repute in the literary history of France, but he will be remembered by his Memoirs of Saint-Martin, even if his work on the Jewish Kabbalah passes into the limbus.

These early examples may be taken to stand in summary form for the existence otherwise and later of a not inconsiderable literature which has grown up on things Martinistic and has been grouped naturally and inevitably about a central figure, being that of the only French Mystic who can be held to count at his period, and he of whom Joubert said long ago that "his feet are on earth but his head is in Heaven." Now the precursor of this cultured and illuminated teacher was Martines de Pasqually, and the environment of his earlier life—from which, moreover, he never emerged entirely—was precisely that Masonic Rite for the foundation and development of which Pasqually carried a Hieroglyphical Warrant, and Lodges of which were established at Bordeaux, Lyons, Paris, and elsewhere. It was the cornet of a season and burned itself out quickly when the Grand Master passed from this life in 1772. The mysterious Warrant, which no one could read and no one has seen since he voyaged to St. Domingo, may have emanated from Unknown Superiors or may have been his own device. It matters little except on the score of sincerity—and even this might have survived at the period—because Pasqually, his personality, his influence, were the only warrants which counted, and they proved convincing enough for those who knew him.

It happens that all books, monographs, and pamphlets which constitute the critical literature of Martinism are long since out of print, while many are hard to obtain. It is this fact which readers must bear in mind as I pass on to speak of a monumental work which M.R. Le Forestier bas added recently to his Researches on Masonic High Grades, more especially those of France, and to his thesis on the Illuminati of Bavaria. It may be remembered also, if I am permitted to venture for once on a

Personal note, that this article is the work of one who is acquainted with all Martinistic literature, as well as with most references thereto and citations therefrom in French occult reviews and Masonic works. We must be dissuaded, however, from regarding M. Le Forestier's extended record as in authentic correspondence with its title: it is concerned with Pasqually, his Elect Priesthood, his theosophical doctrine and its sources, its organization considered as a Rite of Masonry, its story from that standpoint, and the chief personalities who worked with him for its welfare and progress. It is therefore throughout and only a study of the Order of Elect Priests. The point demands registration because there was a wide field of Occult Freemasonry in France of the eighteenth century outside the Pasqually foundation, and it might require another volume of equal proportions to set forth at full length the pretensions and enthusiasms, the attainments, aberrations and follies of Alchemical, Magical, Kabbalistic, Magnetic, Swedenborgian, and even Mystical Systems which came to birth under the banner of Freemasonry between 1760 and the days of Revolution.

Within the limits of its proper subject, it remains that the author has taken all available materials in printed sources and has made an intensive study therefrom. The result is representative in a plenary sense. It is written with understanding and sympathy, underrates and exaggerates nothing, parades no Personal opinion, and in fine omits nothing. It opens with a clear analysis of Pasqually's notable treatise entitled Reintegration, which contains the theosophical reveries of the Order in the form of a Commentary on Genesis. It unfolds therefrom the occult practices of the Priesthood, which constituted its title to existence, and subsequently goes in search of an origin for both in Bible and Talmud, Jewish Kabbalism, and the occultism of Christian centuries in Europe, including Rituals and Grimoires of Magic. Sidelights are sought and found in Pasqually's relation as a Theosophist with Catholic Christianity, old Gnostic heresies, and the Mysticism of the eighteenth century. The story of the Order follows, including a valiant attempt pursued in all directions to shed light upon the Priestly Rituals. There is no question in my own mind that M. Le Forestier's treatise is and will remain a standard work on its subject. It is to be regretted that in one instance, but, as it would seem, in one only, he has been content to derive at second-hand. It should have been possible surely to consult in France that important contribution to the subject which was made in 1801 by Abbé Fournié, seeing that I have been able to meet with it here in England;

but M. Le Forestier derives from Matter. It is to be regretted also, or is at least by myself, that there is so little understanding of Saint Martin; but the reason is not far to seek; the author has none practically for that inward and mystical way which drew le philosophe inconnu from the Ceremonial of Divine Magia, so-called, to the experience of Divine Union.

It has been made plain that M. Le Forestier owes nothing to unpublished sources, but such have been known to exist, and that in considerable proportions, since Matter wrote on Saint Martin in 1862. Some portions of these have been published by Dr. Papus, Steel-Maret, Albéric Thomas, and others. It is assumed or suspected that M. Joanny Bricaud, as custodian or president—so far as it survives—of the Ordre Martiniste, founded by Papus, has important unprinted memorials, and others in private hands are heard of from time to time. Presumably the most important of all—among those known to survive—came into the hands of Papus, being the archives of Jean Baptiste Willermoz, a part only of which relate to Pasqually and his occult foundation. While M. Le Forestier was at work on his memorable undertaking, it would seem that these documents were placed in the hands of M. Paul Vulliaud, author of La Kabbale Juive and a monograph on Joseph de Maistre, both of which were noticed long ago in the Occult Review. It has come about, therefore, that the publication of Le Forestier's volume was followed quickly by that of M. Vulliaud on the Rose-Croix of Lyons in the eighteenth century. The practical simultaneity may seem at first sight ill-starred, but the theses are not in competition, nor can a serious student of one dispense with the other. M. Vulliaud presents from his archives the correspondent of Martines de Pasqually with Willermoz and certain instructions to Elect Priests, all belonging apparently to the year 1774. His chief personal contributions to the subject are a notice of Pasqually, another on Abbé Fournié, and an extended study of Willermoz in respect of his Masonic career. M. Vulliaud has been challenged in Le Voile d'Isis for the ridicule which is heaped upon his subject and for reproducing all Pasqually's grammatical and orthographical mistakes. It matters little to myself, because he gives the documents, now in extenso and now in summary form. He gives them also in respect of several activities outside the present consideration—Protocols of the Strict Observance at Lyons, the Register of the Masonic Congress at Lyons, Records of a Society of Initiates arising out of Le Loge de la Bienfaisance, also at Lyons, and a prolonged account of séances at which a subject in the magnetic trance was not only placed in communication with departed spirits, but gave answers to questions, some of which belong to Masonry. Willermoz was one of the sitters but did not entrance the subject. Taken altogether, the collection is priceless, that is to say, on the side of history and of French Freemasonry on its occult side at the period. In conclusion, my readers must not suppose that we have come to the end of all knowledge regarding the Elect Priesthood. By the orders of Las Casas, its last Grand Sovereign, then abdicating, the Archives of the Order were deposited with Savalette de Langes, President of the Great Masonic Lodge of Philalethes. They were delivered in sealed parcels and are not to be confused with the Willermoz dossier. What has become of them? May not these also in the time to come see the light of day? As one who has devoted his life to research, I tend to believe that a star over-watches research and in most unexpected manners sees at last to its reward.

FINIS

AUTHOR AND MANAGING EDITOR

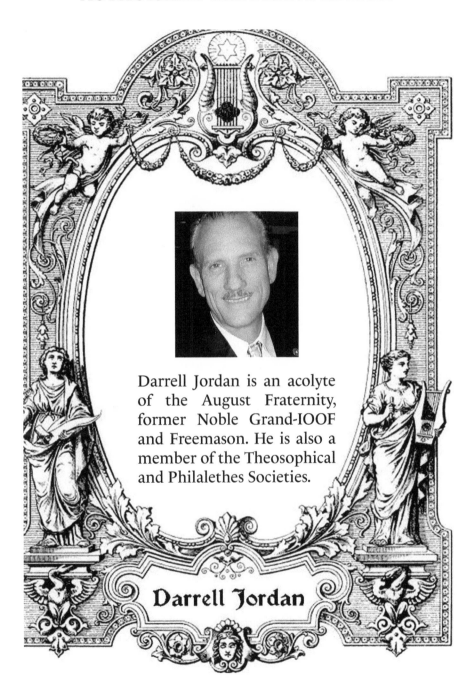

Darrell Jordan is an acolyte of the August Fraternity, former Noble Grand-IOOF and Freemason. He is also a member of the Theosophical and Philalethes Societies.

Darrell Jordan

BOOKS BY THE AUTHOR

- Illustrations of Masonry
- Surviving Document of the Widow's Son
- The Undiscovered Teachings of Jesus
- The Initiates
- Jefferson's Bible
- Master Masons Handbook
- Forgotten Essays - W.L. Wilmshurst
- Forgotten Essays - Waite
- Forgotten Essays - H. Stanley Redgrove
- The Writings of Sigismond Bacstrom M.D.
- Forgotten Essays – Reincarnation
- Masonic Writings of George Oliver
- Masonic Lectures by Wellins Calcott
- The Fellowcraft Handbook
- Secret Societies
- Vibration and Life
- Key to the Rosicrucian Characters
- The Revelation of John
- Life and the Ideal
- The Mystic Key
- The Philosophical History of Freemasonry
- The Magic of the Middle Ages
- Musings of a Chinese Mystic
- The Life of the Soul
- Christian Mysticism
- Krishna and Orpheus
- The Eleusinian Mysteries & Rites
- The Crucifixion Letter
- You Paid What?
- The Illustrated Pioneer History of the America
- Montana Freemasons 19th Century
- Washington Freemasons 19th Century
- Idaho Freemasons 19th Century
- Rock Metaphysics
- Emblems: Jean Jacque Boissard and Otto van Veen
- Emblems: Nicholas M. Meerfeldt
- Alchemy Art: Manly P. Hall
- Emblems: Manly P. Hall
- Alchemy Art & Symbols
- Splendor Solis

For the latest information, please visit author's site:
Parallel47North.com/collections/esoteric-books
If you have any question or feedback, please contact:
info@Parallel47North.com

Hand-drawn Illustration of Book Cover Art by Jessica Naomi.

The Artist Portfolio: JessicaNaomiDesigns.com

For those interested in Rosicrucian or similar Esoteric teaching.

Soul.org

Theosophical.org

Whiteaglelodge.org

PTTHfoundation.com

Milton Keynes UK
Ingram Content Group UK Ltd.
UKHW040809200324
439740UK00002B/20